WHY ⫶⫶⫶⫶ ⫶RMS FAIL

American Politics and Political Economy
A series edited by Benjamin I. Page

WHY CONGRESSIONAL REFORMS FAIL

Reelection and the House Committee System

E. SCOTT ADLER

The University of Chicago Press   Chicago and London

E. Scott Adler is assistant professor of political science at the University of
Colorado, Boulder.

The University of Chicago Press, Chicago 60637
The University of Chicago Press, Ltd., London
© 2002 by The University of Chicago
All rights reserved. Published 2002
Printed in the United States of America

11 10 09 08 07 06 05 04 03 02   1 2 3 4 5

ISBN: 0-226-00755-3 (cloth)
ISBN: 0-226-00756-1 (paper)

Library of Congress Cataloging-in-Publication Data

Adler, E. Scott.
   Why congressional reforms fail : reelection and the House committee system /
E. Scott Adler.
       p.   cm. — (American politics and political economy)
   Includes bibliographical references and index.
   ISBN 0-226-00755-3 (cloth : alk. paper) —
   ISBN 0-226-00756-1 (paper : alk. paper)
       1. United States. Congress. House—Committees.   2. United States.
Congress. House—Reform.   I. Title.   II. Series.

JK1429 .A52 2002
328.73′0765—dc21

                                                              2002018969

♾ The paper used in this publication meets the minimum requirements of the
American National Standard for Information Sciences—Permanence of Paper for
Printed Library Materials, ANSI Z39.48-1992.

To Pam and Annie Bea

Contents

Acknowledgments

IN RETROSPECT, I AM TRULY OVERWHELMED BY THE LARGE NUM-
ber of individuals who went beyond the call of duty in helping me
to complete this book. The endeavor began while I was at Columbia University and bears the imprint of my advisors Chuck Cameron, Bob Shapiro, and Jim Caraley. Chuck and Bob remained involved in my work well after I left Columbia and did more for
me than anyone has a right to ask of his advisors. Several others at
Columbia provided comments, suggestions, or occasionally just a
sounding board for my ideas, including Sunita Parikh, Ed Mansfield, Ira Katznelson, David Epstein, Charlie Riemann, and Eric
Reinhardt. Above all, John Lapinski's assistance was critical in com-
pleting what eventually became part of chapter 3, and he turned out
to be an excellent coauthor.

The study really took shape once I arrived at the University of
Colorado and benefited from the input of several colleagues: David
Leblang, John McIver, Sven Steinmo, Mark Lichbach, and Dan
Drezner. Of particular note, Walt Stone not only read multiple
drafts of chapters but tolerated my loud music. In addition several
other scholars offered extensive assistance at different stages of the
project, many of whom read and commented on the entire manuscript. They include Sarah Binder, Ken Bickers, Greg Bovitz, Tom
Carsey, Roger Davidson, Larry Evans, Tim Groseclose, Tom Ham-
mond, Jeff Jenkins, David King, Walter Oleszek, David Rohde,
Chuck Shipan, Bob Stein, and Rick Wilson. I would also like to
acknowledge the valuable input from seminar participants at the

University of Washington, the University of Maryland, the University of California at Davis, the University of Colorado, Ohio State University, and particularly the Political Institutions and Public Choice Program at Michigan State University.

As the reader will discover, I employ a massive amount of data for this study—some of it my own and some of it borrowed. The project would not have been possible without the generosity of those who not only lent me their valuable data sets but also tolerated my incessant questions. These charitable individuals include Charles Stewart, Ken Bickers, Bob Stein, Frank Baumgartner, Bryan Jones, and Michael Dubin. My own data collection required the assistance of an army of students. Seana Day, Jennifer Gandhi, John Halpin, Angeline Koo, Sharon Karmon, Lisa Luttbeg, Dennis Still, and Chris Walker all provided superb research assistance. Moreover, several individuals were extremely helpful and patient while I struggled through the process of accessing and formatting many of these data sets, particularly the often difficult to use Census data, including Tim Byrne, Greg Strizek, Greg Haley, the consultants at the Columbia University Electronic Data Services Center, and the University of Colorado and Columbia University government documents librarians.

A number of current and former members of Congress and Hill staffers graciously provided me with some of their time and occasionally with access to their files that helped me flesh out the quantitative work. I wish to thank those individuals whose names appear throughout the study; and to those whose remarks were not for attribution, well, you know who you are. Among those who gave of their time and experiences, one deserves special thanks—not only was David Skaggs's door always open for me, but he was quite helpful in opening other people's doors as well.

I gratefully acknowledge the generous financial support of the National Science Foundation (grant SBR-9409451), Frank Mackaman and the Dirksen Congressional Center, the Carl Albert Congressional Research Center at the University of Oklahoma, and the Council on Research and Creative Work at the University of Colorado.

Chapter 3 draws on material from two articles that appeared in the *American Journal of Political Science:* "Demand-Side Theory and Congressional Committee Composition: A Constituency Characteristics Approach," with John Lapinski (41, no. 3 [July 1997]: 895–918, © 1997); and "Constituency Characteristics and the 'Guardian' Model of Appropriations Subcommittees, 1959–1998" (44, no. 1 [January 2000]: 104–14, © 2000). Both are used by permission of the University of Wisconsin Press. The rest of the book aims to move my argument beyond what is covered in those articles. Among the individuals who patiently assisted in the editing and formatting of the book were Dave Underwood, Nancy

Mann, Anne Ford, and particularly Nick Murray—who helped me exorcise those writing ghosts. John Tryneski deserves special thanks for shepherding the manuscript through the obstacles in the publication process. Despite the association of those named above, none of them is to blame for my errors, omissions, or occasional reluctance to take their better advice.

My parents, Sheldon and Lucille, and my brother, Brent, were very generous with their support, encouragement, and companionship on much-needed hiking and rafting trips over the years that this project took. Finally, I could not have completed this book without the love and support of Pam and our collaborative project, Annie Bea, who, thankfully, arrived *after* most of this was done. If anyone went above and beyond the call of duty, it was the two of them.

Chapter 1

Introduction:
Why Is Congressional Structure So "Sticky"?

THE ELECTION OF A GOP MAJORITY IN 1994 OFFERED THE PROM-
ise of a "Republican revolution" that would lead to dramatic changes
in the House and Senate. "The American people will see more reform in 24 hours on the very first day . . . than they've seen in
decades," promised House Republican Conference Chair-elect John
Boehner of Ohio, the day before the opening of the 104th Congress.
Speaker-elect Newt Gingrich (GA) shared this view of the rules and
structural changes his new majority party was preparing to impose
on the House of Representatives and called the planned implementation of new chamber organization and procedures a "historical
[*sic*] occasion" (Associated Press 1995). Thus, not only had the Republican leadership pledged profound legislative changes as part of
their *Contract with America,* but they also vowed historic institutional alterations to bring about those policy changes. Among the
most striking proposals was the elimination of one in every three
House committees. Soon after the election, the *Contract* became the
focus of the national political agenda. The pledge to profoundly alter the business of Congress was nearly unanimous among Republican legislators and would-be legislators—it was signed by 367
GOP candidates for House seats, and signers subsequently composed 97 percent of the Republican House majority.

The *Contract* was not the first sign that the new Republican leadership supported structural changes in congressional operations.
During the previous term, Gingrich had repeatedly expressed wishes
for substantial change in Congress's committee arrangements. For

example, in a 1993 bipartisan meeting of chamber leaders to consider reform proposals to be offered by the Joint Committee on the Organization of Congress, Minority Whip Gingrich said he was disappointed that the reform panel had done little on "the jurisdictional cleanup issue." He advocated bringing to the House floor a bill that would recommend alterations to existing jurisdictional arrangements, and he wanted to leave this bill open to amendment by any member of the House.[1] Despite Gingrich's past attempts to score points with Republican faithful through political bomb-throwing, we can infer some sincerity in his desire for congressional reforms from the private forum in which it was expressed. There were few obvious political gains for Gingrich from advocating jurisdictional restructuring among such a small group of chamber leaders.

Yet the changes ultimately made in the House committee system at the start of the 104th Congress were less than revolutionary and fell far short of the elimination of one-third of the House standing committees that had been promised in the *Contract*. Even though a number of panels were placed on the chopping block, Republicans dissolved only three standing committees (14 percent of the existing committees) and redistributed their jurisdictions to other related panels. Among the remaining nineteen committees, only a small fraction of policy domains were reshuffled, most visibly by reallocating portions of the Energy and Commerce Committee's jurisdiction. Although it was frequently declared that this change affected 20 percent of the panel's jurisdiction—a statement that originated with the Republicans' chief for the committee restructuring effort, David Dreier (R-CA; see Victor 1995; Drew 1996)—a study of committee hearings reveals that the change actually affected less than 5 percent of the panel's policy domain (King 1997, 74).[2] Among other changes to the chamber's committee system were caps on the number of subcommittees within full committees, abolition of proxy voting in committees, term limits on committee chairs, and elimination of independent subcommittee staffs.

The relative failure of the loudly trumpeted GOP proposals to modify the system of House committee jurisdictions should be no surprise. The unfulfilled promise of profound organizational change is part of modern congressional history. Since the mid-1940s, numerous reform advocates have repeatedly attempted to effect meaningful and permanent change in a system of legislative committees that is often claimed to be inefficient, outmoded, unaccountable, and even corrupt. Usually their efforts result in little if any change, as members of Congress who are generally satisfied with existing arrangements obstruct what can be fairly seen as relatively innocuous committee reforms.

Why do attempts at congressional committee restructuring so often fall short of the objectives of reformers? Rather than seek historically specific explanations for why representatives oppose committee reform movements at a particular moment, I set out to test one theory of legislative organization that can plausibly explain the recurring failure of initiatives at committee reorganization. The perspective I offer on legislators' opposition to rearrangement of committee powers and jurisdictions is based on their reelection imperative and the legislative structures they create in order to fulfill that ambition. First I analyze the composition and outputs of House committees since the mid-1940s and seek to establish the boundaries of this reelection theory of congressional organization. Then, using reform implications derived from this perspective on congressional structure and development, I analyze the outcome of the three efforts considered by scholars to be the most important attempts at House committee reorganization in the modern era.

Why Study Committees and Jurisdictional Change?

Political scientists continually document the importance of committees to the duties of the U.S. Congress, particularly its House of Representatives.[3] In the academic literature on American politics, graduate student Woodrow Wilson perhaps obtained more mileage from his statement "Congress in session is Congress on public exhibition, whilst Congress in its committee-rooms is Congress at work" (Wilson [1885] 1981) than did President Woodrow Wilson from any speech he delivered or document he penned during his term of office. The prominence and importance given committees is not unwarranted. In many ways congressional committees are the essential machinery that propels the legislative process. The House rules stipulate that the Speaker must refer each bill, resolution, or other measure to a committee in accordance with the subject matter of the act and the jurisdictions of chamber panels (House Rule XII, Section 2). Almost no bill is passed by the House that is not first acted upon by at least one committee, if not multiple panels.[4] Though the proportion varies by congressional term, usually 90–95 percent of non-commemorative enactments are addressed in some way by either a House or a Senate committee.[5]

Moreover, standing committees are often seen as implicitly setting the legislature's policy agenda by reporting out bills in whatever form they prefer and not reporting out those proposals that they wish to prevent from further consideration. Hence, it is not the personalities or individual policy agendas of committee members that distinguish one panel from the next; it is the jurisdictional boundaries of committees that really define their importance in the legislative process. Almost every landmark legislative battle fought in Congress over the last fifty years has at one point included a skirmish between two or more committees over policy turf—the civil rights struggles of the late 1950s and 1960s (Berman 1966), the battles over control of energy policy in the 1970s (Rosenbaum 1981), and the fracas over the Clinton Health Care Plan (Evans 1995) are just a few good examples. As we will see, the process of delineating jurisdictional boundaries—particularly in an institution like the House of Representatives, where strict rules of deliberation make it difficult to skirt around such structures—is in many ways equivalent to defining the direction of policy and a matter not taken lightly by members of Congress.[6]

Despite the significance of these legislative bodies, the position that standing committees hold in the congressional policy process today is very different from their role in chamber deliberation shortly after the nation's founding. For many years following the ratification of the Constitution, policymaking in Congress rarely included the input of standing committees. Initially, both chambers of Congress formulated policy by first arriving at the general principles of the legislation in the Committee of the Whole, and then appointing a select, or "spot," drafting committee to determine the details and present the bill back to the chamber for enactment. Once the bill was passed, the committee was dismissed (Cooper 1970; Gamm and Shepsle 1989).

Not until the 15th Congress (1817–18) did the bulk of the legislature's work include the efforts of permanent standing committees that operated in much the same way as we know them today (Jenkins 1998). During the next century, the House committee system underwent tremendous upheaval. The chamber created more than forty-five different standing committees of varying sizes and importance (Cooper 1970; Galloway and Wise 1976). Control of the congressional policy agenda shifted from party leaders to committee chiefs. And authority over critical federal appropriations was reallocated among committees several times over the course of a hundred years. Finally, in 1920, with the passage of the Budget and Accounting Act on the horizon, the House overhauled its appropriations process by removing this spending authority from six standing House committees and consolidating budgetary control back into the existing Appropriations Committee (Stewart 1989).

Yet since the 1920s there have been few perceptible changes in the duties of standing committees in the House of Representatives. Committees hold essentially the same position in the policymaking process as they did for most of the twentieth century. In large part the modification of policy property rights has been small, gradual, and mainly concurrent with the evolving policy needs of government and the governed.

But this stability has not prevailed for lack of attempts at change. Over the last six decades politicians, journalists, and even the public have frequently been heard to lament how the existing committee jurisdictions or rules of procedure inhibit the enactment of whatever pressing legislation is being obstructed or facing alteration at the moment. Critics have charged that control of policy arenas is too fragmented among numerous House committees or too concentrated in one obstructionist panel, that committees overrepresent special interests or underrepresent certain political orientations. The list of complaints seems endless. Such protestations have prompted the creation of no fewer than five formal panels within the House of Representatives since World War II to review and propose changes in the existing committee system (including joint efforts with the Senate): the La Follette-Monroney Joint Committee on the Organization of Congress (1945–46), the Monroney-Madden Joint Committee on the Organization of Congress (1965–66), the Bolling-Martin Select Committee on Committees (1973–74), the Patterson Select Committee on Committees (1979–80), and the Boren-Domenici-Hamilton-Dreier Joint Committee on the Organization of Congress (1993–94).[7] In addition, there have been several informal attempts at reorganization, including a decade-long struggle within the Democratic caucus from the mid-1960s to the mid-1970s over sweeping changes of chamber rules, including those governing committee hierarchy and procedures, as well as the Republican efforts at the start of the 104th Congress (1995–96).

Yet, even counting a few name changes and the consolidation of mostly inactive committees in the mid-1940s, the structure is barely any different than it was during the New Deal. Reform efforts, frequently proceeding under the banners of policymaking efficiency and the equalization of workloads, have been largely unsuccessful in accomplishing either. For instance, take workload: if we examine just the days of committee hearings held by each House panel (including their subcommittees) per Congress, we find that the incongruity between the least and most active committees that existed in the late 1940s still exists today. In fact, to a great extent the same committees remain on opposite ends of the workload continuum. House Administration, Government Reform (formerly Expenditures in the Executive Departments), and Veterans' Affairs are among the least active, while Appropriations, Energy and Commerce (formerly Interstate and Foreign Commerce), and Education and the Workforce (formerly Education and Labor) are the most active. The livelier committees hold five to ten times more hearing days per year than the less active panels.[8]

The changes that have occurred in House jurisdictional arrangements have resulted as much from slow and infrequent modifications to structure and "common law" policy property rights during less tumultuous times (King 1997) as from sanctioned efforts at organizational change. Accordingly, scholars have begun to ask the obvious question, paraphrasing Gordon Tullock and other formal political theorists: Why is there so much stability in critical legislative institutions like the House committee system?[9] If reform advocates continually try to initiate reorganization in the House committee system and its jurisdictional arrangements, why is there so little change in the existing structure? What prevents reform proponents from achieving their organizational objectives?

By focusing specifically on the critical policymaking institutions of committees in the U.S. House of Representatives, this book explores when and why a legislature alters its rules and decision-making structures. In particular, I concentrate explicitly on legislators' motives for opposing structural changes and analyze why designs for legislative alterations so often fall short of their goals. What is it about the House committee system that makes it so "sticky"? This question involves a number of other important issues in politics and congressional studies: What are the principles underlying the legislative committee system? How do we measure institutional change? Has meaningful structural change occurred in the committee system? Why is substantial change so difficult to achieve? And, if efforts at profound structural alterations are taken up in the future, what can reform advocates do differently to increase their likelihood of success?

Scholars are now using positive theories of legislative structure to explain changes in congressional rules and procedure. The emerging wisdom is that principles useful in understanding the existence of specific rules and institutions should also be valuable in explaining why the same institutions and rules change or evolve. Similarly, consideration of the reasons for the success or failure of efforts at committee restructuring embodies many of the motivations that define the structure of legislative institutions. Therefore, a study of the "stickiness" of committee jurisdictions under reform pressures should illuminate the underlying principles of congressional organization.

The Legacy of Research on Congressional Reform

The study of legislative change has a relatively long and rich tradition, particularly that which examines the U.S. Congress. For decades, academic work treating the causes and consequences of change in congressional structures would swell following periods of particularly active debate over proposed institutional modifications. Early literature on legislative change, while rich in historical detail, was largely descriptive rather than theoretical (Galloway 1946, 1951). As the field of political science became more analytical and quantitatively oriented, so too did the study of congressional reform (see, for example, Davidson and Oleszek 1977; Sheppard 1985; and works in Ornstein 1975). In recent years, when research in American politics, and particularly on Congress, shifted in a more theoretical direction, so did work examining legislative change (Evans and Oleszek 1997). Yet much of this research on congressional reform has employed theory in a relatively inductive fashion, using models of legislative organization as post-hoc tools for discerning the meaning of institutional outcomes and legislators' behavior.[10]

Another avenue of work on congressional reform, however, is grounded in political science research begun in the 1970s that develops formal models of political institutions and behavior. Borrowing the economic theories of rational actors (as in the works of Riker; Black; Buchanan and Tullock; Olson; and Downs), a group of legislative scholars introduced a more positivist orientation to studies of congressional organization and output.[11] For a number of years, they confined themselves to theoretically based examinations of *stylized* legislative bodies; but as competing models of legislative structure emerged, scholars could not avoid substantiating their theoretical contentions with empirical evidence.

Even when researchers began to test their more formal theories with quantitative and anecdotal evidence, they still confined themselves to investigating the *presence* of specific legislative structures or rules. Internal legislative institutions and rules of procedure, like the committee system and policy jurisdictions, were still considered exogenous or previously determined (Binder 1997, 4). The matter of structural change had not been broached, since scholars were primarily—and rightly—interested in laying an initial theoretical foundation for the organization of political institutions before beginning to treat procedural and institutional modifications.

Over the last decade or so, a new line of research has developed wherein scholars apply theories of congressional structure to our knowledge of historical change and development in congressional institutions. Using positive theories of institutional organization to guide them, researchers explore the evolution of congressional rules and procedure to gain a fuller understanding of how and why members of Congress have reconfigured the structures through which they legislate. The prevailing question has been, If there is nothing to prevent the legislature from reorganizing itself except for the preferences of its own members, under what circumstances does this occur and for what reasons? Research by

Binder; Dion; Schickler; Schickler and Rich; Stewart; and King has enhanced our knowledge of the historical development of Congress as it tests more extensively the rationally based models of legislator behavior.

Binder (1997) contends that changes in the rules governing the powers and privileges of minority parties have been conditioned on the state of interparty political divisions and the existence of cross-party cleavages. Similarly, Dion finds that "small majorities are more cohesive, cohesive majorities lead to minority obstruction, minority obstruction leads to procedural changes on the part of the majority to limit obstruction" (1997, 245). Conversely, Schickler and Rich's (1997) study of changes in House rules from 1919 to 1994 (including committee jurisdictional alterations) calls into serious question the ability of the majority party to control the extent or direction of structural modifications in the policy process, at least until the more recent period, when the majority party became more homogenous and unified. Even then the majority caucus has been constrained in what types of structural arrangements it can implement. Schickler (2001) further argues that no one theory of legislative organization can explain the institutional development of Congress. Rather there exists a "disjointed pluralism," in which different interests influence the process of change in legislative arrangements during different periods. Stewart's (1989) examination of budget reform politics between the Civil War and World War I shows that a combination of environmental and membership pressures, including the electoral incentive to seek targeted benefits for members' districts, shaped the aggregate decisions made about the changing structure of the budgetary process in Congress.

Perhaps most relevant for the current study is King's examination of changes in "common law" jurisdictions: committee policy boundaries as determined by the precedent of bill referrals made by the House Parliamentarian. King contrasts these with what he refers to as "statutory" jurisdictions: the list of policy issues written into the chamber rules delineating committee boundaries (1997, 19). King claims that "most of the organizational action"—significant change in policy property rights of House committees—occurs via common law rather than statutory jurisdictions. His argument is that the principal jurisdictional modifications happen not as a result of formal efforts to alter the structure of committee arrangements written into the chamber rules, but as informal encroachments by committees on other panels' turf or through adoption of emerging policy arenas. I have no intention of disputing the claim that formal efforts at committee restructuring often fail. I believe that King is largely correct that policy entrepreneurs tend to rely on jurisdictional expansion through bill referrals because system-wide and sanctioned reform efforts are more often than not doomed to failure. Where we are most likely to disagree is in the extent to which any jurisdictional changes have altered the House committee system, if at all.

Yet, even though the jurisdictional action that does occur is likely to be informal, this does not mean that what occurs in the more formal instances is inconsequential. To the contrary, we will see that if the chamber-sanctioned reform efforts had succeeded to any significant degree in their proposed reorganization, the result would have been substantial rearrangement of committee responsibilities and powers. To wit, the very reasons for the failure of such reform movements will lend us even greater insight into the underlying motivations of the existing legislative structure.

A New Direction for the Study of Congressional Change

The present study continues in the rational-choice vein, returning to the study of formal efforts at system-wide jurisdictional reforms in the House of Representatives—the kinds of changes in legislative structures that previous legislative scholars have often considered to be among the most important for shaping congressional procedure and the policymaking process. The phrase "congressional reform," however, is not an easy one to define and can mean different things to different people. Davidson and Oleszek perhaps described this phrase most succinctly in their study of the Bolling-Hansen reorganization debate in the 1970s: "One person's reform is another's stumbling block" (1977, 2). Though scholars continuously probe the intent, causes, and consequences of "reform" movements in Congress, they frequently cannot produce any better definition for the phrase than "a change for the better." [12] For purposes of this study, I am agnostic on the meaning of the word *reform* and accept its definition as "any suggested changes in the existing congressional structure."

I specifically examine one type of congressional reform—proposals for the formal relocation of policy issue property rights between committees. I chose to focus on efforts intended to alter committee policy jurisdictions because such chamber-wide reform movements seem to recur continuously over the span of modern congressional development. While the details of the specific proposals may vary in different time periods, the articulated objectives of reformers are almost always the same—rationalize committee jurisdictions, eliminate useless panels, equalize committee workloads, and improve the efficiency and effectiveness of the policy process in Congress. If reformers are simply advocating something as seemingly innocuous as the improvement of policy decision making through restructuring of these essential legislative panels, why are such efforts so persistently and bitterly contested? Obviously there are other

kinds of reforms that I do not consider here—changes in leadership powers, alterations in the structure and authority of subcommittees, modifications in the rules governing minority party rights, and so on. Other
scholars have examined the success and failure of such reform movements
(see, for example, Binder 1997; Schickler 2001; Rohde 1991). I conclude
this study with a few words about how the lessons drawn from this analysis can help us to understand other types of reform efforts directed at
structures other than legislative committees.

What is different about my study of efforts at jurisdictional restructuring (although it is similar in many ways to more recent research on other
types of organizational change in Congress) is the use of positive models
of rational legislators in a more systematic analysis of institutional outcomes. Following the established principles of the rational-choice literature, I analyze member preferences in combination with organizational
structures to develop an understanding of institutional resilience in Congress. Given that "the rules of the game" are controlled by the legislators
themselves, positive theories explaining the *presence* of specific legislative
institutions should also explain the *persistence* of the same structures.

I take issue with some previous literature on congressional reform in
two important ways. First, I do not assume that efforts during prominent
reform periods necessarily change organizational structures. More to the
point, I challenge the notion that certain historical modifications in committee jurisdictions resulted in substantial and enduring change in the policy responsibilities of individual House panels. George Galloway noted
that the Legislative Reorganization Act of 1946 was thought of as a "legislative miracle . . . [that] added up to the most sweeping changes in the
machinery and facilities of Congress ever adopted" (Galloway 1953,
646).[13] Similarly, contemporary scholars have referred to the changes imposed by the Republicans at the start of the 104th Congress as "sweeping
institutional reforms" (Gimpel 1996, 38) or "landmark" organizational
alterations (Deering 1999, 93).[14] I show that despite minor alterations in
committee names and the reshuffling and merger of largely overlapping or
marginal jurisdictions, there have been no "sweeping" or "landmark"
changes in the arrangement of the policy property rights of committees.
The essence of the House committee system and the legislative responsibilities of individual committees have remained essentially the same over
the last half-century or more. Therefore, what I set out to explain is not
why or when certain committee structures change, but rather why, under
significant and direct pressure for change, they are so resilient. In the process my approach implicitly explores why legislators find some institutional alterations tolerable while rejecting others.

Given that the U.S. Constitution clearly grants each chamber the freedom to "determine the rules of its proceedings" (Article 1, Section 5), there appear to be two possible reasons for the committee system's resilience in the face of the sincere and determined efforts of reformers: either some faction within Congress—a chamber or party elite, for example—has the gatekeeping power to stifle reform efforts, or the majority of members are satisfied with the existing structures. This study supports the latter hypothesis and attempts to explain majority acceptance of the committee system by expanding on one of the fundamental underpinnings of legislative organization—the electoral connection. My second major challenge, then, is directed at observers who agree that little change has occurred in committee jurisdictions but who attribute the stability to other factors and pressures—to legislators' institutional motivations (protection of internal organizational turf and positions of influence) or even to partisan policy objectives (defense of legislative structures that facilitate passage of policies desired by the majority caucus).

I contend that a primary and constant force hindering committee restructuring movements has been the electoral objectives of members of Congress. Under pressure to bolster their reelection prospects in order to achieve long-term legislative and personal goals, rational politicians with the ability to shape legislative structures utilize the arrangement of rules and procedures to secure targeted government benefits for needy constituency groups and voting blocs. Any widespread change in the established order of policy deliberation—particularly its centerpiece, the committee system—would create far too much uncertainty in members' electoral strategies and therefore would be broadly opposed from the start.

The notion that politicians are electorally motivated was the unsurprising core assumption in Mayhew's study of the essence of congressional structure. His distinctive contribution was to use this fundamental instinct of politicians as the critical building block in theorizing on the structure and procedures of Congress. Foremost, he recognized that, while reelection was not the only objective of members of Congress, it was "the *proximate* goal of everyone, the goal that must be achieved over and over if other ends are to be entertained. . . . Reelection underlies everything else" (1974a, 16–17). Mayhew revealed how structures within Congress, many of which are inherently endogenous, were remarkably well suited to serve members' electoral needs for advertising, credit-claiming, and position-taking (81).

Predictably, legislators invest considerable time and staff resources in work on committees that consider issues of particular importance to their home districts. The first half of this book maps the theoretical and empirical boundaries of this investment. I document the consistency with which, across a half-century, legislators have gravitated to House panels of special interest to their constituents. Then I explore how district characteristics and committee membership affect members' ability to bring home disproportionate shares of particularized federal benefits. Given the recent scholarly attention to the importance of parties and party leadership in congressional operations, I examine closely how the distributive aspects of committee composition and policy output change with the rising conditions of strong party polarization and caucus influence over the legislative agenda.

The second half of the study examines how the nature of the constituency/electoral investment in the existing committee structure drives legislators' resistance to changing committee arrangements. That is, I extend the notion of the "electoral connection," suggested by Mayhew (and others), to the important subject of congressional jurisdictional reform. If legislators arrange the committee system so that it meets members' electoral needs, the same motive should propel their preferences and actions when confronted with proposals to alter the committee system.

To explore my contention about the electoral connection, I examine the most significant and celebrated occasions when the modern Congress contemplated fundamental restructuring of its committee system.[15] They are (1) the efforts surrounding the Legislative Reorganization Act of 1946; (2) the work of the House Select Committee on Committees (the Bolling Committee) in 1973–74 and the substitute proposal of the Democratic Committee on Organization, Study, and Review (the Hansen Committee); and (3) the efforts of the Joint Committee on the Reorganization of Congress in 1993–94 and the subsequent actions of the Republican leaders when they took control of the House in the 104th Congress. As should already be evident, the outcome of each of these institutional junctures is almost exactly the same—little to no change in the extant powers and policy arrangements of House committees. From a social science perspective, this research design presents a bit of a problem for my examination of reelection theory: there are no contrary cases here. That is, no committee reform proposals succeeded. This is not to say that there have never been successful reform movements in Congress, but, because I limit my scope to decisions about jurisdictional rearrangement of committees, I necessarily must examine the failure of reform movements, since there were no other outcomes. Therefore, the critical question is not whether committee reforms failed, but what theory best explains why such reforms incessantly fail. On this point, I contrast the electoral approach with whatever theory seems most appropriate or plausible for the time period at hand. Moreover, the periods do offer considerable diversity in the political and institutional circumstances of Congress. For instance, through study of three reform eras that span fifty years, we find variations in the party control of the Houses, cycles of weak and strong parties, eras of substantial membership turnover before reforms and eras of negligible turnover, and instances where congressional reforms were a publicly salient issue and others where the electorate was largely unaware of efforts at institutional reform.

Scholars lately have remarked how much Congress and its membership have changed since Mayhew wrote, noting the diminished impact of the electoral motivation vis-à-vis the impact of parties (Aldrich and Rohde 2001). Since some of this recent work on institutional changes in Congress has argued that legislators' reactions to structural alterations can take on different forms depending upon the partisan conditions in Congress at the time, I explore in detail how the reelection theory plays out in periods of partisan strength or change in party control of the chamber. To the extent that I dispute the claim about the diminished influence of the "electoral connection," it is a matter of degree—parties are more influential in Congress at the start of the twenty-first century, but the electoral motivation has anything but disappeared.

Thus, when parties are particularly weak and members are more or less left to their own devices in determining policy choices and reelection strategies, I contend that representatives protect legislative arrangements, like committee structures, that help them provide for the specific social and economic needs of their districts. Electoral motivations take a slightly different shape under a strong partisan regime. In eras where co-partisans are staunchly similar in their policy preferences, but preferences between parties diverge and party structures are more influential in determining the form of legislative rules and procedures, reform is still unlikely. Under such conditions the reform preferences of individual legislators are more likely to be driven by a *combination* of individual constituency/electoral needs and the collective electoral needs of party candidates.

To support my contention, I draw on a substantial amount of information from the public record, archival material, and quantitative data. The quantitative analysis investigates how congressional district interests determine legislators' committee memberships; whether or not panel membership and district need relate to the provision of disproportionate federal benefits; and how these factors drive individual preferences on jurisdictional restructuring. Data on members' reform preferences are taken from roll-call votes and public and private statements concerning specific structural or jurisdictional changes. The more qualitative evidence, such as archival materials and participant interviews, shows as thoroughly as possible how key political actors viewed the overall structural effects of reform efforts on the institution's policy decision making.

One word of caution: I do not contend that the theoretical perspective offered in this book is the *only* explanation or a *complete* explanation for committee organization, output, or change. Nothing in the social sciences, specifically in the study of politics, is that simple. I offer here what I believe to be an important ingredient in our understanding of congressional structure. The critical question, therefore, is *how much* can be explained by this approach. After laying out the theoretical propositions for both the existence and alteration of relevant committee structures, I test their limitations as a model for House organization, using congressional data since World War II. Knowing the empirical boundaries of this electoral/constituency approach to legislative organization helps us to probe more precisely how the model merges with other theoretical approaches for a more accurate portrayal and clearer understanding of Congress.

Overview of the Book

The book is divided in the following way. In the first part I examine the constituency approach to committee structure. Chapter 2 elaborates a distributive/electoral theory of congressional committee organization and reorganization. I review the relevant literature on electoral theories, or what will more accurately be referred to as "gains-from-exchange" models of legislative behavior and congressional structure, and establish explicit hypotheses regarding committee assignments and output. Drawing on the underlying tenets of the distributive theory, I also suggest several propositions regarding how members of Congress will react to proposals for profound structural changes in the system of legislative committees. Finally, I address the ways in which these theories should or should not be adjusted for periods of heightened partisanship and party polarization.

In chapters 3 and 4 I conduct an explicit examination of the evidence relating to the recruitment/composition and benefits hypotheses of distributive committee structure and operations. Chapter 3 explores the nature of committee assignments and uses newly compiled data on the characteristics of congressional districts to analyze the relationship between constituency needs and the appointment of representatives to standing committees and Appropriations subcommittees from the early 1940s to 1998. In chapter 4, I test the effect of committee membership and district needs on outlays falling under the jurisdiction of several standing committees and Appropriations subcommittees for a number of congressional terms, during both Democratic and Republican chamber majorities.

The second part of the book investigates the reaction to and the ultimate failure of jurisdictional reorganization efforts in the three major reform eras since World War II, using the knowledge about the prevalence of distributively oriented committee structures. In chapter 5 I argue that the changes made by the Legislative Reorganization Act of 1946, sometimes considered the most substantial revamping of congressional committees in history, were simply cosmetic. By exploring in depth four principal elements of the Act, I demonstrate that legislators purposely avoided any alterations that would impair the distributive capacity of the committee structure, which was already well established as a useful reelection tool; indeed, in many ways, jurisdictional and procedural changes simply augmented the institution's gains-from-exchange potential.

Chapter 6 explores the committee reforms considered during the 93rd Congress (1973–74), sometimes referred to as the Bolling-Hansen reforms. Specifically, I examine the consideration of seven distinct jurisdictional changes, including roll-call votes for several of these reforms, as well as the final passage of the Hansen package, which was significantly weaker than the proposed Bolling reforms. Quantitative and archival evidence shows that even when one controls for the institutional interests of legislators (established committee position and panel seniority), which are frequently blamed for the failure of the Bolling proposal, constituency factors substantially affected members' reform preferences and behavior.

The third reform effort, spanning the Democratic 103rd Congress (1993–94) and the transition to the Republican-controlled 104th Congress, is the subject of chapter 7. Unlike those of earlier periods, this reform moment was characterized by considerably more party unity and by active caucus involvement in the shaping of congressional structures and provision of electoral resources. While such influences do alter the manner in which reforms are considered, constituency and reelection considerations are still clearly among the most important factors in the decision. Contrasting the distributive explanation for reform outcomes with two others—one based on institutional efficiency and another grounded in party policy objectives—I find that, while profound changes in committee jurisdictions remain quite unlikely, under conditions of increased partisanship individual-level constituency factors become less important than broader party constituency motivations as the caucus contemplates jurisdictional reforms. In addition, I explore how changes in the way congressional campaigns are financed in the modern era have served to alter the electoral needs of legislators and in part redefined the meaning of the term *constituency*.

In the conclusion, chapter 8, I summarize the findings and clarify what we have learned about the limits of a distributive notion of committee organization and restructuring. I evaluate how much a gains-from-exchange principle of legislative structure teaches about congressional organization over the last six decades and what it explains in the realm of congressional reform. I also assess the prospects for future efforts at comprehensive jurisdictional reorganization and offer some recommendations regarding issues that must be considered by procedural entrepreneurs.

Chapter 2

Understanding a Gains-from-Exchange Theory of Committee Structure and Change

ON MAY 21, 1999, ALMOST TWO MONTHS INTO THE MILITARY BOMBING campaign in Yugoslavia, President Bill Clinton signed into law the 1999 Emergency Supplemental Appropriations Act.[1] The primary purpose of the bill was to fund U.S. troops and equipment deployed with other NATO forces waging an air war against the Serbian military, which had recently invaded Kosovo. Clinton's original request to Congress was for $6 billion. The final tally for the legislation was two-and-a-half times that—almost $15 billion. How the price tag attached to this bill went through the fiscal roof is in part a study in the distributive nature of congressional politics.

Two aspects of the legislation helped members of Congress to treat this bill as a vehicle for additional government benefits to home constituencies: (1) its primary purpose was to fund military operations in Kosovo, and (2) it had emergency status. The urgency of its purpose made it unlikely that the measure would fail to pass both houses in a timely manner, and because that purpose was largely perceived domestically as Clinton's initiative, the president would be compelled to sign it. Moreover, since it was considered emergency legislation, most of the spending provisions put into it would not be limited under the spending caps agreed to in the 1997 balanced-budget legislation.[2] Knowing this, legislators added a number of district-serving amendments. Among those included in the final language were the following:

- $70 million for livestock assistance, with a provision broadening the definition of livestock to include reindeer, which are farmed in

Alaska, and $26 million to compensate crab fishermen hurt by federal limits placed on crabbing in Glacier Bay, Alaska. Republican Senate Appropriations Chair Ted Stevens is from Alaska.

- $500,000 added by Steny Hoyer (D-MD), a member of the House Appropriations Committee, to extend a crime fighting unit along the District of Columbia-Prince George's County, Maryland border.
- $1.5 million for the purchase of water for fish and wildlife purposes at San Carlos Lake, which is just outside the district of Jim Kolbe of Arizona, Republican member of the House Appropriations Committee. John Kyl (R-AZ) is a member of the Senate Appropriations Committee.
- Language added by Kay Bailey Hutchinson (R-TX), a member of the Senate Appropriations Committee, that prevented the Interior Department from raising the wellhead tax on oil and gas companies.
- Language added by Representative Doc Hastings (R-WA) and Senator Slade Gorton (R-WA), the latter a member of the Senate Appropriations Committee, that put an end to the Clinton Administration's obstruction of a gold mine project in eastern Washington.
- $2.2 million added by Bob Bennett (R-UT), of the Senate Appropriations Committee, for improved sewers in Salt Lake City for the upcoming 2002 Olympic Games.

The padding of the emergency Kosovo appropriations is a superb example of the instinctive drive of elected officials to provide for the economic and social needs of their constituencies. What made the above example relatively uncomplicated was that funding provided in the act would not force Congress to reduce spending in other budget areas—indeed, it would "free up" more fiscal room in the regular appropriations bills (Baumann 1999). The revenue to pay for the emergency outlays was mostly to be taken from the Social Security budget surplus. Within some unspecified limit, the president would almost assuredly sign whatever language Congress brought before him as long as it included funding for the Kosovo military operation. This must have seemed like an ideal opportunity for legislators to add a little extra for their districts.

Though this supplemental appropriation is not an ordinary enactment, the effort exhibited by members of Congress to obtain targeted benefits for their constituencies is quite ordinary. While such enterprises do not occupy all their time, legislators are continuously angling for such opportunities to improve their electoral prospects. This chapter lays out some theoretical elements of a distributive notion of committee structure and change that will be tested throughout the book. I begin by recounting some of the well-established principles of legislative structure predicated on gains-from-exchange theory and explaining what this notion of congressional organization should mean in terms of committee composition and budgetary outlays. Then, taking this approach one step further, I explore the implications that a distributive/reelection underpinning to the legislative committee system has for members' preferences concerning jurisdictional rearrangements and chamber-wide reform proposals. Recognizing the dramatic increase in partisanship and the authority of party leaders to control congressional organization in recent years, I address what theoretical differences, if any, we should expect in an environment of extreme party polarization and active party caucus leadership. Finally, I say a few words about the potential for committee reform proposals to emerge even in the context of a legislature where reelection is the dominant collective goal.

Reelection and the Role of Committees

The foundations of a gains-from-exchange theory of legislative organization should be familiar to most students of American politics, but to ensure that the reader fully understands the underlying motivations for my electoral approach to congressional stability, I return to the somewhat mundane assumption that legislators usually pursue reelection. Indeed, as Mayhew (1974a) pointed out a generation ago, representatives *must* secure reelection in order to pursue many of their other goals. For instance, some politicians have explicit policy agendas, like tougher crime laws or more effective environmental protections. If enacting new policies is as difficult as some scholars profess (Kingdon 1995)—and this is not hard to imagine, given that Congress is composed of 535 elected officials who have 535 different configurations of policy preferences—it is reasonable to assume that most House members will need more than two years to accomplish their policy goals. Likewise, if the goal is higher political office or at least more influence within the policymaking body, a representative will require time to build a reputation as an accomplished and reliable politician and legislator and to foster good relations with voters and colleagues (Wawro 2000).

If members of Congress are reelection maximizers, we reasonably expect them to behave in ways that increase their likelihood of winning at the polls. Like other candidates, incumbents may want to improve name recognition by traveling in the district to meet voters or purchasing radio, television, and newspaper advertisements (Fenno 1978), or to create a large and diverse campaign staff and group of supporters to get their messages out to different communities within their district. But of course incumbents have an electoral advantage—not just privileges such as franked mail and better access to free media, but influence over the wide-ranging powers and deep pockets of the federal government (Fiorina 1989). If, for example, the home district has long-term needs for money to assist struggling farmers, to repair damaged roads and bridges, or to bolster the local economy with small business loans and grants, the incumbent legislator is well positioned to secure it—and to claim credit with constituents when it comes. Some theorists argue not only that incumbent legislators *can* use this privilege to maximize their electoral support, but that it is their *obligation* as "representatives" to provide for the pressing needs of their home constituency (Eulau et al. 1959).

The question for members, therefore, is how best to situate themselves in the legislature to secure benefits for the district. With the exception of a very small number of leadership posts, the most promising sources of long-term influence over specific policy arenas are the authorizing and appropriating committees. Membership on a panel with jurisdiction over a relevant federal agency increases a legislator's ability to pull the purse strings for government programs important to her constituents. Awareness of the utility of committee assignments to representatives is at the heart of legislators' resistance to changes in committee jurisdictions.

Shaping Committees and Jurisdictions
for Maximum Electoral Advantage

Previous studies using a more formal analysis of the role of committees and their jurisdictional boundaries in a legislative body have shown that these institutional subunits can help induce legislative equilibria in what would otherwise be chaotic majority vote cycling (Shepsle 1979). Building jointly from this recognition that committees offer *structure-induced equilibria* (SIE) and from Mayhew's observation that congressional organization and rules are appropriately arranged to promote incumbent reelection, Weingast and Marshall (1988) clarify how the congressional committee system can help to advance members' electoral prospects. Employing concepts and empirical analyses familiar from earlier congressional research, they lay out the theoretical foundations that explain why legislators would foster a committee system that facilitated gains from exchange, and how this structure would not only be self-enforcing but also generate constituency benefits for members.

The essence of the committee system, according to Weingast and Marshall, is that policies that confer particular benefits on specific constituencies or types of constituencies require the assent of a majority of legislators for enactment; thus, in a diverse legislature, supporters of these policies need some mechanism to facilitate the necessary logrolling for passage of bills. One such mechanism in an institution composed of members with heterogeneous tastes is to enforce bargains and trades among legislators by granting jurisdictional property rights to each committee. The successful operation of such a system requires the following: committees must have exclusive issue authority; a seniority system and property rights to committee seats must exist for panel members; and vacancies must be filled through a process of bidding, the highest bidder being (presumably) the one most desiring the assignment for electoral reasons. For further exposition of these points, see Weingast and Marshall (1988).

Hence, the committee system and its arrangement of jurisdictions are critical for distributive policymaking because they coordinate a legislative division of labor in which representatives are granted increased control over policies in areas of keen interest to their constituencies in exchange for relinquishing authority over other less important jurisdictions. Legislative bargains are enforced implicitly through this "live and let live" trade-off (Shepsle and Weingast 1981; Weingast and Marshall 1988). Majority rule procedures prevent any one committee from extracting too many gains at the expense of other legislators (such as excessively costly construction projects in committee members' districts), since, at the extreme, nonmembers can reject policy proposals that impose undue costs on nonbenefiting constituencies. Most important, the utility received by any one legislator (passage of her preferred policies) exceeds the burdens she must bear in support of other legislators' preferred policies (Shepsle and Weingast 1994). In other words, distributive policies concentrate benefits but disperse costs.

This policymaking structure, of course, allows members to distribute government benefits among themselves above and beyond what may be socially necessary for the general welfare. That is, "locally targeted expenditures are counted by the local constituency as benefits. . . . [T]he districting mechanism in conjunction with the taxation system provides incentives to increase project size beyond the efficient point by attenuating the relationship between beneficiaries and revenue sources. A cooperative legislature has no incentive to remove entirely these sources of inefficiency" (Weingast, Shepsle, and Johnsen 1981, 658). Nevertheless, the endogenously determined institutional arrangements may still be in equilibrium because they serve legislators' most basic imperative—reelection. Why would any member of Congress, therefore, want to alter a committee system that so efficiently addresses the electoral needs of politicians?

A Digression on the Meaning of "Gains from Exchange"

Before going any further I want to clarify the phrases *gains from exchange* and *distributive policies,* since the two are often used interchangeably. Provisions included in the Kosovo appropriations, such as sewers for Salt

Lake City and water purchase for an Arizona lake, are classic examples of what are traditionally considered distributive policies. These are political decisions "that concentrate benefits in a specific geographic constituency and finance expenditures through generalized taxation" (Weingast, Shepsle, and Johnsen 1981, 644; see also Lowi 1964). Strictly speaking, distributive policies are government projects that purposely target a single district or a relatively small number of congressional districts narrowly defined in the language of the legislation.

Mayhew offers a similar definition for "particularized government benefits," although his emphasis is on "credit-claiming" with constituents. In general terms, legislators act

> so as to generate a belief in a relevant political actor (or actors) that one is personally responsible for causing the government, or some unit thereof, to do something that the actor (or actors) considers desirable. The political logic of this, from the congressman's point of view, is that an actor who believes that a member can make pleasing things happen will no doubt wish to keep him in office so that he can make pleasing things happen in the future. (Mayhew 1974a, 52–53)

Mayhew's "actors," of course, are constituency and interest groups who desire some pecuniary compensation or special consideration from government. Thus legislators seek policies that benefit their constituents *and* that they can claim they helped produce.

However, successful credit-claiming with constituents does not require that the benefits be provided exclusively (or semi-exclusively) to their group or locality. And with the use of legislative logrolling, pursuit of government assistance is not inevitably a zero-sum competition for scarce funds.[3] Therefore, for purposes of this examination, I broaden the "distributive" propositions about the role of legislators and the system of committee jurisdictions to include all policies that benefit or have the potential to benefit constituencies with particular characteristics.

This is precisely the view that Weingast and Marshall take in their "gains-from-exchange" model of congressional organization and committee structure. They emphasize that members solicit support from the politically responsive interests within their districts through attention to their needs from government. In order to position themselves to better serve the requirements of miners in West Virginia and Pennsylvania or the elderly in Florida and Arizona (to draw from their examples), politicians assume greater control over these political matters in exchange for relinquishing control over issues of little concern to their constituents (1988, 136–37). Weingast and Marshall believe that politicians do not necessarily desire a single new project to claim credit for, but generally want credit for a disproportionate amount of relevant benefits—whether they are crafting new programs for this purpose or securing a greater amount of funding from existing federal programs.

Strictly speaking, the distributive ability of legislators is the capacity to provide their constituencies with narrowly targeted governmental benefits beyond the "normal" allocation for that kind of district, and the benefits are made available through broadly collected tax revenue. However, the term *distributive* is often used to connote something more like a "gains-from-exchange" political arrangement, as Weingast and Marshall define the term—that is, any political structure (existing or new) through which legislators funnel government benefits to constituencies with a particular set of social, economic, or geographic characteristics. Certainly gains from exchange may include the targeted or distributive benefits— what are sometimes referred to as "pork barrel"—but Weingast and Marshall do not restrict the legislative output in their stylized political structure to just such benefits. Despite the subtle distinction, I yield to accepted vernacular and occasionally use the term *distributive* as a shorthand for the concept of gains-from-exchange political arrangements.

The Electoral Connection and Institutional Stickiness

To some researchers it was not so clear that established legislative institutions, like committees, really offer stability in policy decisions. In response to Shepsle's seminal work on structure-induced equilibrium, Riker raised a critical question for the notion that policy equilibria may be reached through endogenous legislative structures and rules.

> [R]ules or institutions are just more alternatives in the policy space, and the status quo of one set of rules can be supplanted with another set of rules. Thus the only difference between values and institutions is that the revelation of institutional disequilibrium is probably a longer process than the revelation of disequilibrium of tastes . . . institutions are probably best seen as congealed tastes. We ought, I think, to be thoroughly aware that the distinction between constitutional questions and policy questions is at most one of degree of longevity. If institutions are congealed tastes and if tastes lack equilibria, then also do institutions, except for short-run events. (Riker 1980, 445)

Riker asserts that legislative structures, particularly those in a setting where the rules are established by members, simply inherit the same instability that policies face through majority rule vote cycles. If endogenously determined institutions are the only mechanism preventing political actors from forming new coalitions in order to alter a policy (and possibly leading to chaotic vote cycles), what is to prevent those same actors from simply altering the constraining structures and then constituting new coalitions when they find themselves on the losing end of policy outcomes? Essentially, this is the question that has been at the core of current research on the development of congressional rules and structures.

In a series of articles, some coauthored with Weingast (Shepsle and Weingast 1981, 1984a, 1984b), Shepsle suggests that legislative institutions are stickier equilibria than Riker intimates. Drawing upon his earlier work, Shepsle first proposes that structures such as committees are critical for ensuring the cooperation necessary for the enactment of policy (Shepsle 1986). Legislative panels with well-defined policy jurisdictions can prevent shirking between two (or more) political actors who strike a logrolling agreement to ensure passage of desired legislation. Committees facilitate cooperation of individual legislators across policy subjects, since these larger working groups of representatives with similar policy interests are more likely to persist even after a specific legislator has departed from the institution and thus permit reciprocity on a larger scale. The trades are not simply individual-level; whole committees are able to logroll through the exchange of policy control.

Shepsle accounts for the stickiness of the congressional committee system, or the reluctance of members to accept changes, by differentiating between how the body considers policy changes and how it considers rules and structural changes. The durability of such institutions derives partly from the reliance of legislators on committees as a means for pursuing the objectives of the legislature (passage of legislation and governing), but even more from the high transaction costs of attempting to alter existing structures, which are conceived of as "equilibrium institutions." [4] For various reasons, the long-range policy and political uncertainty associated with new institutional arrangements is a cost that most legislators are unwilling to bear, even if they are not completely satisfied with the current system (Calvert 1995; Shepsle and Weingast 1981, 1984b). North (1981) notes that there is good reason to believe that high transaction costs lead to the persistence of even inefficient institutional structures. The enemy we know is somehow less intimidating than the enemy we do not know.

The transaction costs of changing the committee system are high because the institution has to some extent been fine-tuned over many decades to fulfill members' varied distributive or reelection needs. This, of course, has meant that over time the system of committee jurisdictions has had to adjust in small ways as the economic and social needs of constituencies have changed. For example, as science and high-technology research and manufacturing grew, it became increasingly necessary for Congress to have a subunit for handling such policy matters. But a comprehensive reorganization, even if it might prove more efficient at distributing benefits to members' constituencies, would require establishing new relationships with different configurations of legislators or specialized interests. This process is far too uncertain and risky, especially for politicians facing a short election time horizon (a maximum of two years for all House members and the same for at least one-third of the Senate).

Consequently, the stickiness of certain institutional arrangements in Congress is derived partially from the reelection motivations of legislators. Unlike other studies of change in congressional structures, this view anticipates not only that certain structures are more highly resistant to change than others, but that this institutional stability is also resistant to the effects of partisan or membership changes. Previous researchers have often contended that the endogeneity of legislative structures makes them susceptible to enormous turnover in membership or shifts in the partisan control of the legislature (e.g., see Ainsworth and Sened n.d.; Calvert 1995, 259; Diermeier 1995). New dominant coalitions of legislators seek new rules for policy decision making in order to enact their preferred policies. For instance, Schickler, McGhee, and Sides's (2001) study of reform preferences in the early 1970s found that the support for institutional alterations came from junior and liberal members seeking to advance policy proposals obstructed by more conservative and senior legislators. In contrast, I argue that, while marginal adjustments may occur as economic needs change or as a dominant coalition (e.g., a new majority party, etc.) attempts to court a slightly different reelection constituency (Fenno 1978), such changes are relatively minor. In most districts, the prevailing economic, social or geographic needs develop very slowly, and no arrangement of rules or policy jurisdictions offers more certainty that the representative can meet these demands, regardless of tenure or partisan affiliation, than does the time-tested existing structure. Furthermore, any changes in committee structure that do occur will in large part have the same distributive character. Any alterations in congressional rules and procedures that are acceptable to the body must meet the requirement that they have no net negative effect on members' reelection probabilities. The only exception to this imperative will occur under conditions of heightened party polarization and very active party leadership. (This will be treated in detail below.)

Implications of a Distributive Theory of Legislative Committees

From this gains-from-exchange notion of committee organization one may draw several important implications as to how committees should be composed and what we should expect them to do. The simplest way to conceptualize the elements of the model is to classify them as *demand* and *supply* elements. On the demand side are conjectures concerning the linkage between constituency characteristics and legislators' committee membership—Rundquist and Ferejohn (1975) refer to these as the *recruitment* and *overrepresentation* hypotheses.[5] On the supply side are propositions about the linkage between committee membership and the rendering of federal benefits to congressional districts. The propositions I present about committee composition and output are not necessarily new, but I use them to formulate some new ideas about how legislators would approach the issue of change in committees.

A Distributive Hypothesis of Committee Composition

If legislators pursue benefits for their home districts and committees are the institutional nuclei for parceling out those benefits, then we should not be surprised that committees attract representatives from districts with a specific economic or social interest in the federal programs and policy matters under their authority. Assuming that members themselves play a large part in the selection of panel assignments, committees will overrepresent constituencies with a stake in their subject matter.[6]

It is not difficult to find examples of legislators ruminating about their efforts to obtain committee slots in order to serve the special needs of their constituents. In his diary of activities during the 100th Congress (1987–88), Representative Bill Lehman (D-FL) recounts an example not only of self-selecting onto committees for constituency purposes (in this case, an Appropriations subcommittee), but of trading such rights to reward a colleague for cross-issue legislative logrolling:

> JANUARY 8 THURSDAY
> In the Democratic Caucus of the full Appropriations Committee in choosing subcommittee assignments on the third round of choices, I was first in line to choose a vacancy on the Military Construction Subcommittee, but I passed so that [Rep.] Vic Fazio of California, who wanted this assignment to protect a military installation in his district, could have it [*sic*]. Vic is a good ally when it comes to protecting the transportation subcommittee legislation on the House Floor against off-budget resolutions, and I owed him. (Lehman 2000, 6)

The distributive model predicts that committees addressing policy arenas that are of particular interest to narrow constituency types or are geared toward delivery of policy benefits to specific groups of constituents (this would exclude committees such as House Administration or Rules), will be composed of "homogeneous high-demanders or preference outliers" (Krehbiel 1991). That is, the preferences of such committee members on issues under the committee's jurisdiction will be extreme and in the same direction, and thus will stand out compared to the preferences of nonmembers. For example, the Agriculture Committee will draw representatives from farming-oriented areas, and the Merchant Marine and Fisheries Committee will attract legislators with significant ports or water commerce at home. Since many of the benefits that legislators seek for their constituents are pecuniary, I expect, as do Rundquist and Ferejohn (1975), that this proposition and all of the following hypotheses will hold not just for standing committees but also for the important Appropriations subcommittees.

> **Committee Composition Hypothesis:** *House committees, especially those with constituency-oriented jurisdictions, are composed of members from districts with acute interests in the particular policy benefits within the panel's jurisdiction and thus will exhibit an aggregate level of constituency demand that is significantly different from that in the chamber as a whole.*

Krehbiel further suggests that the distributive model may predict a second type of outlier committee: the bipolar outlier (1991, 124). In these "heterogeneous" committees all members have extreme preferences, but they differ in their orientation—some Agriculture Committee members, for example, may desire large subsidies to dairy farmers but could care less about wheat farmers, while other panel members want large subsidies for wheat farmers but have little or no interest in serving dairy farmers. The empirical implication of a committee composed of members with bipolar preferences is far different from that just presented. If a committee attracts legislators with contrary constituency interests, the panel's combined preference should tend toward a moderate position and in all likelihood be quite similar to the central tendency of the chamber.[7]

A Distributive Hypothesis of Committee Output

In general, districts with high demand for specific benefits should garner a larger share of the outlays. For instance, we expect that poor urban districts receive more benefits from Housing and Urban Development programs than other districts. This suggests an observable hierarchy among legislators with respect to policy-relevant outlays. But beyond this general presumption, the gains-from-exchange premise suggests that committee membership should also be an important factor in securing targeted benefits for constituents; a supply hypothesis of committee *output* will follow quite reasonably from the demand notion of committee *assignments*. Not only will committees be composed of high-demand outliers, but there should be clear indications that assignment to a particular committee comes with an identifiable payoff. That is, one should see evidence that members are actually capable of providing for district needs through such institutional positions.

More precisely, Rundquist and Ferejohn's (1975) *benefits hypothesis* contends that, relative to those of other representatives, the districts of committee members benefit disproportionately from the distribution of expenditures under their jurisdiction (see also Weingast and Marshall 1988). Their contention is that committee membership does not merely allow for the protection of federal programs important to the individuals and businesses within the district, but can indeed offer opportunities to increase the amount of government moneys aimed at the locality in precisely those sectors of greatest social, economic, and geographic need. Using the Resources Committee as an example, the theory contends not only that extant federal Resources programs that are helpful in providing funds to panel members' districts should be safe from elimination or even reductions in funding, but also that Resources Committee members should be proficient in garnering greater benefits, like Bureau of Land Management or Bureau of Reclamation funds, than they would obtain if they were not committee members.

> **Committee Output Hypothesis:** *The members of House committees, especially those whose committee jurisdictions match constituency demands, will gain a disproportionate share of federal benefits under the jurisdiction of their panel.*

Even among committee members, there may exist a continuum of benefits. All committee members are well positioned to ensure that their districts will garner disproportionate federal funds, but representatives of especially high-need districts have a strong incentive to work especially hard. Because funds from such targeted programs are the benefit most likely to appeal to voters at home, these legislators should stand out as the biggest winners. For example, among Agriculture members, those with the highest constituent dependency on a farming economy are likely to gain a larger proportion of relevant federal benefits than any other group within Congress.

This hierarchy of committee benefits goes beyond just panel membership. Not all representatives with acute district interests in programs under the control of a specific committee will gain assignment to that panel. First, a committee with a finite number of available slots may not always be able to accommodate all members with intense district demands. Conversely, chamber- or party-imposed limits on the number of committee assignments a member may have might come into conflict with the numerous district and personal demands on a legislator. Therefore, legislators who need benefits from panels to which they do not belong should be most apt to foster relations with members of those panels and most aggressive in pursuing those benefits. Though unlikely to receive as much in the way of district benefits as committee members from high-demand constituencies, they should profit beyond the level of the average non–committee member.

Distributive Approaches to Structural Change in a Legislative Setting

The gains-from-exchange perspective outlined here predicts resistance to changes in committee jurisdictions. Institutional stickiness is grounded in the linkage between legislative structure and the reelection motivation. Over time members of Congress have tailored a legislative structure that is effective for pursuing many collective goals, the most common of which is reelection. This structure includes not just formal institutions and rules like committee jurisdictions, assignment property rights, and enactment procedures, but also more informal phenomena like long-term relationships with government agencies and important bureaucracies that command the implementation of federal programs and have the discretion to direct government benefits to one district or another (Fiorina 1989). An additional part of this linkage is that legislators frequently cultivate associations with prominent organized groups and individuals in their constituencies who have intense concern for the policies controlled by the committee. Furthermore, legislators who have intense interests in matters under a panel's jurisdiction but are not members build strong and interdependent relationships with panel members: nonmembers depend upon their committee patrons to ensure that their districts are provided for, while committee members rely on support among the general chamber membership to ensure passage of their bills. Such support is easiest to find among members whose own districts will benefit from committee bills.

Such existing relationships make the transaction costs of upsetting long-standing institutions like committee jurisdictions prohibitively high. Committee members are in the best possible position to provide for district needs, and interested non–committee members will not want to incur the costs of initiating new relationships with a different set of committee members if the relevant jurisdiction is transferred to a different or new panel. While it may be possible to improve on the distributive capacity of the existing committee layout, the current jurisdictional alignment offers significantly more *certainty* with respect to outcomes than one that has undergone reforms. Ultimately, jurisdictional change can be electorally dangerous to legislators. To illustrate, Transportation and Infrastructure Committee members are quite familiar with the officials and procedures within relevant agencies like the Department of Transportation and the Army Corps of Engineers, and their construction-oriented constituents know they can rely on them to look after local economic interests and intervene effectively with government decision makers. Representatives from high-demand districts who are not members are likely to have built relationships with Transportation members whose decisions they can influence. Thus, individual members will resist reforms that alter the existing jurisdictions of such committees.

> **Individual Committee Restructuring Hypothesis:** *Legislators with intense district interests in the programs under a panel's purview will actively oppose alterations to that committee's policy jurisdiction.*

The theoretical exercise up to now has largely focused on the individual level—members pursue their own reelection, they seek committee assignment where they can influence policies of import to their constituents' interests, and they resist changes that upset the issue authority of those self-interested panels. But the individual-level hypothesis has clear and easily derived implications for large-scale reform packages that impact a large number of legislators. Proposals for simultaneous reform of numerous committee jurisdictions are likely to arouse the opposition of a *widespread* coalition of legislators protecting the existing jurisdictions. The more committees targeted for reorganization, the greater the number of high-demand legislators facing disruption of the status quo. For instance, an omnibus proposal to reform both Agriculture and Interior panels will galvanize opposition both from representatives of farming districts and from legislators whose districts have significant Native American populations or large amounts of public lands.

> **System-wide Committee Restructuring Hypothesis:** *Broad committee reorganization proposals affecting a wide array of legislators will provoke widespread opposition and thus are likely to be defeated.*

Similarly, members of Congress will resist changes that impair the degree of control a committee has over matters within its policy boundaries, for example, its control of authorizing or appropriating legislation, or its oversight of relevant federal programs. As ideological coalitions evolve and attempt to control the legislative agenda, or as partisan divisions arise between chambers or between the legislative and executive branches, reformers will advocate rules and structural modifications that can alter the powers of committees with respect to the programs and agencies in their bailiwick. For example, an emerging party caucus organization may wish to give a party policy committee the power to determine the types and content of bills considered by individual committees. Alternatively, procedural entrepreneurs or party leaders under divided government[8] may find themselves dissatisfied with the current ability of the legislature to oversee the implementation of enactments by the executive branch and may wish to impose administrative reforms, such as centralizing bureaucratic oversight in one committee.

From the same underlying distributive motivations, legislators will resist such changes. Members of Congress may support increased authority for a party caucus or a structural rearrangement that gives the appearance of more efficient law-making or oversight, but not at the expense of committee control over issues relevant to their constituency needs.

> **Restructuring of Committee Authority Hypothesis:** *Reorganization proposals that diminish the authority of committees to legislate or to oversee programs and agencies under their jurisdiction will be resisted by members who fear loss of authority over federal benefits important to their district's needs.*

A Partisan Theory of Congressional Committees and Structural Change

Until now I have said relatively little about the effect of increased party polarization and a strengthened party apparatus on the composition and operations of committees or on committee reorganization. These matters are critical for two reasons. First, notwithstanding research questioning the influence of parties in motivating legislative behavior (Krehbiel 1993, 1999), much recent evidence has documented the increasing policy division between the major parties in Congress (Groseclose, Levitt, and Snyder 1999; Poole and Rosenthal 1997; Rohde 1991) and the mounting influence of caucus organization and leadership in shaping legislative behavior and institutions (Aldrich and Rohde 1997b; Cox and McCubbins 1993). Although the evidence of escalating partisanship and interparty policy divisions is compelling, I question the extent to which strengthened party organization substantially influences committee composition, committee output, and choices regarding the reorganization of congressional structures.

The second reason, in large part related to the first, is that much of the literature on contemporary congressional structure and change in the last decade or more has adopted a partisan model of organization in one form or another as a basis for its analysis of legislative structure (e.g., see

Aldrich and Rohde 1997b; Binder 1997; Cox and McCubbins 1993; Dion 1997; Kiewiet and McCubbins 1991; Rohde 1991). I too rely on a theory of strong party influence in my examination of the reforms in the 1990s, but, in a fashion similar to the work of Aldrich and Rohde (and colleagues), I add a potent distributive element to this understanding of committee organization and change. As in the earlier periods, I explore the extent to which the reelection needs of legislators—in the context of strong parties and partisan polarization—explain the outcomes of reform choices in the 1990s.

Partisan Approaches to Committee Composition and Output

At the risk of oversimplification, I summarize here some of the more important work on partisan theory. This model of legislative structure posits that parties are the key mechanism through which members of Congress reach their individual goals—most importantly, their goal of reelection (see Cox and McCubbins 1993; Kiewiet and McCubbins 1991; Rohde 1991; Aldrich 1995). We can think of a legislator's reelection prospects as a combination of her personal characteristics, the issues of particular interest to voters, and her party's characteristics. Party characteristics and reputation are built largely on legislative success or proven ability to govern effectively. Since Congress is controlled by the majority party, that party will try to manipulate the composition of committees so that they produce legislation that will gain partisan electoral advantage. But the fundamental objective of the party and its leadership is not to erect an impeccable, collective public reputation, but to maintain its majority status through the electoral process. The congressional committee system, therefore, is an institutional mechanism for assuring that governmental policy maximizes the electoral prospects of majority party candidates.

In the "cartel theory" of partisan legislative organization (Cox and McCubbins 1993), caucus leaders' concern for the makeup of their committee contingents varies with the committee's external effects, that is, the bearing that "committee decisions have on the probabilities of victory of party members not on the committee" (191). They distinguish three classes of jurisdictions based on the "uniformity and skewness" of a committee's external effects. Committees with *uniform* externalities are those whose jurisdictions on average affect the districts of all non–committee members about equally and thus "need the most careful regulation" (228). Such committees, which "will tend to have contingents that are microcosms of their party caucuses" (198), include those considered to be the House's most important (Appropriations, Commerce, Rules, and Ways and Means); those that may authorize projects and grants on a national scale (Public Works and Transportation; and Science); those with jurisdiction over capital equipment, construction or constituencies that exist in every district (Post Office and Civil Service; and Veterans' Affairs); and those that perform management or "housekeeping" functions (House Administration and Government Operations).

Committees with *targeted* externalities have jurisdictions that affect only a small subset of non–committee members. Caucus leaders are more likely to permit these panels to be composed of legislators with extreme preferences on the relevant policy dimensions, and such panels are thus likely to be unrepresentative of the party caucus (Agriculture, District of Columbia, Interior and Insular Affairs, and Merchant Marine and Fisheries). Finally, committees with *mixed* externalities have jurisdictions that are partially uniform and partially targeted (Armed Services, Banking, Education and Labor, Foreign Affairs, and Judiciary). Cox and McCubbins make no definitive claim about the partisan contingent composition of mixed panels, saying merely, "The closer they are to the uniform externalities end of the spectrum, the more representative they should be; the closer they are to the targeted externalities end, the more unrepresentative they may be" (1993, 199).

Aldrich and Rohde offer a slightly different theory of parties, contending that the place of parties in congressional politics and structure is not fixed and that their influence ebbs and flows over time. Specifically, partisan dominance over decisions about legislative organization is most prominent in periods when legislators "grant their partisan institutions—their party conference/caucus, leaders, and other such institutional mechanisms—more powers and resources, and more latitude to use these powers and resources, to achieve collectively desired outcomes" (Aldrich and Rohde 1997a, 3). This is likely when two conditions exist: (1) there is a large degree of preference agreement *within* the membership of the major party caucuses and (2) there is considerable preference conflict *between* the parties. Aldrich and Rohde use these two conditions to define the level of "conditional party government" (hereafter CPG).

Despite the surrender of authority over chamber operations to caucus leadership in times of heightened partisanship, Aldrich and Rohde do not lose sight of the reelection imperative that often operates at the individual level. In some ways similar to cartel theory, CPG allows that committees have latitude in certain instances with respect to the composition of their membership and their legislative output. However, CPG theory contends that such autonomy may vary with time or even from issue area to issue area within a committee's jurisdiction. Rohde and coauthors explain that committee autonomy most likely occurs

> when certain issues within the jurisdiction of a particular committee are of great import to its members but not to the rest of the House, the committee will use its influence in various ways to ensure that the outcome on the floor accords with its policy preferences.... Preferences on these distributive issues will cut across party lines on the basis of geographic or economic interests, and the committee may be able to affect the legislative outcome if the preferences of its members are both sufficiently strong and homogenous. (Hurwitz, Moiles, and Rohde 2001, 912)

Like Aldrich and Rohde, I take the position that during periods of heightened partisanship and influential party organization, caucus leaders are interested in constructing committee contingents that will generate legislation reflecting positively on the party as a whole but may still allow for the congregation of representatives from districts with acute interests in panel jurisdictions. It is to the party's advantage to tread the fine line between caucus policy needs and members' constituency needs. Ultimately, the party may find itself in the minority if it does not allow its members the flexibility to pursue policy outputs important to their districts and thus maximize their electoral prospects. Since the bulk of legislation that most committees produce is opaque to the general population and has a trivial effect on overall party reputation, there is relatively little harm in allowing party contingents within some committees to consist of members with extreme district needs. The risk of outlier committees can be far outweighed by the advantage conferred on members who will enhance their electoral chances through service to district policy demands. Hence, I test the same empirical contention about committee composition that I proposed under eras of weak parties: Even in periods of heightened partisanship and increased caucus control of congressional structure, committees will be composed of members representing districts with extreme needs for the programs under their jurisdiction.

Similarly, the caucus can benefit collectively from condoning disproportionate provision of targeted government benefits to committee members' districts if those benefits in turn increase the member's value to important groups within the constituency. In regard to constituency-related matters, Mayhew states that "the best service a party can supply to its congressmen is a negative one; it can leave them alone" (1974a, 99–100). The majority party will do so as long as it has relatively little impact on public perception of the party's ability to control federal spending. Furthermore, the majority party can be disproportionately advantaged at the ballot box by incumbents' allocation of certain particularized government outlays to congressional districts. This is especially true for constituency groups with definite partisan leanings. For instance, if districts with heavy economic dependence on waterborne commerce and port activity more often elect Democrats than Republicans, a Democratic majority will find electoral profit in providing these districts with government maritime funds and subsidies. High-demand members of the majority caucus need not even attempt to diminish outlays to high-demand minority party districts, since such efforts will hinder the creation of coalitions necessary to pass legislation. Thus I examine the limits of the proposition stated earlier that members of House committees will gain a disproportionate share of federal benefits under the jurisdiction of their panels in conditions of heightened partisanship and increased caucus control of congressional structure.

Although there is little substantive change in the committee output hypothesis under strong versus weak partisan influence, there may be one distinction regarding the constituency base of different party regimes. Assuming that the two major parties try to appeal to different groups of voters, change in party control of the legislature is likely to result in shifts in distributive committee output. For example, a Democratic legislature that wishes to cultivate support from federal employees is inclined to permit members of the Post Office and Civil Service Committee to benefit from district-directed outlays, but the same may not be true for members of the Small Business Committee, since independent and small business owners tend to vote Republican. Change in majority control of the chamber might reverse this trend and allow Small Business Committee membership to become distributively profitable, while disproportionate outlays for Post Office members dry up.

Partisan Theory and Committee Reform

Though I suggest that there may be limits to party influence over the composition or output of individual congressional committees, parties can more significantly affect system-wide committee restructuring. Again, no matter which party dominates Congress, a substantial majority of legislators are likely to oppose changes in committee jurisdictions and authority. Schickler and Rich propose that "[t]he reason that partisan coalitions have put through few major revisions in committee jurisdictions may well be that membership on committees creates a source of cross-cutting cleavages that is generally viewed as a legitimate basis for opposing party leaders" (1997, 1359).

Nevertheless, increased party polarization might make members of Congress more receptive to certain structural changes—provided that they enhance the collective electoral prospects of copartisans without helping candidates from the opposing party. Given that committees are a means of protecting or procuring greater government benefits for needy constituency groups and thus maximizing legislators' reelection prospects, altering the structure of the committee system may seem valuable as a way to increase the majority party's electoral edge. By increasing the visibility of policy matters of concern to important, partywide constituency groups or groups potentially supportive of majority party members, the caucus may help to shore up its electoral coalition. There is no better way to embrace an important constituency group than to elevate its pet issues within the jurisdiction of an existing standing committee (or, potentially, to give them a new committee).

Conversely, an effective way to cut into the traditional reelection coalition of the opposing party is to demote the policy interests of its supportive clientele groups within important committee jurisdictions or, even more radically, to eliminate the relevant committees altogether. A majority caucus that pursues this partisan electoral advantage must, nevertheless, be careful not to hinder a sizable number of its own party members whose electoral constituents resemble those of the opposing party, or to damage its relations with groups whose allegiances are less clear. Thus party-imposed committee reforms will involve only those panels whose jurisdiction affects clientele groups with clear, identifiable partisan leanings.

> **Committee Restructuring under Strong Party Government Hypothesis:** *In periods of heightened partisanship and increased caucus control of the committee system, the majority caucus will protect the jurisdictions of panels that serve the needs of groups within, or potentially part of, its electoral coalition and will target for restructuring those committees whose jurisdictions serve the interests of the opposing party's constituents.*

The Origins of Congressional Committee Reorganization and the Recognition of Profound Change

Thus far I have outlined several motives for resistance to changes in committee jurisdictions, but I have provided no reasonable mechanism for the emergence of those reform proposals, nor any criteria by which to recognize when significant change has actually occurred. Why would such reform proposals ever arise, particularly appeals for system-wide committee rearrangements, if most legislators rely on the committee system for their own reelection prospects? Why would any member pursue organizational alterations that are likely to result in net electoral losses, if not for herself, at least for a significant number of colleagues? Similarly, on what basis can I contend that alterations in the committee system do not constitute *fundamental* restructuring?

The answer regarding the origins of reorganization efforts may lie in the electoral connection. For instance, even though distributive theory hypothesizes that most legislators seek particularized benefits for their districts in order to maximize their reelection prospects, some scholars have suggested that there are also legislators whose reelection hinges on their reputations as "pork busters." That is, some representatives may actually strengthen their standing with voters by a consistent stance of fiscal conservatism and the elimination of particularized government benefits to individual districts (Sellers 1997; Bovitz 1999). The same phenomenon can just as well exist in the realm of institutional reforms—some legislators may find that their electoral edge can come from being "procedural entrepreneurs" rather than protectors of existing committee powers.[9] Davidson describes them as members of Congress who cultivate a lively interest in the institution itself: how Congress works, how its virtues can be nurtured, and how its effectiveness can be improved (1990, 360). Several members come to mind when one thinks of procedural entrepreneurs in the modern House of Representatives—A. S. "Mike" Monroney, Ray Madden, Richard Bolling, Phillip Burton, Frank Thompson, Barber Conable, and David Dreier.[10]

Second, by what criteria do I contend that profound alterations in committee arrangements have never occurred? There is no easy answer to this question. It would be difficult to establish a quantifiable measure to distinguish committee rearrangements that are overwhelming and fundamental from token, superficial changes. Nevertheless, certain factors are significant in recognizing profound alterations in committee structure: Do institutional rearrangements result in severe disruption of the existing policy agenda of a committee or group of committees? That is, do changes modify the configuration of issue areas within a committee's jurisdiction in a substantial way? Are the powers of a panel (or panels) altered so that its place in the policy deliberation process is far different than it was previously? An obvious and suitable example of committee reforms that clearly fit these criteria would be the elimination of a sizable number of panels with active policy agendas and the redistribution of the issue property rights to existing or newly created committees. Of course, to a large extent the institutional "significance" or "impact" of such structural alterations is in the eye of the beholder. I will try to make the case that most often these criteria are not met by the types of committee rearrangements adopted.

Conclusion

The theory presented here provides a relatively comprehensive view of committee restructuring and the reaction of legislators to proposals for rearranging jurisdictions and committee powers. Instead of analyzing the outcome of various reform movements in an ad hoc fashion, I perceive the common failure of ambitious plans for committee restructuring as resulting from one of the more enduring principles of congressional politics— the reelection factor.

On the basis of a familiar gains-from-exchange model of legislative behavior and congressional structure, I offered details regarding recognizable hypotheses as to the makeup of House committees and the kinds of policies they should produce given this membership composition. Because members of Congress are elected officials with their own political survival foremost in their strategic calculations, they will oppose any alterations in the policymaking process that disrupts their ability to provide for important constituency needs. Thus, modifications of existing jurisdictional arrangements will be contested by members who are protecting their distributive authority. The more ambitious the reform effort, the more widespread the opposition. These electoral motivations are largely unaffected by periods of deep partisan divisions and strong party organization in Congress. Constituency considerations have a similar dampening affect on the outcome of reform efforts during these partisan eras.

To appreciate fully how this reelection motivation has influenced the outcome of reform efforts over the last half-century, I first investigate the boundaries of the theory to simply explain a committee system in equilibrium. In the following two chapters I examine the evidence for the gains-from-exchange hypotheses of committee composition and output for much of the postwar period. Chapter 3 examines the proposition that House committees will be composed of members with acute district concern for the specific benefits under the panel's purview. I gather evidence on the aggregate constituency characteristics for a large number of standing House committees dating back almost five decades. Additionally, I investigate the effect of change in the majority party on the makeup of House committees.

In chapter 4, I explore the gains-from-exchange hypotheses on committee output. Using considerably better data on the distribution of federal outlays and a more sophisticated model of the budgetary process than have been employed in most previous studies of distributive politics, I examine the effect of committee membership and district needs on the allocation of government benefits to constituencies across four congressional terms in the 1980s and 1990s. I also explore the effect of a new majority party on this relationship. The findings from these two chapters support the notion that the structural foundation of the House committee system is, at least in part, grounded in legislators' reelection imperative.

Chapter 3

Demand-Side Theory and Congressional Committee Composition: A Constituency Characteristics Approach

THE TWO MONTHS BETWEEN THE NOVEMBER ELECTIONS AND the opening day of any new Congress is an extremely busy period for those fortunate enough to have won their seat. Incumbent representatives have to shift from campaign mode back to the business of legislating, which may include participating in the formulation of new caucus or chamber rules, replacing departing staff, or even moving to a bigger suite of offices. This assumes that little or no legislative action remains for the congressional session that is coming to a close.[1] For new members, this period can be even more hectic, with "freshman" orientation, familiarizing oneself with colleagues, putting together an entirely new office and staff, and finding housing in Washington for oneself and possibly family. Amid this commotion, all members must make critical decisions concerning the committee assignments they will seek and hold for the next two years if not for the remainder of their congressional careers. Among all the actions legislators take between election and the start of a new congressional term, perhaps no decision has more long-term ramifications than the choice of committee seats.

The formal procedure of assigning representatives to committees in the House has been relatively constant in the postwar period. Generally speaking, the parties coordinate the details of the assignment process by establishing a few official guidelines (such as limitations on the number of total assignments or assignments to "exclusive" committees), gathering the request letters from members (including both new-member assignment requests as well as requests for transfers by continuing representatives), and creating a formal committee on committees to process requests and make assignment recommendations to the party caucus, who then votes on the slate of assignments.[2] The parties have made a few changes in this process over the years, including alterations in the composition of the committee on committees, modifications in the types of committee assignments that come up for ratification by the party (such as assignments to the Appropriations Committee), and adjustments to the individual limitations for assignments to certain "privileged" committees.

Though parties coordinate much of the committee assignment procedure, many different factors must be considered when doling out seats, not the least of which are the electoral needs of the individual representatives. Deering and Smith report that among the criteria mentioned by Democratic Steering and Policy Committee members in making nominations for members' committee assignments in the 97th Congress the "electoral needs of the member" were far and away the most often cited argument (1997, 106). Though other considerations, like regional claims on committee slots or a member's policy views, play a part in the assignment calculus, Deering and Smith argue that the "range of factors taken into account by members of the committee on committees has changed little during the past twenty-five years" (105).

Observe the incoming membership of any pending Congress, and one will find a flurry of jockeying for the "right" committee slot by both seasoned veterans and freshman legislators alike. Much of the maneuvering and negotiating goes on behind the scenes, in face-to-face meetings and telephone conversations. However, members' concerns and preferences for desired committee slots are evident in the stacks of assignment request letters and memoranda that legislators send to their party leaders and the caucus committees responsible for coordinating the assignment process. A perusal of such letters[3] reveals one consistent and overwhelming theme in members' committee preferences—they are very concerned with landing a slot or slots that serve the needs of their district *and* doing so, they believe, will assist in their reelection efforts.

Requests for assignment to specific panels based upon district characteristics and interests run the gamut from traditionally considered constituency-oriented committees, like Agriculture and Public Works, to those more often deemed policy-oriented, such as Judiciary, Education and Labor, or Banking. For instance, during late 1974 Representative-elect Floyd Fithian of Indiana wrote that a seat on Agriculture "would allow me to better serve my constituents . . . [and] is the first major step toward reelection in 1976." Similarly, the first request of Representative-elect Allan Howe of Utah was assignment to the minor committee, Interior and Insular Affairs, because of his constituents' concern for issues under its jurisdiction, like "public lands, parks, energy and Indian problems." Representative-elect Phil Sharp of Indiana indicated that he had promised in his campaign for the Tenth District to address the area's unemployment and housing issues and thus was seeking an assignment to the Banking, Currency, and Housing Committee. Representative-elect Mark Hannaford of California pursued a seat on Education and Labor because his Los Angeles district includes "the largest University in the West" (California State University–Long Beach).

Of course, it is not just the member who benefits from assignment to a particular panel. Since neighboring colleagues and especially constituents potentially profit when a legislator gains a choice committee seat, both frequently lobby on a member's behalf for a desired assignment. It is not surprising, for example, to find senior incumbent members advocating a specific panel slot for a neighboring representative. Such action seems quite reasonable and even prudent. If a legislator is denied an assignment that might benefit his district due to limits on total assignments, the next best thing is for the member representing the adjacent district to gain a seat on that committee. There is nothing to keep government benefits resulting from a legislator's committee work from flowing across district lines. Moreover, constituency groups—those with a direct interest in the work assignment of their representatives—also lobby party leadership to help a member land a choice panel slot.[4] For instance, the Oklahoma Wheat Growers Association wrote to Speaker Carl Albert in 1974 to support Representative-elect Glenn English's (Sixth District of Oklahoma) pursuit of an assignment to the Agriculture Committee. This was undoubtedly an effective strategy for such a group, since the Speaker was also an Oklahoman.

The linkage among district interests, members' committee assignments, and their evolving strategies for reelection seems a relatively routine feature of the process of composing legislative panels each term. The question is how pervasive this experience is across committee types and over time. Answering this question is a first step in recognizing the influence of reelection motivations on committee stability. As expressed in the previous chapter, a gains-from-exchange, or distributive, structure to the congressional committee system should result in two empirical regularities: (1) committees with relatively well-defined spheres of influence should attract representatives from districts with acute economic or social interests in the programs and policies under their jurisdiction, and (2) the structure of the policymaking process in combination with committees disproportionately composed of high-demand representatives should result in policies that unevenly impart targeted benefits to the districts of committee members and high-demand nonmembers.

This is the first of two chapters that examine the aforementioned propositions of the gains-from-exchange theory of House committee structure. To test the hypotheses of committee composition, I tread through a well-worn field of recent congressional scholarship—the committee outlier debate—but do so with a new approach to the question of member preferences. This approach, I believe, addresses more directly the question of the overrepresentation of concentrated constituency interests on House committees. I examine a number of empirical and methodological debates in previous literature, including questions concerning the measurement of member preferences and procedures for testing preference outliers. I also describe how I constructed the new measures of constituency demand and the outliers tests used for separate analyses of the authorizing committees and Appropriations subcommittees, using data covering almost fifty years.

Prior Research on Committee Composition

Committee assignments and composition have long been the subject of speculation and study by congressional scholars, and this research has largely taken the same empirical and theoretical direction as other work on legislative structure. For years, researchers would make suggestions about the makeup of different committees and offer assertions concerning the process of assigning members to panels with little systematic basis for their accuracy or consistency (Goodwin 1970; Morrow 1969). For the most part, this speculation was based upon anecdotal or qualitative evidence. In many ways these data supported the distributive contention as to committee structure. Certain committees were frequently noted as being composed of representatives from districts with disproportionate concern for the federal programs under their specific jurisdictions.

In the 1960s speculation about the committee assignment process gave way to more focused study and data collection on the subject. Scholars such as Masters (1961) and Bullock (1976) began to provide evidence as to legislators' motivations in pursuing specific committee seats and the party objectives in granting those assignments. Though these studies offered insights into a structural feature of Congress for which there was little concrete or long-range evidence, the research was more motivated by the behavioral revolution sweeping the field of political science than by examinations of theories about legislative structure or legislator conduct.

The study of committee composition changed considerably in the late 1970s with the publication of Shepsle's (1978) exploration of House

Democratic panel assignments. The research was inspired in many ways by findings in two realms of congressional scholarship. The first consisted of work on the subject of committee structure and operations, and the distinctiveness of various panels as identified through those features. The second included individual-level research on the factors influencing legislators' goals, preferences, and behavior. Probably the most influential work in both areas was by one of Shepsle's mentors, Richard Fenno (1973). Shepsle's model of committee assignments shows that while the specific factors influencing assignment to various panels may differ by type of committee or member seniority, the overwhelming consistency is that the Democratic committee on committees generally tries to accommodate the individual "interests" of rational legislators.

Since Shepsle's seminal work, numerous authors have viewed the topic of committee assignments and resulting membership composition as fertile ground for tests of their theories of congressional organization and committee structure. Through analyses of the preferences and characteristics of committee members and their relationship to parent bodies, such as the full chamber or party caucuses, scholars have tried to find support for their most preferred model of legislative structure. At the core of the more prominent positive theories of congressional organization is an assumption about the principles upon which legislative committees are congregated. For instance, the proposition concerning committee membership posed by most distributive theorists follows logically from the theory presented in the previous chapter and often resembles the assertions made by Weingast and Marshall:

Weingast and Marshall's Distributive Prediction on Committee Composition: *Committees are not representative of the entire legislature but instead are composed of "preference outliers," or those who value the position most highly (1988, 148–49).*

Researchers such as Weingast and Marshall, Ray (1980b), and later scholars like Hall and Grofman (1990) and Londregan and Snyder (1994) conducted tests showing that committees are often dominated by members with extreme policy preferences. These findings, scholars claim, comport with the principles of a distributive model of committee structure.

Reacting to the work of distributive theorists, particularly that of Shepsle and Weingast, Gilligan and Krehbiel (1989, 1990) question this claim regarding committees with extreme aggregate preferences and pose their own assumptions about panel composition based on the tenets of the informational model of legislative organization. They assume that legislative committees with vastly different preferences from those of the parent body (in this case, the entire chamber) are informationally inefficient, and thus the legislature will discourage their development. Krehbiel offers an alternative prediction about the makeup of committees:

Krehbiel's Informational Prediction on Preference Outlying Committees: *Legislative committees will* not, *as a matter of practice, be composed predominantly of high demanders or preference outliers (1991, 95).*

Krehbiel's research supports the claim that the preferences of committees are largely representative of the chamber as a whole and thus comport with an informational understanding of the role of committees in the policymaking process. Subsequent examinations of the same question using slightly different data and statistical techniques support Gilligan and Krehbiel's findings (Groseclose 1994a, 1994b; Poole and Rosenthal 1997).

Purveyors of a partisan theory of legislative organization, of course, could not avoid this debate over committee composition. The most thorough treatment has been presented by Cox and McCubbins, who assert that "assignments to committees are made in order to further some collective goal, such as the number of seats that the party will win at the next election" (1993, 189). However, the translation of this conjecture into specific hypotheses for the composition of committees is slightly more complicated than in the previous theories. Cox and McCubbins, as described in chapter 2, offer a typology of committee assignments according to the breadth of congressional districts affected by the decisions made by each panel. For example, committees with "uniform externalities," those whose decisions affect all non–committee members about equally,[5] can be thought of as "public goods" suppliers and will, therefore, be intensely scrutinized to ensure that each party's contingent is representative of the caucus as a whole. Alternatively, committees with "targeted externalities," those whose policy decisions are "concentrated on a narrow set of constituents in a small number of districts,"[6] can be seen as providers of "private goods," and thus their party contingents are not as closely monitored for policy preferences corresponding with those of the caucus generally. Finally, the powers of "mixed" committees can reach both concentrated populations and broad groups of constituencies.[7] While it is hard to identify exactly where the party contingents of this last group of committees should be on the caucus "representativeness" continuum, Cox and McCubbins assert that the closer they are to targeted externalities panels, the less representative they will be, while the closer they are to uniform externalities panels, the more parallel will be their party contingents.

Though varying by committee and era, studies such as those by Cox and McCubbins and Kiewiet and McCubbins (1991) find that for the most part the central tendencies of Democratic and Republican contingent preferences are analogous with those of their parent caucus. Again, using slightly different measures of policy preference and varied methodologies, the findings in support of the partisan model are further strengthened by the research of Poole and Rosenthal (1997) and Maltzman (1997).

Despite the mounting evidence disputing distributive preference outlying committees, I maintain that previous research has focused on the wrong measures of legislator "preference" (elaborated below) for distributive hypotheses of panel composition. I begin with the standard gains-from-exchange claim that committees are composed of legislators representing districts with similar and high-demand interests:

> **Committee Composition Hypothesis:** *House committees, especially those with constituency-oriented jurisdictions, are composed of members from districts with acute interests in the particular policy benefits within the panel's jurisdiction and, thus, will exhibit an aggregate level of constituency demand that is significantly different from that in the chamber as a whole.*

As noted in chapter 2, I apply a liberal interpretation to the potential for standing committees to serve the constituency interests of representatives. That is, I test the distributive capacity of panels beyond those traditionally considered to be "constituency-oriented"—(Agriculture, Armed Services, Interior and Insular Affairs, Merchant Marine and Fisheries, Public Works and Transportation, Science, Small Business, and Veterans' Affairs; see Deering and Smith 1997, 64). Other House panels have the ability to provide monetary or other forms of special consideration from government for influential groups within members' districts, and these do not always resemble the traditional "pork barrel" project. For example, a seat on the Banking, Finance, and Urban Affairs Committee may allow a legislator to influence the agenda on a new urban redevelopment program important to her struggling inner-city neighborhoods, or may offer an opportunity to shape more favorable legislation for depository insurance to help the large bank holding company in her district. Alternatively, an assignment to Foreign Affairs, with its influence over the massive foreign aid bills, may be important to a member whose district has a large immigrant population from countries dependent upon development funds from the United States Agency for International Development. Finally, assignment to Education and Labor might be useful for representatives from industrial areas with politically active, working-class communities, since the panel controls policy decisions regarding such things as fair labor standards and labor-management relations.

I contend in a similar fashion that Appropriations subcommittees hold the same distributive attraction to members of Congress because of their direct authority over spending decisions and their relatively concentrated jurisdiction (see also Rundquist and Ferejohn 1975). Therefore, we should also find that Appropriations subcommittees are composed of legislators with high concentrations of district demand for the programs within their policy boundaries. This assertion conflicts directly with Kiewiet and McCubbins's declaration that Appropriations subcommittees are so broad and heterogeneous that it is impossible to define specific constituency characteristics that would identify a district as a "high-demander" for the programs under the jurisdiction of a particular subpanel (1991, 130–31). I argue just the opposite: that the jurisdictions of these subcommittees are often as narrow as those of standing committees, and in some cases even more so (e.g., Military Construction, Energy and Water, etc.).

Finally, rather than assuming that parties will automatically try to seize control of committee contingents on certain panels during periods of heightened partisanship, as Cox and McCubbins's cartel theory would contend, I let the existing hypothesis stand and test how well the distributive propositions hold under such changing partisan conditions. If House committees exhibit fewer distributive characteristics with respect to membership during these highly partisan eras, then this would support the notion that a gains-from-exchange committee structure is conditional on the state of member partisanship and strong caucus authority over committee makeup. Alternatively, I assert, in a fashion similar to the Aldrich and Rohde (1997a) conditional party government theory, that parties can benefit by allowing members freedom in choosing committees with district relevance. Therefore, I contend that electorally driven preferences over congressional organization and committee membership in many ways transcend partisanship and party politics, and this analysis will measure their scope.

> **Committee Composition under Conditional Party Government Hypothesis:** *In periods of heightened partisanship and increased caucus control of congressional structure, committees will be composed of members representing districts with extreme interests in the programs under their jurisdiction.*

Measuring Member Preferences

On the issue of measuring member "preferences," I argue that existing literature on committee composition has not adequately treated the

implications of distributive theory. Most recent studies of committee composition gauge the policy preferences of legislators by using some variation on ideology scores culled from roll-call votes. Normally ideology
scores place members on a liberal-conservative continuum according to
their voting patterns during a specific period of time or for a set of relevant roll-calls. Often scholars employ a measure of general political ideology such as that generated from a small number of key roll-call votes,
like the scores produced by the Americans for Democratic Action (Cox
and McCubbins 1993; Groseclose 1994b; Krehbiel 1991; Weingast and
Marshall 1988), or they use a rating constructed from the entire universe
of recorded votes in a given congressional term, like Poole and Rosenthal's NOMINATE scores (Poole and Rosenthal 1997; Kiewiet and McCubbins 1991; Londregan and Snyder 1994).[8] Occasionally scholars dissatisfied with general ideology ratings utilize more issue-specific measures
of policy preferences generated from appropriate roll-call votes, like the
agriculture-oriented ratings produce by the National Farmers Union or
the defense and military-support scores of the American Security Council
(see, for example, Krehbiel 1991). Similarly, Maltzman created his own
measures of committee "congruence" and "divergence" with the preference of parent bodies from a selection of jurisdiction-specific roll-call
votes (Maltzman and Smith 1994; Maltzman 1997).

While roll-call-based ideology scores may be adequate for certain studies of committee composition, particularly those aiming to specifically assess the congruence of committee and floor ideological positions, they are
not adequate for the main premise of distributive theory. A primary tenet
of the gains-from-exchange model of legislative organization is *not* that
congressional committees are composed of members with extreme *ideological* preferences, but that they are composed of members who seek to
provide for the specific social or economic needs of their constituencies,
and that this is best done through assignment to a particular panel. The
argument is not ideological, but is based on a notion of distinct constituent or district policy demands. "The basic assumption of the distributive
theory is that congressmen are motivated to serve the economic interests
of their constituencies. The theory states simply that congressmen are best
able to benefit their constituencies if they are members of standing committees with jurisdiction over government activities that affect their constituencies" (Rundquist and Ferejohn 1975, 88). Committees, according
to this view of outlier panels, should be primarily composed of legislators
from constituencies with high demand for that specific panel's policy jurisdiction rather than having extreme aggregate ideological preferences.
This may explain why a large percentage of studies using ideology scores

failed to detect a significant number of committees with outlying preferences.[9] The lack of evidence for wide-spread, homogeneous high-demand
panels has led many scholars to conclude that the distributive model of
congressional committees is incorrect.

I propose that a more suitable test of the gains-from-exchange model
of committee composition uses data on the characteristics of congressional districts rather than the ideological scores of members of Congress.
The critical assumption here is that we can draw some inferences about
legislator preferences or at least gain a better understanding of some of
the strong motivating factors behind their actions from the characteristics of the people and places they represent (see Hall and Grofman 1990,
157–58).

Krehbiel disputes this notion of constituency-induced legislative preferences on the premise that it "ignores the prospect that modal preferences among geographic and reelection constituents may differ substantially" (1991, 117). As an example, Krehbiel points out the different
reelection constituencies of former California Senators Alan Cranston
and Pete Wilson. It is easy to see how two senators in the largest and most
diverse state in the union might rely on different coalitions of voters for
their elections while ignoring the political concerns of other sizable voting groups in the state. On the other hand, a representative of a considerably smaller constituency (as of the 1990 Census, most congressional districts comprise little more than one-half million constituents) is unlikely
to disregard the policy demands of, say, farmers and farm workers in a
district where they are 20 percent of the population, as they are in Cal
Dooley's district in the San Joaquin Valley of California. Nor would a representative disregard the legislative interests of the military in a district
with a military population of 15 percent and seven major military installations, such as Owen Pickett's Virginia district, which is home to the U.S.
Navy's Atlantic fleet.[10] I employ a measure of constituency demands that
captures the relative size of relevant constituent groups in congressional
districts for each committee examined.

I am not the first to propose the use of constituency characteristics to
gauge the "representativeness" of congressional committees (see Arnold
1979; Cowart 1981). For example, Arnold examined the location of military installations and the size of military employment in the districts of
Armed Services Committee members versus the entire chamber. Hall and
Grofman (1990) studied the extent of Senate Agriculture subcommittees'
divergence from the position of the chamber using government commod-
ity and agriculture-related payments to congressional districts. However,
up to now no one has devised a method of contrasting the constituency

characteristics of committee members with those of the chamber using some of the more sophisticated statistical techniques developed within the current debate, nor has anyone explored members' district characteristics and committee assignments for numerous committees over long periods of time. This is what I do in this chapter.

The Methodological Debates

The previous discussion concerning measurement of legislator preferences raises an obvious question: If the data used to measure legislator preferences in most prior studies of committee membership has essentially been the same, then why would there be any variation in the findings? What has differed among the studies are the quantitative methods used to measure central tendency and to compare principal (the chamber or caucus) and agent (the committee or party contingent on the committee) preferences.

The first question raised in this debate over statistical methods, which seems to have been largely settled, is whether to employ *means* or *medians* as the measure of central tendency. Several studies comparing the mean of a committee and "floor" on various general ideological scores use standard, two-sample, difference-in-means or *t*-tests (Cox and McCubbins 1993; Hall and Grofman 1990; Krehbiel 1990, 1991; Londregan and Snyder 1994). However, since the focus of these studies is to explain differences in preferences in a policy decision-making environment, means have less theoretical significance as a measure of the central tendency of legislative bodies like congressional committees. Most theoretical studies of decision-making institutions stress the importance of the *median* voter in a majority-rule committee setting for determining policy outcomes (Black 1958; Shepsle 1979). That is, it is not the *average* of the distribution of member preferences that determines the aggregate policy position of the winning coalition in this environment, but an actual median individual who is the critical actor in determining a policy equilibrium.

Moreover, the standard, two-sample, difference-in-means test cannot actually test the null hypothesis of $\mu_F = \mu_{C_i}$, where μ_F is the mean score of what is often called the floor, or chamber, and μ_{C_i} is the mean score of committee i. The reason for this is that committee members must be excluded from μ_F, or else the two samples would not be truly independent of each other, and this violates a basic principle of the two-sample t-test (Hogg and Craig 1995; Rice 1995). Consequently, the actual null hypothesis being tested under the two-sample framework is whether or not members of a particular committee are different from the *rest of the chamber* (non–committee members). The chamber-minus-committee-members is not the appropriate decision-making body for comparison.

Thus, as the debate over committee composition has intensified, the theoretical and methodological importance of medians has quickly penetrated the discussion. However, the shift from the use of committee and floor means to medians has necessitated more varied and sometimes rather ingenious tests of principal-agent differences. At the start the only seemingly acceptable statistical test of "difference-in-medians" was the Wilcoxon signed-rank test, which Cox and McCubbins (1993) used in combination with NOMINATE scores.[11] Dissatisfied with the existing median tests (or more appropriately, the *lack* of adequate tests), a number of researchers devised their own methods of evaluation based upon basic principles of sampling distribution and Monte Carlo simulation techniques. For instance, Londregan and Snyder (1994), assuming that some measurement error is always involved in any ideological gauge of members' preferences, employ a bootstrapping technique (see Mooney and Duval 1993) to create a distribution of median ideal NOMINATE points that are used to measure the "statistical significance" of preference disparity between committees and the chamber. Similarly, Poole and Rosenthal (1997) employ a Monte Carlo sampling technique to create standard errors for the floor medians that are utilized in devising *p*-values for the measurement of outlier committees. Their technique takes into account the actual distribution of membership slots (number of possible seats) on each committee for both parties every congressional term. To further model the process of committee assignments, Poole and Rosenthal also account for members who have multiple committee positions in their process of creating randomly composed committee rosters. Finally, Groseclose (1994b) devised a more straightforward test of difference-in-medians based upon the same Monte Carlo techniques and principles of sampling distributions. He simply runs a simulation that constructs thousands of "sample" committees of randomly selected members (without replacement) from the entire chamber membership for each real committee and then reports each of their medians. Using these sample committee medians as a distribution, Groseclose determines whether or not a committee is a preference outlier by comparing the actual median with that of the distribution, applying a rejection region, or *p*-level, of .05 or less (a committee is considered an outlier if its median is greater than 95 percent or more of the sample medians).

Affirming the knowledge gained through numerous innovative studies, I incorporate many of the methodological advances in my tests of committee composition. First, I employ committee medians rather than means as my measure of central tendency.[12] Second, I utilize a difference-in-medians test based on a Monte Carlo sampling technique in order to create a distribution of medians. The methodology, similar to the Groseclose analysis, samples from the chamber populations ten thousand times to create a distribution of committee medians that can be used for comparison with the actual panel median.

The Question of Committee *Assignment* versus *Request* Data

One common critique about many of the above-mentioned studies of committee composition is that they employ data on the actual *granted* assignments rather than the *requested* committee assignments. Essentially, the critique is that received assignments may not be a good indication of legislators' assignment preferences. The argument is that panel seats granted may depend more on vacancies available than on members' expressed desires. Notwithstanding such critiques, I employ assignment rather than request data (for such data see Canon, Nelson, and Stewart 1994), but offer several justifications for doing so. First, while *assignments* are tempered by the obvious restrictions of limited committee size (not all "high-demanders" can be on their first-choice committee), and although assignments and transfers are not the results of a pure self-selection process, *requests* suffer from an equally important "sincerity" problem. That is, requests, because of the same restriction of limited vacancies and an assignment process facilitated (to a greater or lesser extent) by party caucuses, are not always a true representation of members' actual assignment preferences (Shepsle 1978; Munger 1988).

Evidence of the strategic behavior of committee requests can be observed by returning to the assignment request letters and memoranda sent to party leaders and the caucus Committee on Committees. These documents reveal explicitly that representatives have tempered and readjusted their committee assignment requests according the availability of open panel slots. For instance, soon after her election in 1974, Marilyn Lloyd expressed a ranked preference ordering of Agriculture, Appropriations, and Education and Labor assignments that would help her to provide for the needs of her eastern Tennessee district and ensure her reelection. Three weeks later, in a second letter to Speaker Carl Albert, she readjusted her assignment preferences, which were now Public Works and Veterans' Affairs. No doubt the metamorphosis occurred after Lloyd realized that she would have little chance of receiving at least the first two of her original choices, since more senior Tennessee Democrats already had seats on those panels. Again Lloyd indicated that her preferences and ranking were based upon her constituency needs. Representative-elect John Krebs of Fresno, California, experienced a similar change of heart, changing his request for a slot on Foreign Affairs to a new preference for a seat on Judiciary, after a conversation with Speaker Albert. As for Representative-elect Mark Hannaford, who had requested Education and Labor because his district included California State University–Long Beach, a conversation with retiring California legislator Dick Hanna convinced him that he could better serve his district, particularly its concern with the "activities of the Long Beach harbor," as a member of the Commerce Committee. He subsequently changed his request assignment.[13]

Second, if the critique is that requests are a "better" representation of legislators' constituency interests than the actual assignments, then one should be less likely to find outlier committees when using assignments data. If members who most "need" particular committee assignments (the ones who presumably would make such requests) are not necessarily the ones *granted* the assignments, then there is a greater likelihood of heterogeneity in the constituency characteristics of both committee and floor memberships and a smaller probability of finding outlier committees. This would bias tests in favor of "representative" committees and make results in the other direction that much more convincing.

Finally, the overriding reason for the use of assignment rather than request data is that gathering request data for long periods of time is prohibitively difficult. For example, Shepsle's study of sixteen years (eight congressional terms) of request data required the generosity of three other political scientists and two congressional staff members to allow him to inspect information on assignments for just one party (Shepsle 1978, 7, n. 4). For the current study, I would have required request data for both parties over fifty years, including requests for Appropriations subcommittee assignments.

Hypotheses of Committees as High-Demanders

Standing Committees

The "textbook" classification of congressional committees, which is largely based on the pioneering research of Richard Fenno (1973), places committees in one of three categories on the basis of the reasons members give for seeking a specific assignment (see also Deering and Smith 1997). *Prestige* panels, often considered the most desirable assignments, are those regarded as the "movers and shakers" of the chamber. They are responsible for many of the most important matters considered by the legislature—devising spending legislation (Appropriations), devising taxing legislation (Ways and Means), and directing legislative traffic (Rules). *Policy* committees, on the other hand, attract representatives with a personal interest in managing public policy of national importance. These include panels with a wide range of policy jurisdictions—Banking, Finance, and Urban Affairs; Energy and Commerce; Foreign Affairs; Judiciary; and Government Operations. The third category includes *constituency* or *re-election* committees, which are preferred because they serve a critical district need (as described above). Agriculture; Armed Services; Interior and Insular Affairs; Merchant Marine and Fisheries; Public Works and Transportation; Post Office and Civil Service; Science, Space, and Technology; Small Business; and Veterans' Affairs offer members numerous opportunities to influence specialized policy matters of potential importance to their constituents.[14]

However, these committee categories are not entirely inflexible. For example, Deering and Smith's most recent set of interviews concerning members' motives for committee assignments, conducted for the 100th (1987–88) and 101st Congresses (1989–90), found that preference for membership on two of the chamber's most important panels, Appropriations and Energy and Commerce, were more driven by constituency than prestige or policy considerations. Similarly, other policy committees (e.g., Banking, Education and Labor, etc.) often have many members who are driven by constituency motivations (Deering and Smith 1997).

Rather than assuming that only a few committees traditionally considered "constituency-oriented" can provide government benefits to legislators' districts, I argue that a much larger number are capable of attracting members whose purpose is to supply benefits or policy outputs for re-election purposes. Thus, many more panels are potentially composed of members with special constituency interests in the policy benefits under their control. Accordingly, I use each committee's policy jurisdiction to derive "profiles" of congressional district characteristics that would indicate greater demand for the policy benefits that a panel controls (the methodology is described in more detail below).[15]

Table 1 provides a general sketch of congressional district profiles expected to be "high demanders" with regard to the jurisdiction of thirteen standing House committees. The demand characteristics for most committees are straightforward. For example, agriculture districts are likely to want a representative on the Agriculture Committee; coastal districts will prefer a representative on the Merchant Marine and Fisheries Committee. High-demand district types for some other committees can be much less intuitive, like Commerce and its "business-oriented" districts or even Foreign Affairs and its ethnic constituencies.

Appropriations Subcommittees

My expectations for the composition of Appropriations subcommittees are generally quite similar to those for House standing committees; however, the theoretical debate within which they are embedded is slightly different. The traditional belief about the composition of Appropriations subcommittees, which conforms with the notion that members are guardians of the federal treasury, is that subcommittee assignments are made through a practice of "non-advocacy" (Fenno 1966, 141–42). That is, these "guardians" are granted seats on subcommittees in a manner intended to avoid possible conflicts of interest resulting from their gaining control over budgets for federal programs that matter to their constituencies. This perspective is frequently attributed to the Appropriations Committee prior to the budgetary reforms in the mid-1970s, and is often referred to as the "Cannon-Taber norm." [16] Robert Wallace's understanding of Appropriations subcommittee assignments was typical of many who studied the committee in 1950s and 1960s: "Those who serve on the House [Appropriations] subcommittees represent regions that have little stake in the appropriations under their subcommittee's jurisdiction and thus subcommittee members do not quaver at the thought of substantial [budget] reductions" (Wallace 1960, 29). As late as 1983, Maass held that in spite of the changes in the budgetary process, the membership of the Appropriations Committee has retained many of its traditional norms, including those of budget cutting (1983, 130–35).

The "guardian" notion of Appropriations subcommittee composition conforms to one of the main predictions of Krehbiel's informational theory—the outlier principle. Krehbiel states that in order to avoid informationally inefficient and/or distributionally nonmajoritarian committees, a legislature will purposely try to prevent the formation of panels with drastically different or high-demand preferences. This standard is even more likely for a committee whose powers are as far-reaching and important as Appropriations. In fairness, however, Krehbiel does not insist that committees must be composed of "disinteresteds," but he does argue that they will be heterogeneous and representative of the spectrum of preferences in the chamber as a whole (Krehbiel 1991, 95–96).

More recent claims about Appropriations, particularly since the budgetary reforms of the 1970s, contend that its subcommittees are composed of legislators seeking to benefit their congressional districts through assignment to panels with jurisdiction over relevant federal programs and agencies (LeLoup 1980, 122). Schick posits that one of the primary reasons for this change in the early 1970s was that members no longer

Table 1 Committees, High-Demand Congressional Districts, and Demand-Side Measures

Standing Committee/ Appropriations Subcommittee	District Types with Highest Expected Demand	Demand-Side Measures
Agriculture Committee *Agriculture, Rural Development, and Related Agencies Appropriations Subcommittee*	Agriculturally-oriented districts	Percentage employed in farming, fishing, and wildlife (*Census Occupational Code*) Percentage living in rural farming areas
Armed Services Committee *Defense Appropriations Subcommittee Military Construction Appropriations Subcommittee*	Districts with military installations and/or high levels of military employment	Number of military installations Number of major military installations (fort, base, air force base, etc.) Size of "military workforce" (noncivilian labor force)
Banking, Finance, and Urban Affairs Committee	Destitute urban districts or those with large numbers of constituents employed in banking/finance	Percentage living in urban areas Percentage African-American Percentage unemployed District contains one of the fifty largest cities (dummy) Size of the state's banking assets Percentage employed in finance, insurance, and real estate (*Census Occupational Code*, only from the 1970s–90s)
Education and Labor Committee *Labor, Health and Human Services, Education and Related Agencies Appropriations Subcommittee*	Districts with underfunded school systems or those with strong union interests	Percentage employed in blue-collar industries (*Census Occupational Code*) Percentage of state workforce unionized Percentage attending public elementary and high school Median family income

Energy and Commerce Committee	Districts with high levels of employment in commerce or transportation	Percentage employed in wholesale and retail trade Percentage employed in transportation and public utilities (*Census Industry Code*)
Commerce, Justice, State, and the Judiciary Appropriations Subcommittee	Districts that are poor, in urban areas, with large percentages of minorities and immigrants, have high crime rates or maritime concerns	Percentage African-American Percentage living in urban areas Percentage self-employed Percentage foreign born District borders a coastal area or the Great Lakes (dummy) District is in a city with one of the twenty-five most active ports (dummy)
Foreign Affairs Committee	Districts with populations interested in large foreign aid or foreign policy programs	Percentage foreign born Total percentage of Irish ancestry Total percentage of Italian ancestry Total percentage of Polish ancestry Total percentage of Russian ancestry
Government Operations	Districts with high levels of federal employment	Percentage employed by the government (*Census Class of Worker Code*) District within 100 miles of Washington, D.C. (dummy)
Interior and Insular Affairs Committee *Interior and Related Agencies Appropriations Subcommittee*	Rural districts with large land areas controlled by the Interior Department or large numbers of Native Americans	State acreage owned by the National Park Service and Bureau of Land Management Population density
Judiciary Committee	Districts with high levels of interest in civil rights and legal issues	Percentage African-American Percentage living in urban areas District contains one of the fifty largest central cities (dummy)

(*continued*)

Table 1 (continued)

Standing Committee / Appropriations Subcommittee	District Types with Highest Expected Demand	Demand-Side Measures
Merchant Marine and Fisheries Committee	Coastal districts, particularly those with large ports and districts with maritime academies	District borders a coastal area or the Great Lakes (dummy) District contains Merchant Marine, Coast Guard, or state maritime academy (dummy) District is in a city with one of the twenty-five most active ports (dummy)
Post Office and Civil Service Committee Treasury, Postal Service, and General Government Appropriations Subcommittee	Districts with high levels of postal or civil service employment	Percentage employed by the government (Census Class of Worker Code)
Public Works and Transportation Committee	Districts with high levels of interest in large public works projects, particularly those which safeguard against natural disasters	Percentage employed in transportation and public utilities (Census Industry Code) Percentage employed in construction (Census Industry Code) Relative flood-potential level Percentage unemployed
Energy and Water Appropriations Subcommittee	Districts with high flood potential or interests in energy research and development	Relative flood-potential level Location of nuclear power facilities. Location of top 100 research universities

Transportation and Related Agencies Appropriations Subcommittee	Districts with many workers in transportation, or with urban or coastal areas	Percentage employed in transportation and public utilities (*Census Industry Code*) Percentage employed in construction (Census Industry Code) Percentage unemployed Percentage living in urban areas District contains one of the fifty largest central cities (dummy) District borders a coastal area or the Great Lakes (dummy)
Veterans' Affairs Committee	Districts with a substantial number of veterans or large facilities administered by the VA	Percentage of state population who are veterans (male only) Number of beds in district VA hospital
VA, HUD, and Independent Agencies Appropriations Subcommittee	Districts in urban areas with large poor populations, or substantial numbers of veterans, or large facilities administered by the VA.	Percentage living in urban areas District contains one of the fifty largest central cities (dummy) Median family income Percentage of population who are veterans Number of beds in district VA hospital

needed approval for subcommittee assignments from the committee leadership, but could pick their seats in accord with a seniority-based procedure. Moreover, Schick goes so far as to argue that "[e]ven in the heyday of fiscal control, Appropriations subcommittees tended to be dominated by program supporters; the forced placement of 'indifferents' on the subcommittees was an exceptional practice" (1980, 432; see also White 1989).[17] The "claimant" notion of Appropriations members conforms with our accepted understanding of reelection-oriented politicians using congressional institutions to enhance their electoral prospects (Fiorina 1989; Mayhew 1974a).

Changing Expectations of Committee Composition under Conditional Party Government

In 1994, the established understanding of the composition of both standing House committees and Appropriations subcommittees was challenged by the Republican takeover of the House in the 104th Congress. With the intention of drastically altering the operations and output of committees, Newt Gingrich and the GOP leadership changed the process of granting standing committee assignments for Republican Party members. In order to ensure that all of the party rank-and-file would conform to the leadership agenda, conference leaders assumed a substantially larger percentage of votes for committee assignments in what was being called the Steering Committee, with the Speaker and Majority Leader together controlling almost one-quarter of the votes (Aldrich and Rohde 1997b).

Moreover, the House GOP leadership's desire to reduce federal spending and alter the existing bipartisan and self-serving patterns on the Appropriations Committee manifested themselves in two ways (Aldrich and Rohde 2000). First, Gingrich selected Robert Livingston (R-LA) as the full committee chair, leap-frogging several more senior Republicans largely because they were perceived as not being partisan or aggressive enough to cut federal spending (Evans and Oleszek 1997, 87). Second, Gingrich required that all GOP Appropriations members sign a "letter of fidelity" that bound them to follow the leadership's plan of budget cutting (Evans and Oleszek 1997, 120). Finally, Republican rhetoric during the transition was intended to signal to potential Appropriations assignees that it would no longer protect pet programs and funnel benefits to congressional districts (Aldrich and Rohde 2000; Deering and Smith 1997, 67–68).

The objectives set forth by the Republican leadership through management of committee assignments and the congressional agenda correspond with the principles of partisan control over legislative structure as expressed in Cox and McCubbins's cartel theory. Nevertheless, the explicit implication about the composition of committees during this partisan era is similar to that of the information and guardian models in one very important way—narrowly focused standing committees and Appropriations subcommittees should *not* be made up of legislators acting as constituency advocates. Gingrich and the GOP leadership saw constituency-oriented Appropriations subcommittees as an impediment to pursuing their partisan policy program. Therefore, under the conditions laid out in this partisan perspective, a period of strong partisanship and dominant caucus authority should reveal committees that are *not* composed of representatives seeking to provide for constituency needs. That is, committees will not be outliers with respect to district characteristics.

Determining Measures of Distributive Need

Because the level of analysis for studying hypotheses concerning House committee composition is the congressional district, I required relatively detailed data of the characteristics of each members' home district. The district-level data, while not explicitly differentiating "geographic" from "electoral" or "primary" constituencies (Fenno 1978), do provide for adequate identification of the relative size of "core constituencies" for each member. In other words, I cannot know with certainty the characteristics of the voters a legislator specifically relies upon for her reelection, but I can compile knowledge of the magnitude or relative importance of certain constituency groups likely to be critical to members for electoral reasons.

General Committee Jurisdictions

The standing committees I chose to examine had to meet at least two criteria. First, for consistency, a committee had to have persisted at least from the Legislative Reorganization Act of 1946 to the end of the 103rd Congress (1993–94).[18] Second, the committee had to have a jurisdiction that included responsibilities other than purely "housekeeping" duties.[19] In addition, I exclude the Ways and Means Committee and the *full* Appropriations Committee because of their broad policy property rights and ability to influence outcomes in a wide range of issue areas considered by the legislature. This left me with thirteen standing House committees that existed between 1943 and 1994, which account for about two-thirds of all standing House committees in this period and provide ample evidence for the analysis. Similarly, I chose to examine the Appropriations subcommittees that appropriate the vast majority of the funds that fall under the control of the full Appropriations Committee. For example, the regular appropriations bills considered by the ten subcommittees chosen for the study made up 98 percent of the funds appropriated by all thirteen subcommittees for FY1998.

Devising measures of "demand" that correspond with the general policy jurisdictions of committees is not a simple task. It requires first determining the general jurisdictions of each congressional committee and then creating acceptable district-level measures to capture the major policy matters under a committee's sphere of influence. The objective in establishing each committee's general jurisdiction is not to capture the entire policy property rights of each one, but to determine which constituencies or characteristics of the electoral district would prompt a representative to have a compelling interest in the authority of a specific committee.[20] This task is obviously much easier for committees whose "statutory" and "common law" (King 1997) jurisdictions serve very specific constituencies (like Agriculture or Merchant Marine and Fisheries) than for those with much broader jurisdictions appealing to universal constituencies (like Energy and Commerce or Judiciary).

I used a combination of primary and secondary sources to construct the general policy jurisdiction of each committee. For the statutory jurisdictions, I examined the House Rules and bill referral as specified in Cannon's (1963) and Deschler's (1977) compilations of referral precedents. Then, to identify the more vague "common law" jurisdictions, I examined case studies of committees in the political science literature for references to the less official, yet still important, dimensions of each committee's policy turf. These included reference works that track committee histories (Anderson 1989; Nelson 1994; Tiefer 1989), as well as specific committee studies (e.g., Henderson 1970; Jones 1961; King 1997; Munger and Fenno 1962; and Perkins 1980). By examining the major issue areas considered and legislated by a specific committee, I then identified key economic, social, and geographic traits that might indicate a particular attraction or "need" for representation on the committee. Note that I treat the general jurisdictions of the committees as largely static over the length of the study. (This assumption is debatable, but as the reader will note, I will ultimately affirm that it is largely correct.)

District-Level Measures of Policy Demand

Once district profiles were established, measures were selected to gauge each congressional district's level of "demand" for representation on a specific committee. If a committee had jurisdiction over multiple policy areas of interest to individual constituencies, then several measures were chosen to capture each dimension. The measures draw quite heavily on

Census information, so that updated data for each district were only calculated every ten years in accord with the schedule of the Census. This inevitably led to some imprecision in the district profiles in the latter part of each decade. Three exceptions to the decennial data occurred for the 1960s, 1980s, and 1990s, when many states underwent court-ordered redistricting (or a threat thereof) due to gross inequalities in district size and when boundaries meant to increase minority representation were found unconstitutional (Butler and Cain 1992, 26–41). New Census data were included for several states that experienced significant redistricting on off-years.[21] County-level Census data for the 1940s and 1950s were aggregated into congressional districts using detailed maps and descriptions of congressional districts.[22]

I supplemented Census information with demographic and geographic data compiled from other sources. In some instances data were gathered using information provided by federal departments and agencies or private institutions. For example, the locations of major Department of Defense installations were identified using maps provided in a biennial publication (United States Department of Defense various years). Various sources were used to identify other such relevant locales, including the location and size of Veterans Administration Hospitals; the twenty-five most active ports; the fifty largest central cities; and the location of maritime academies. Placing these sites in their proper congressional districts for various decades was accomplished using a combination of Census *Congressional District Atlases; Congressional Directories; Congressional Quarterly's Congressional Districts in the 1970s, 1980s, and 1990s; Rand McNally Road Atlases;* a military road atlas (Crawford 1993); U.S. Geological Survey maps; and maps of congressional districts in the 1940s and 1950s provided from a private collection.

A few of the measures adopted come from state-level rather than district-level data. Several scholars have made compelling arguments for the use of state-level data in this type of analysis, mostly based upon the cohesion of state delegations and the representation of state interests on committees. Ferejohn (1974), for example, argued that delegation members can maximize their bargaining advantage and hence their ability to exact projects for their districts by working together en bloc (see also Born 1976; Bullock 1971; Deckard 1972; Fiellin 1970; Rundquist, Lee, and Luor 1995). Nevertheless, state-level information does not always capture the possible conflicting interests of statewide versus district populations. To account for this potential problem, I try to avoid creating additive district need scales that are made up exclusively of statewide measures.

In order to create a single measure of interest in a committee's jurisdiction that can be used in the tests described below, the component measures were combined into one score. The combined scores of committee or
subcommittee "need" were created by standardizing all component measures (a mean of zero and a standard deviation of one) and then summing.[23] For example, the measure of district demand for the jurisdiction
of the Agriculture Committee is an additive scale of standardized measures of both the percentage in each district employed in farming and the
percentage living in rural farming areas. Therefore, members who rank
high on both measures have a greater "need" for the policy benefits provided by the Agriculture Committee than a member who ranks high on
only one of the two components.[24]

Tests of Committees as High-Demanders

Monte Carlo difference-in-medians tests were conducted to examine the
extent to which committee members represented congressional districts
with higher than average demand for particular policy benefits. This simulation procedure allows for tests of the preference-outlier hypothesis for
standing House committees with different distributions of preferences.
The nonparametric technique is not influenced by outliers or the underlying distribution of the data. As previously mentioned, such an approach
usually produces results similar to those of standard means tests; however, violations of parametric assumptions can result in surprisingly different findings between the two analyses. In such cases, the Monte Carlo
simulations produce more reliable results.[25]

For the simulation, the computer constructs ten thousand committees
of randomly selected members from the entire House each term between
the 78th and 105th Congresses. For each simulation, the program saves
the median of a simulated committee of the same size as each actual committee. The ten thousand sample medians for each Congress are used to
derive an approximate distribution of the committee median for the inference tests. For example, to derive the median for the Armed Services
Committee in the 89th Congress, the computer would randomly select
the demand scores of thirty-seven House members (the actual size of the
Armed Services Committee in the 89th Congress) from the entire chamber membership, without replacement.

Perhaps the most important and contentious step in the median tests
is defining the rejection region. Julnes and Mohr (1989) suggest that traditional p-value levels of .05 or less do not adequately protect against
Type II errors, which would imply that past studies using such levels may
have reported results biased in favor of accepting the null hypothesis of

random committee selection. Although concerned with the possibility of Type II errors, I wanted a stringent test for whether a committee is a preference outlier. Thus, I chose a traditional p-value of .05 or less in order to minimize Type I errors. If any bias exists in the tests it would be toward finding *less* evidence in support of outlier theories than actually exists.

In practical terms, the null hypothesis of random committee composition is rejected if less than 5 percent of the simulated medians are as extreme as the actual committee median. For example, the median demand score for the Armed Services Committee of the 87th Congress generates a p-value of .048. That is, I found that out of ten thousand simulations for this particular committee, 480 instances had a median for the randomly assembled committee that was greater than or equal to the actual median demand score of the committee. I would identify this committee as a significant preference outlier, since only 4.8 percent of the randomly created committees had median values that were equal to or greater than the actual committee median.

Notwithstanding the ".05 criterion," there is nothing to prevent one from exploring broader trends in the data even if they do not meet this level of significance. To be sure, a "tendency" in the direction of extreme panel constituency demands might be sufficient evidence to reject a hypothesis that committees are composed of disinterested legislators. Moreover, it may be reasonable, at least for Appropriations subcommittees, to argue that the null hypothesis is not "representativeness," but actual "disinterest." That is, the median member of the Appropriations subcommittee, according to the Cannon-Taber norm, should exhibit even less interest in the programs under the panel's jurisdiction than the median of the chamber. Therefore, I provide the p-values for each committee for the reader to make her own judgment, and I offer some interpretations of my own.

Analysis of House Standing Committees

The preference-outlier hypothesis is that a committee is composed of members representing constituencies who are among the most extreme with respect to demand for the committee's policy benefits. Hence, we should expect the median policy demand score for members of such committees to be higher than the majority of "unbiased," or random, committees. Table 2 provides the results of the Monte Carlo tests for the committee medians for all thirteen committees from 1943 (78th Congress) through 1998 (105th Congress).[26] Most apparent from the analysis of standing committees is that, in a large proportion of cases, committees appear to be composed of members who, on average, rank higher in terms of constituency demand for the programs under their jurisdiction than the

Table 2 Tests of Distributive Outliers for House Committees, 1943–1998

| | Congress (year) | | | | | | | | | | | |
Committee	78th 1943	79th 1945	80th 1947	81st 1949	82nd 1951	83rd 1953	84th 1955	85th 1957	86th 1959	87th 1961	88th 1963	89th 1965
Agriculture	.00	.00	.00	.00	.00	.00	.00	.00	.00	.00	.00	.00
Armed Services						.15	.43	.43	.08	.05	.03	.00
Banking			.69	.13	.43	.63	.00	.58	.00	.00	.03	.02
Education & Labor			.59	.54	.54	.92	.86	.90	.77	.51	.53	.25
Education & Labor (labor-only)	.54	.48	.46	.14	.60	.28	.28	.34	.05	.00	.06	.02
Energy & Commerce	.23	.41	.68	.53	.71	.46	.49	.39	.43	.49	.68	.75
Foreign Affairs	.21	.16	.05	.02	.07	.28	.27	.27	.12	.01	.01	.00
Government Operations	.46	.64	.30	.21	.13	.60	.23	.48	.75	.83	.85	.52
Interior			.00	.00	.00	.00	.00	.00	.00	.00	.00	.00
Judiciary			.45	.57	.29	.45	.38	.12	.05	.14	.48	.27
Merchant Marine	.00	.00	.00	.00	.00	.13	.00	.13	.13	.09	.18	.00
Post Office			.97	.33	.42	.51	.50	.46	.56	.34	.12	.78
Public Works			.19	.04	.05	.08	.02	.02	.22	.11	.02	.01
Veterans' Affairs			.57	.57	.63	.52	.66	.52	.67	.66	.88	.42

NOTE: Figures in the cells are the *p*-values from the Monte Carlo difference-in-medians tests.

chamber as a whole. Furthermore, the committees composed of members from high-demand districts are not necessarily the ones traditionally considered to be constituency-oriented.

High-Demand Constituency Committees

Three committees—Agriculture, Armed Services, and Interior and Insular Affairs—are composed of members whose demand scores are almost always significantly different from that of the floor. It is not surprising that these three committees, so commonly thought of as being constituency-oriented, would be outliers. As a group, Agriculture and Interior committee members always represented districts with aggregate levels of policy demand (actual median demand scores) greater than all of the randomly assembled committees. As expected, Agriculture members have consistently higher proportions of constituents employed in farming and living in rural farming areas than do non–committee members, even as the number of legislators representing traditional "farming" districts has dwindled in recent years (Browne 1995). Similarly, Interior consistently draws its membership from states with enormous amounts of acreage under the authority of the Interior Department (traditionally in the West) and, particularly in recent years, from districts with very low population

Table 2   (continued)

	Congress (year)														
90th 1967	91st 1969	92nd 1971	93rd 1973	94th 1975	95th 1977	96th 1979	97th 1981	98th 1983	99th 1985	100th 1987	101st 1989	102nd 1991	103rd 1993	104th 1995	105th 1997
.00	.00	.00	.00	.00	.00	.00	.00	.00	.00	.00	.00	.00	.00	.00	.00
.00	.00	.00	.00	.00	.00	.00	.00	.00	.00	.00	.00	.00	.00	.00	.00
.02	.06	.03	.00	.11	.11	.04	.04	.09	.50	.43	.77	.83	.05	.00	.38
.17	.16	.22	.06	.79	.87	.24	.77	.02	.04	.10	.00	.00	.05	.36	.13
.04	.00	.00	.00	.04	.02	.13	.52	.02	.00	.00	.00	.00	.02	.26	.18
.51	.51	.50	.05	.19	.28	.20	.64	.40	.27	.27	.21	.18	.65	.62	.62
.00	.00	.00	.05	.01	.01	.05	.01	.00	.00	.00	.00	.00	.01	.01	.01
.78	.87	.80	.84	.68	.68	.12	.86	.61	.69	.74	.70	.47	.79	.81	.87
.00	.00	.00	.00	.00	.00	.00	.00	.00	.00	.00	.00	.00	.00	.00	.00
.67	.53	.25	.37	.17	.42	.36	.44	.05	.04	.04	.17	.25	.07	.01	.44
.13	.16	.12	.00	.00	.00	.00	.20	.10	.07	.07	.09	.06	.06	—	—
.73	.46	.54	.26	.16	.01	.85	.38	.13	.41	.61	.85	.31	.35	—	—
.01	.01	.01	.04	.43	.05	.04	.04	.07	.00	.12	.09	.11	.04	.05	.04
.45	.44	.48	.20	.74	.74	.30	.63	.73	.72	.67	.46	.51	.17	.39	.19

densities. The Armed Services Committee, while not quite as consistently extreme in the mid-1950s, has since steadily attracted members whose districts have large or important military installations with sizable numbers of military personnel.

Three more committees appear to have compositions similar to the previous panels; notably, however, not all are traditionally considered constituency-oriented. For example, for the majority of the period since the early 1950s, Foreign Affairs Committee members as a group have had a much higher proportion of foreign-born constituents than would be expected if the committee were randomly congregated. The Monte Carlo simulations show that twenty-one out of twenty-eight Foreign Affairs Committees are significant outliers at the .05 level or better.[27] The Merchant Marine and Fisheries Committee also draws its membership from a very high-demand constituency, but this seems to fluctuate over time. While in most congressional terms the committee's membership does seem to represent a disproportionate number of districts that are likely to demand more benefits from the maritime panel, in portions of the 1950s, 1960s, and 1980s the *p*-value is frequently between .15 and .06 (greater than 85–94 percent of the random committees), not always meeting the .05 criterion. Finally, the long tradition of "pork barrel" projects handed out by the Public Works Committee suggests that demand attributes of districts will emerge in its membership composition, although this panel is not traditionally thought to serve one particular type of constituency. I discover that Public Works members do commonly rank much higher than most members on employment and flood-control measures for most congresses, and this difference is below the .05 level for seventeen of twenty-six congressional terms.

Finally, two more committees—Banking, and Education and Labor—exhibited characteristics suggesting that they were frequently composed of high-demand members, even though both are usually thought to attract legislators seeking influence over broad federal policy. The median demand score for the Banking Committee is regularly greater than the vast majority of randomly drawn committees, and the p-value is at or below the .05 level for many congresses between the late 1950s and the 1970s, and part of the 1990s. That is, in many years, Banking members disproportionately come from poor urban areas or districts with interests in banking and finance.[28] On the other hand, the broad set of constituency groups interested in issues under the jurisdiction of Education and Labor may have contributed to the non-outlier results for its combined measure of "policy demand" over most of its life until the mid-1980s. However, examining only its labor components (percentage of districts employed in blue-collar industries and percentage of state labor force unionized) reveals that in the majority of congressional terms, starting in the early 1960s, members of the Education and Labor panel have come from blue-collar districts in highly unionized states. Using this "labor-only" measure, Education and Labor's median demand score shows a committee more extreme than 95 percent of the randomly assembled committees in sixteen of twenty congresses since the late 1950s.

Uniform-Demand Constituency (Duty) Committees

As a contrast, more "public goods" committees are seen as offering relatively few opportunities for legislators to provide particularized benefits for constituencies; therefore, it is likely that these panels will only rarely be found to be outliers. Consequently, measures of constituent demand are less likely to tell us much about their makeup. Two committees that Unekis and Rieselbach (1984) characterize as "duty committees" are also the two whose natural constituencies draw most heavily from the pool of federal employees—the Government Operations and Post Office and Civil Service committees. Accordingly, neither panel shows much effect of distributive politics influencing membership composition. The Government Operations Committee, whose jurisdiction encompasses the oversight of executive branch agencies, does not seem to be overrepresentative of legislators with large contingents of federal employees in their districts, nor do its members more frequently come from districts around the Capitol. Members of the Post Office and Civil Service Committee, a panel whose jurisdiction spans federal agencies more broadly, also do not exhibit strikingly different constituency characteristics from the House in most congressional terms.[29] I obtain similar results for the Veterans' Affairs Committee. Tests show that statewide counts of veteran populations or the location of VA hospitals in congressional districts did little to improve our understanding of membership on the Veterans' Affairs Committee.[30]

Other Uniform-Demand Committees

Finally, there are two committees for which it might be possible to discover evidence of high-demand memberships, but for a number of reasons the tests conducted here reveal no such story. The findings of the tests on the Judiciary Committee show a panel that is only periodically composed of members from high-demand districts. This result could arise from one of two factors. First, the demand measures used here, percentage black and percentage urban per district, are a bit narrow when trying to gauge constituent interest in the work done by this committee over the life of this study. Judiciary's jurisdiction was much broader than just the civil rights issues this demand scale captures. Second, it may simply be that Judiciary does not attract members for purposes of distribution of particularized policy benefits to begin with. Although the legislation this panel considers may resonate with a locality's economic or social relations, the policy issues before Judiciary are rarely directed at particular districts or areas. Civil rights, capital punishment, and legal reform are issues that have nearly equal effect on the constituencies in all home districts.

Similarly, the findings for the Energy and Commerce Committee—*p*-values meet the .05 significance level only once (in the 93rd Congress)—may also result from component measures that do not nearly capture the myriad issues and policy arenas that come before this panel. Especially considering the growing common-law jurisdiction of Energy and Commerce in the last twenty years (King 1997), it is difficult to establish a narrow set of constituency characteristics that translate into a distinct interest in a particular part of this committee's policy jurisdiction. In contrast to the policy orientation of the Judiciary Committee, however, the Commerce panel is frequently thought of as offering *numerous* opportunities for legislators to provide for the economic needs of a home district. Therefore, the difficulty in discovering any consistent trend in the constituency

Table 3   Tests of Distributive Outliers for House Appropriations Subcommittees, 1959–1998

	Congress (year)								
Subcommittee	86th 1959	87th 1961	88th 1963	89th 1965	90th 1967	91st 1969	92nd 1971	93rd 1973	94th 1975
Agriculture	.01	.36	.19	.00	.00	.00	.00	.00	.00
Commerce, Justice, State	.16	.65	.78	.76	.66	.80	.85	.50	.95
Defense	.50	.59	.29	.18	.76	.76	.21	.65	.55
Energy & Water	.77	.77	.43	.28	.02	.19	.19	.39	.13
Interior	.61	.78	.11	.27	.18	.18	.09	.00	.58
Labor, HHS, & Education	.22	.22	.12	.06	.31	.31	.44	.70	.19
Military Construction	.26	.24	.01	.18	.13	.17	.13	.20	.02
Transportation					.44	.20	.20	.17	.12
Treasury & Postal Service		.76	.12	.07	.12	.02	.04	.25	.18
VA, HUD & Ind. Agencies	.14	.14	.38	.28	.56	.58	.51	.60	.36

NOTE: Figures in the cells are the *p*-values from the Monte Carlo difference-in-medians tests.

characteristics of members may be a result of this committee's distributive attraction to representatives from *all* congressional districts, rather than its inability to supply particularized benefits.[31]

Analysis of Appropriations Subcommittees

Table 3 provides the results of the Monte Carlo simulations on the Appropriations subcommittee medians for all ten panels from 1959–60 (86th Congress) through 1997–98 (105th Congress).[32] Several subcommittees appear to be composed of representatives from districts with disproportionate interest in the programs under their jurisdiction.[33] Using the .05 level of significance, we find that five of the ten subcommittees are preference outliers with respect to their district profiles at least 25 percent of the time. Like its standing committee counterpart, the Agriculture subcommittee is almost always disproportionately composed of members who represent rural farming districts. The Energy and Water subcommittee frequently has significant membership representing districts with high flood potential or concerned with energy policy; this is most often the case from the mid-1980s to the early 1990s. The VA, HUD, and Independent Agencies subcommittee is frequently composed of members representing urban poor districts or those with extreme interest in veterans' issues— again, this is true mostly for the 1980s. Not surprisingly, Military Construction has members from districts with high military populations or numerous military installations, and these extreme panels are sprinkled throughout the entire forty years of the study. Similarly, the Treasury,

Table 3 (continued)

				Congress (year)						
95th 1977	96th 1979	97th 1981	98th 1983	99th 1985	100th 1987	101st 1989	102nd 1991	103rd 1993	104th 1995	105th 1997
.00	.00	.00	.00	.00	.00	.00	.01	.04	.01	.05
.95	.75	.95	.91	.99	.99	.99	.99	.99	.66	.59
.55	.91	.97	.43	.34	.34	.58	.65	.36	.16	.28
.37	.27	.97	.02	.02	.02	.02	.04	.70	.35	.35
.17	.45	.47	.99	.60	.60	.60	.51	.44	.12	.15
.03	.06	.41	.18	.61	.58	.58	.28	.96	.96	.99
.18	.08	.42	.10	.06	.03	.03	.12	.04	.32	.12
.18	.23	.25	.73	.93	.72	.72	.99	.98	.62	.82
.46	.31	.35	.25	.02	.02	.41	.51	.69	.01	.01
.75	.03	.05	.01	.02	.02	.08	.08	.50	.51	.60

Postal Service, and General Government subcommittee also had a number of panels that were significant outliers in terms of their districts' concern for issues involving government employees that were spread from the 1960s to the 1990s.

Expanding the examination of extreme committees to look for those with disproportionate leaning—that is, for sake of argument, an actual subcommittee membership that tends to be more extreme than 85 percent of the sample panels (a p-value of .15 or less)—I find that two more committees have a trend toward memberships representing relatively high-need constituencies. For example, at different times during the 1960s, 1970s, and 1990s, the Interior subcommittee frequently had a membership representing states with low population densities and large amounts of public land acreage. Also Labor, HHS, and Education members in the mid-1960s and late 1970s tended to represent blue-collar areas or districts with poor public schools.

Furthermore, there is evidence that the overall constituency alignment of Appropriations subcommittees was less probable during the Cannon-Taber era (for the period examined—1959–64) than subsequently. Using the .05 significance level, we find that in two of the three Cannon-Taber terms examined here,[34] only one subcommittee was an outlier, and in one term there were no outliers. Even when I relax the definition of outlier subcommittee membership ($p < .15$), we only begin to see trends toward more widespread outlier contingents in the last of these three terms (the 88th Congress; the Interior; Labor, HHS, and Education; and

Treasury and Postal Service subcommittees). The Cannon-Taber era also includes the only congressional terms when the consistently extreme Agriculture Subcommittee was not an outlier.

Moving beyond the 88th Congress, one finds little evidence that the overall tendency of Appropriations subcommittees to attract high-demand representatives changes significantly (no matter what level of statistical significance one uses). Alterations such as seniority bidding for subcommittee seats, budgetary reforms in the early 1970s, or the takeover by Republicans in 1995 do not lead to any significant changes in the overall trends of these panels. In almost all congressional terms, at least two subcommittees are composed of members with extreme constituency interests—usually Agriculture and some other panel—and a few others have similar, but not quite as extreme, trends. The mid-to-late 1980s cover one period where the overall tendency of outlier panels is altered slightly—increasing to 3–5 subcommittees as outliers.

Committee Composition Changes after the "Republican Revolution"

The change to Republican control of the House in 1995 seems to have had only minor effects on committee composition. Only a few standing committees show any kind of shift in the trends of the district characteristics of members in the 104th or 105th Congresses. The most pronounced change occurred in the Education and Labor Committee (which subsequently changed its name to the Economic and Educational Opportunities Committee). Democrats representing heavily industrial and manufacturing districts lost a large number of seats, contributing to the steep decline in the number of "labor-oriented" members on the committee. This traditionally liberal panel was undoubtedly a target for radical agenda change under a conservative Republican majority. However, for the most part, committees with long-term trends of attracting members with acute constituency interest in the programs under their authority—Agriculture, Armed Services, International Relations (formerly Foreign Affairs), Resources (formerly Interior and Insular Affairs), and Transportation and Infrastructure (formerly Public Works and Transportation)—continued to do so even after the Republican takeover.

On the composition of Appropriations subcommittees, the new majority party and policy agenda had an equally weak effect, although there was one additional wrinkle—a few subcommittees began to show signs of slightly more extreme membership. For instance, members representing military-oriented districts are more evenly distributed between the Defense and Military Construction subcommittees than previously—

Defense becomes more extreme and Military Construction becomes less extreme. Furthermore, two panels, Commerce and Interior, experience rebounds in their high-demand membership at the start of the 104th Congress, which neither had seen since the mid-1970s (although neither reaches the .05 level of significance). Commerce, in particular, seems to have been a panel whose membership for many years was largely composed of "disinteresteds." Treasury, which had a high-demand membership in the mid-1980s also experiences a resurgence of such members with the Republican takeover. Interestingly, two subcommittees, Energy and Water, and VA, HUD, and Independent Agencies, continue trends in the 104th Congress from the previous term toward significantly less extreme memberships.

Conclusion

The findings in this chapter suggest that the distributive nature of House committees cannot simply be dismissed with statistical tests on ideological scores derived from roll-call votes. Congressional district-level data provide different results as to the composition of certain standing committees and Appropriations subcommittees than do previous studies using ideology scores. The profiles of members from several of these panels look much more extreme compared to the floor when we examine district characteristics rather than ideological proclivities. The data reveal that for most of the postwar period, House members often gain assignment to panels of specific interest to their constituents, resulting in panels whose membership is overrepresentative of districts with qualities of particular concern to those panels.

More remarkable is that the standing committees traditionally considered constituency-oriented are not the only ones often composed of representatives from high-demand districts (e.g., Agriculture, Armed Services, Interior and Insular Affairs, Merchant Marine and Fisheries, and Public Works and Transportation); the same is true of some committees usually considered to be policy-oriented (Banking, Finance, and Urban Affairs; Education and Labor [for its "labor-only" measures]; and Foreign Affairs), as well as a large proportion of Appropriations subcommittees (Agriculture; and often Energy and Water; Military Construction; Treasury and Postal Service; and VA, HUD, and Independent Agencies). Thus, despite structural changes such as shifts in partisan control, alterations in the process of committee and subcommittee assignments, and budgetary reforms, seats on many House panels still fall prey to the most fundamental force in congressional politics—the reelection motive. As

stated earlier, representatives need to ensure their own reelection in order to pursue almost any other legislative goal and frequently use even
the most influential committee positions to maximize their probability of
returning to office. This chapter has shown us the scope and boundaries
of the distributive notion of committee composition.

This analysis of committee composition has offered a measure of legislator preferences that is an alternative to the standard ideology score.
Both measures have their shortcomings, but the one employed here seems
more appropriate for a study of the distributive notion of committee
structure. The findings do not necessarily prove that committees are unrepresentative of the chamber in all respects—it may still be the case that
several panels are composed of a broad distribution of *ideological* perspectives. It is not surprising from an informational perspective that in
constructing a committee of low-cost experts, the chamber may simultaneously compose a committee dominated by representatives from
distributively high-demand districts. Nevertheless, the data support the
distributive view that many committees are unrepresentative from the
perspective of constituency demands, and therefore I cast some doubt on
the argument that committees are mainly delegates of higher institutional
authorities (the chamber or party caucus).

Hence, this work does in part reject some of the assertions of previous
research on committee composition. If we accept district characteristics
as a gauge of legislator policy preferences, then Krehbiel's contention—
that "the classical homogeneous high-demand committees seems . . . to be
an endangered species"[35] (1991, 130)—is not supported by the evidence
provided here. This does not preclude that other factors can influence the
behavior of legislators with respect to committees and assignments. For
instance, it may be that legislators are responsible for serving the needs of
their party as committee members (Aldrich and Rohde 1997a; Cox and
McCubbins 1993), but part of that duty includes providing for the constituency needs—and consequently the electoral prospects—of partisan
colleagues. Nevertheless, their foremost responsibility may be to ensure
their own reelection.

The findings here lay the groundwork for the reelection notion of committee stability. That is, one can begin to see why representatives would
reject structural changes to committee jurisdictions—such alterations
would upset existing institutional arrangements that help serve many
members' district needs and thus their reelection strategies. One major
concern with this study of committees is that the measure based on constituency characteristics tells us about what legislators *should be doing*
(whether or not they belong to committees that *could* provide for district

interests) rather than what they are *actually doing* as committee members (actually providing for district needs through committee-controlled government benefits). We may get at the latter issue in several ways, and the next chapter pursues one of them—testing the extent to which federal outlays also reflect a distributive character.

Chapter 4

Distributive Politics and Federal Outlays

PROVIDING FEDERAL LARGESSE FOR LEGISLATORS' HOME DIS-tricts had one of its shining moments in May 1998, when Congress sent to President Clinton a $216 billion, six-year surface transportation bill. The Transportation Equity Act for the Twenty-first Century[1] was by far the largest investment the federal government had ever made in transportation policy and infrastructure, representing an increase of approximately 40 percent above existing spending levels, and would reportedly create an estimated four hundred thousand new jobs in construction, maintenance, and operation of highways and mass transit (Ota 1998a). The enactment would affect every aspect of transportation policy—gasoline taxes, the Highway Trust Fund, contracts to disadvantaged businesses, automobile safety regulations, low-income commuting subsidies, grants for low-polluting buses, and so on. Most important for individual legislators, the bill supplied 1,850 highway and road construction projects worth $9.35 billion, an additional $8.2 billion in special mass-transit projects, and $3 billion in bus programs (Ota 1998c). These earmarked funds were to go to forty-nine of the fifty states, and almost every congressional district.

The process of deciding what funds would go to what projects in what localities and, ultimately, the means by which Congress passed such a massive authorization over the strident objections of Republican budget hawks is a lesson in the power of distributive politics. Congress had been considering a reauthorization of the 1991 Intermodal Surface Transportation Efficiency Act since the start of the

105th Congress.[2] House Transportation and Infrastructure Committee Chair, Bud Shuster (R-PA) advocated a $200 billion-plus bill from the start—significantly more than the Senate's approximately $150 billion reauthorization plan (Weisman 1997). Since House and Senate bill sponsors were unable to agree on the terms for restructuring the formulas to distribute certain highway funds and the proper use of portions of the gasoline tax, Congress in mid-November 1997 was forced to pass a $9.8 billion short-term authorization. The hastily constructed measure avoided what would have been perceived as another Republican-initiated partial government shutdown, since state and federal transportation agencies had been operating on reserves following the expiration of the 1991 transportation authorization on September 30 (Weisman 1997).[3]

As the fiscal outlook for the federal government improved in 1998, the perception on Capitol Hill was that more money would be available for a massive transportation reauthorization measure. In mid-1998, with the life-span of the previous year's stop-gap measure coming to an end, House and Senate bill managers shepherded through floor approval two versions of the transportation act that differed by only $4 billion and a few key policy matters. The differences were eventually worked out in conference in May.

Undoubtedly one of the intentions of bill supporters in both soliciting members' requests for special projects in their home districts (Hosansky 1997) and doling out thousands of district-directed grants that varied from a few hundred thousand dollars to tens of millions of dollars was to build a coalition sizable enough to ensure passage of this extraordinary transportation bill. Throughout the debate on the measure, two large factions of Republicans railed against the bill because (1) its cost would exceed the spending cap agreed to in the 1997 balanced budget measure by somewhere in the neighborhood of $20 billion,[4] and (2) many felt that this type of "pork barrel" legislating directly contradicted the essence of the Republican revolution (Koszczuk 1998).[5]

Of course, the enactment had further potential to anger some constituencies by such provisions as delaying requirements for states to comply with the Clean Air Act's haze standards in specially protected areas or a constraint that legislators offset the overspending by a $1.8 billion cut in services to low-income families and a $15.4 billion reduction in health benefit payments to veterans. On the other hand, the bill had tangible and very salient benefits for the quality of life in many districts. Almost every member could go home and claim credit for bringing back somewhere in the neighborhood of $15 million in special projects monies (VandeHei 1998). These funds were for extremely visible and popular projects like highway maintenance, bridge improvements and reconstruction, or road widening.

Moreover, the funding of special projects went not just to the building of a supermajority for bill passage, but also to help provide for the constituency demands of this traditionally high-demand committee membership (see chapter 3). Members of the panel brought home almost three times the average level of earmarked funds. One early estimate was that top committee members, both Republicans and Democrats, secured over $60 million in district-directed funds (VandeHei 1998). Projects included such things as $30.3 million for a new road in New Hartford and Whitestown, NY—in the district of fourth-ranking Republican Sherwood Boehlert—and $22.1 million for an I-85 bypass in Greensboro, NC—part of sixth-ranking Republican Howard Coble's district.

More important from an electoral standpoint, Shuster and Gingrich had reached an agreement that some of the discretionary spending would help bolster the reelection bids of vulnerable Republicans. Among the GOP members given special consideration were a number of Transportation freshman and sophomores, like Asa Hutchinson (AR), John Cooksey (LA), Bob Ney (OH), and Merrill Cook (UT), as well as non–committee members who were targets for defeat by the Democrats, like Robert Aderholt (AL) and Bob Riley (AL; see VandeHei 1998; Pianin 1998). Care for such marginal legislators was not limited to the House. Senator Alfonse D'Amato (R-NY), facing a number of very high-profile Democratic challengers in his 1998 reelection bid, was successful in securing funds for several large construction projects, including $353 million for a tunnel under the East River for Long Island Rail Road trains to reach Grand Central Station (Ota 1998a).

House Democrats naturally engaged in the exactly the same activity, providing very high levels of transportation funding to such precarious members such as Leonard Boswell (IA), Jay Johnson (WI) and Neil Abercrombie (HI; VandeHei 1998). While there is no direct evidence that these funds were the key to reelection for vulnerable members, in at least one example, Bob Ney's Democratic opponents conceded that he had "gotten an important political boost from all the media attention to his pork-barrel prowess" (Pianin 1998). In what was initially speculated to be a tight race, Ney won with 60 percent of the vote. During the latter part of 1998 the Appropriations subcommittee responsible for transportation matters griped a bit but went along with the earlier authorization and appropriated the needed transportation funds. In fact, by Senator John McCain's (R-AZ) count, the FY 1999 transportation appropriations included more than $200 million in additional funds for projects that were not even previously authorized (Ota 1998b).

Conventional wisdom concerning the distribution of some kinds of particularized federal benefits has in many ways resembled the previous example. That is, politicians shore up their reelection prospects by bringing home targeted funds through mechanisms like the system of committee policy property rights and cross-issue vote trades or logrolling. In fact, the perception that legislators in the House of Representatives are responsible for securing federal benefits for the home district is hardly an invention of the modern Congress. Henry James Ford noted before the turn-of-the-century,

> "What has he done for his district?" is a question which applies the test by which ordinarily the value of a representative is gauged. . . . The dominant idea is that it is the proper business of a member to represent his district, and most people would be surprised to hear that any other idea could be entertained. . . . Hence, the long-established practice of "log-rolling," by which many minority interests are united to form an overwhelming majority. This is the way in which extravagant River and Harbor and Public Buildings appropriations bills are passed. (Ford 1898, 239–42)

One frequently cited example from a more recent period involves Mendel Rivers (D-SC), who for many years was a high-ranking member and eventually chair of the House Armed Services Committee (1965–72). Legislators would joke that if Rivers placed any more military installations in his Charleston district the area would sink. Rivers was so serious about this "distributive" aspect of legislating that he would campaign for reelection on the slogan, "Rivers Delivers" (Arnold 1979; Pearson and Anderson 1968).

Yet, in spite of the long-held popular notion that committee membership assures benefits for one's constituents, years of scholarly work have failed to conclusively establish such a relationship. After dozens of studies of the distribution of federal outlays, scholars still cannot agree whether or to what extent the institutional standing of legislators, such as committee membership, alters their ability to "bring home more bacon." Some studies have found links between committee membership and increases in particularized policy benefits (Alvarez and Saving 1997a; Arnold 1979; Carsey and Rundquist 2001; Goss 1972; Gryski 1991; Plott 1968; Ritt 1976). Others have been unable to demonstrate the value of committee membership for legislators' home districts (Anagnoson 1980; Hooton 1997; Ray 1980a; Rundquist and Ferejohn 1975). Like the work on committee composition addressed in the previous chapter, ambiguity as to the effect of committee membership on the distribution of federal outlays has inspired researchers to seek other explanations for congressional behavior and institutional design. For example, scholars have tried to understand if or when legislators seek the passage of legislation through the use of universal or minimum-winning coalitions facilitated by a broad allocation of federal benefits to districts (Collie 1988; Stein and Bickers 1994b; Weingast 1994).

This chapter takes a new stab at an old problem. That is, using improved data, a longer time frame, and more fully specified models than have been employed previously, I seek to better answer the question of the effect of committee membership and district need on the allotment of federal outlays. I begin by reiterating the relevant propositions of the distributive model of congressional structure and uncovering some of the more important issues that have been implicit in the debate over empirical applications of the model. I follow with an explanation of where improvements can be made in model specification and data analysis. Then I offer a fairly broad series of tests on the ability of different committees to provide particularized benefits to their members. Specifically, I examine the outlays for programs under the jurisdictions of six standing House committees over four different congressional terms. The question to keep in mind is not just, Do legislators from high-demand districts garner a larger proportion of the available federal benefits in their area of policy? but Does committee membership offer some additional "kick" above and beyond demand?

Results of these tests indicate that there is more to the conventional wisdom than some research has found. Based upon the more refined reading of distributive theory that ties the effects of committee membership closely to district needs, I make significant improvements in the traditional techniques of previous studies and find that committees considered "constituency-oriented" are sometimes able to target more federal dollars to their members' districts than might normally go to a district with the same geographic or economic characteristics. This finding continues a trend of recent studies that conclude a gains-from-exchange model can be very helpful in understanding committee output. Moreover, the conclusions of this chapter in combination with the previous examination of committee composition give some indication of the extent of distributive structure in the House committee system and suggests important implications for the analysis of committee reforms.

Theory and Debates in the Study of Federal Outlays

As demonstrated in chapter 2, a gains-from-exchange, or distributive, notion of committee structure and operations is grounded in two main premises: (1) some committees attract and are composed of representatives from districts with acute demand for the programs under their authority, and (2) the main reason that members belong to these panels is to protect the flow of targeted federal benefits to their districts and to pursue new avenues for such funds. In the previous chapter I discovered evidence for the committee composition hypothesis. Now I evaluate the validity of the second proposition. Specifically, the chapter uses as a starting point the first hypothesis of committee output:

> **Committee Output Hypothesis:** *The members of House committees, especially those whose committee jurisdictions match constituency demands, will gain a disproportionate share of federal benefits under the jurisdiction of their panel.*

According to the gains-from-exchange approach, members seek specialized benefits for their districts in order to claim credit and foster constituent goodwill and district prosperity. The indirect effect of federal largesse is believed to increase a politician's likelihood of reelection (Mayhew 1974a; Fiorina 1989). This is not a totally unsubstantiated claim. A number of studies have found that increased federal outlays or even the number of new grant awards to localities can substantially boost an incumbent's likelihood of reelection, vote margin, or level of support among voters (Alvarez and Saving 1997b; Levitt and Snyder 1997; Stein and Bickers 1994a).[6]

The most effective federal benefits for one's district are, of course, those directed at the area's particular social, geographic, and economic needs (Rundquist and Carsey 1998). Legislators are expected to devote extra effort in ensuring that federal monies likely to do the most good in their home districts will get there, and membership on committees authorizing or appropriating such government funds significantly aids in this endeavor. Furthermore, distributive theorists hold that the committee system itself facilitates vote-trades, both within committees and among members of different committees, that are necessary for passage of these authorizing and appropriations bills (Weingast and Marshall 1988).[7]

Until recently, the chief problem for scholars has been that adequate data on federal outlays that would allow empirical examinations of this notion of committee power were not available. Scholars frequently developed ingenious methods of collecting information on federal expenditures to test their theories of distributive politics. For many years, they limited themselves to studies that examined only large federal programs, but as a means of understanding an overall theory of distributive politics, such studies would of course suffer from selection bias issues (for examples of such studies, see Gryski 1991; Ritt 1976). Broad data on federal outlays across numerous programs have existed for a number of years but have generally been available only for states or counties, and remapping the data to congressional districts has usually proved too difficult or introduced too much error into individual observations (Webster 1991; Ray 1980a; Owens and Wade 1984). Moreover, the difficulties encountered in data collection, such as gathering information on just one program or set of programs, have made it largely impractical to study the influence of committee membership across a number of panels or over many years.

Bickers and Stein recently took a major step toward solving these problems. By merging detailed programmatic information relevant for identifying the committee of jurisdiction from the Office of Management and Budget's Catalog of Federal Domestic Assistance (e.g., the types of recipients eligible for each program, the form of the assistance, etc.) with the annual number of awards and dollar value of individual outlays going to each congressional district from the Census Bureau's Federal Assistance Awards Data System (FAADS), they created the most comprehensive picture possible of federal spending in each of the 435 congressional districts from 1983 to 1996 (Bickers and Stein 1990). Its versatility and breadth has proven that such data sets are precisely what is needed for many different studies of the distribution of federal benefits to localities. To be sure, the data set is not flawless, but it is a monumental improvement over the data used previously.

Since its creation, the Bickers and Stein data set has been used for research on the effect of political parties (Levitt and Snyder 1995), tenure in office (Halvorson and Elder 1998; Moore and Hibbing 1996), and Senate apportionment (Lee 1998) on the allocation of federal benefits, as well as for studies of how outlays alter constituents' attitudes toward politicians (Stein and Bickers 1994a, 1995) or aggregate vote outcomes (Alvarez and Saving 1997b; Levitt and Snyder 1997).[8] Additionally, these data have been employed in a few studies of the effect of committee membership on the distribution of federal outlays (Alvarez and Saving 1997a; Heitshusen 2001), but the number of such studies is surprisingly small considering the availability of exceptional data and the importance of the question to current debates over legislative structure.

Despite considerable headway on the problem of adequate data, several important and unsettled debates remain inherent in the research on federal outlays. These questions are of related theoretical and empirical natures, and the various ways scholars have treated them contribute to the vastly different conclusions being drawn from similar analyses and data. The major issues in the study of committee effects and district need on the distribution of outlays involve questions about levels of aggregation, units of analysis, and the appropriate program types to be examined. I address each question and show how an adequate resolution of these important theoretical and empirical issues can shape the direction of the current analysis.

Levels of Aggregation

Researchers have examined the uneven distribution of federal benefits with differing assumptions as to the level of program outlays most susceptible to the influences of powerful committee members. The primary dichotomy exists between studies that explore the individual programmatic level—such as Rich's (1991) study of economic development programs (Community Development Block Grants, Urban Development Action Grants, etc.) or Svorny's (1996) study of job-training formula allocations (see also Ferejohn 1974)—and those that examine a much broader, aggregate level. The aggregate studies frequently investigate disparities in some variant of *overall* federal expenditures to localities. Recent studies of this kind (Levitt and Snyder 1995; Moore and Hibbing 1996) use an aggregation of all congressional district outlays from the FAADS database as their dependent variable (for a slightly older example, see Webster 1991). To some extent, the choice of aggregation level of federal programs for these prior studies was prescribed by the research agenda. For example, studies focusing on a particular policy arena often explored outlays at the programmatic level. However, the limited scope of such work may overlook the broader policymaking implications of the gains-from-exchange theory.

Still others contend that, rather than the straight dollar amount allocated to districts, what is truly important is the change in expenditures in districts from one year to the next (Ray 1980a), the increase in per capita dollars (Lee 1998), or even the growth in the total *number* of federal programs (Anagnoson 1982; Stein and Bickers 1994a, 1995). For example, Stein and Bickers claim that a greater number of awards allows a legislator to credit-claim with a broader array of constituency groups than would a single award of a large amount.

Notwithstanding the previous arguments, I contend that the gains-from-exchange theory itself best dictates the appropriate level of aggregation to effectively capture the essence of distributive politics and its most fundamental behavioral prediction—*intra*-committee logrolling. That is, under the gains-from-exchange model of committee membership and output, we are most likely to see members of the same committee with similar district characteristics logrolling within committee legislation for provision of district-directed benefits. If legislators cooperate to provide particularized federal benefits to each other's districts, this will most often be revealed in the programs under the control of a specific committee. That is, it is easiest to work out vote-trades among committee members, since varied issues can be easily wrapped into one large piece of legislation (like annual authorization or appropriations bills), and, as Weingast and Marshall (1988) show, this severely reduces the likelihood of shirking. To account for the existence of the more direct and easily enforceable vote-trades among committee members, I aggregate total outlays for programs under the jurisdiction of a specific authorizing committee.

Units of Analysis

Disputes about the units of analysis are closely related to the question of level of aggregation: Does distributive theory require the study of outlays to congressional districts, states, or some other jurisdiction? Most often scholars have examined federal funding at the district level (Levitt and Snyder 1995; Alvarez and Saving 1997a), but there is no lack of research examining state-level expenditures (Webster 1991; Gryski 1991; Levitt and Poterba 1999).

The use of state-level data on federal outlays is often predicated on the importance of accounting for the shared responsibility for policymaking across both chambers of Congress. This argument for the use of state-level outlays data is often based upon the motivations of individual legislators in two ways: (1) senators represent entire states, not just portions of states, so they promote the interests of more than just one or two districts within the state (if the state has multiple districts); and (2) representatives have reasons to provide benefits to their entire states—usually their ambitions for higher office (senatorial, gubernatorial, etc.)—and are therefore likely to play to wider constituencies than their own congressional districts (Rundquist and Ferejohn 1975, 90–91).

Both of these justifications have elements of truth to them, but they are not sufficient reasons for examining state- rather than district-level federal outlays. Senators clearly seek to represent entire states in the legislative process. However, if I wish to test a committee-centered hypothesis of influence, I could rightly make the case that most states are equally represented in most programmatic decisions in the Senate. Assuming that we consider both the Senate authorizing committee of jurisdiction and the Appropriations Committee relevant to budgetary decisions, the relative size of any one Senate authorizing panel (around twenty members) and the Appropriations Committee (around thirty members) in the period under consideration (the 99th through the 104th Congresses) makes it likely that most, if not all, states have at least one senator on one of these two panels. For example, programs falling under the jurisdiction of the Senate Banking Committee in the 100th Congress could have included the input of senators from thirty-four states that had at least one member on either the authorizing or Appropriations committees.

As for the "progressive ambition" of House members (Schlesinger 1966), this is a realistic assumption for *some* members of Congress in any one congressional term. However, the primary concern of the overwhelming majority of representatives at any specific time is reelection in their own districts. For instance, only fourteen representatives (3 percent of the total House membership) sought a statewide elective office (senator or governor) in 1998, and this figure is about average for most elections. As a whole, members of the House have considerably more to gain from the direct electoral payoffs of providing particularized benefits to their own congressional districts than the potential and somewhat distant rewards of catering to a statewide constituency. Acknowledging that the policy output of Congress is a negotiated agreement between the two chambers (and ultimately the president), but keeping in mind that states have near universal representation on relevant Senate committees, I turn back to the House and individual congressional districts for evidence that panel members enjoy strengthened ability to deliver federal benefits at home.

Program Types

Finally, scholars have hardly agreed on the types of federal programs that should be vulnerable to the vote-trades and benefits exchanges characterized by distributive politics. Researchers who examine the universalism proposition of distributive theory have tried to define program criteria for which the conditions of distributive politics should best apply (Stein and Bickers 1994a, 1994b, 1995; Weingast 1994). Other scholars have attempted to narrow further the programmatic conditions under which one should see committee members apt to deliver particularized benefits, and have examined only outlays for newly created programs for which committee members played key roles in formulating the enabling legislation. Similarly, discretionary or project-oriented programs are seen as extremely vulnerable to the influence of committee members, since each project requires precise statutory language (Alvarez and Saving 1997a; Hird 1991).

While discretionary or new programs undoubtedly offer opportunities to observe the influence of committee action on budgetary decisions, it is possible that *any* federal program which awards money or offers special consideration to individuals, organizations, or local governments can in a similar fashion be used to direct particularized benefits to members' districts. Though this is much less likely under such high-profile entitlement programs as Aid to Families with Dependent Children, any committee that considers annual reauthorizations or reappropriations may alter the criteria for funding or alter the actual funding levels to advantage members' constituencies.[9]

Given this broader view of the gains-from-exchange influence of committees, I apply a relatively stiff test of the distributive hypothesis by aggregating district-directed funding for nearly every program within a panel's jurisdiction to examine the effectiveness of committee membership in bringing home disproportionate benefits. By aggregating into each committee's policy jurisdiction such a large set of federal programs with diverse budget decision-making environments, I bias the tests *against* finding any relationship between committee membership and disproportionate outlays. If increased committee capacity to secure targeted district benefits occurs only for new or discretionary programs—on a term-by-term basis, this is often a relatively small percentage of the total outlays under a committee's jurisdiction—then aggregating such federal programs with other potentially larger outlays under the panel's purview might render the distributive effects imperceptible. However, if gains-from-exchange behavior is visible under these conditions, then there is new evidence that this theory of legislative structure and policymaking goes beyond this small portion of federal outlays.

Plan for This Analysis

Building on the prior controversies, this new analysis of the relationship between the institutional positions of legislators and their influence over budgetary content focuses specifically on the ability of committee members to deliver particularized benefits to home districts. As indicated above, I examine outlays to all congressional districts for almost all federal programs under the jurisdiction of each standing committee. Because of the availability of the comprehensive Bickers and Stein (1990) data, I can examine the political influence of panel membership for several committees across a number of years. Consequently, I investigate the outlays from programs under the jurisdiction of six standing House committees across four congressional terms in the 1980s and 1990s (the 99th–101st and the 104th Congresses).

The committee jurisdictions studied are those of Agriculture; Banking, Finance, and Urban Affairs; Interior and Insular Affairs; Public Works and Transportation; Science, Space, and Technology; and Veterans' Affairs. The panels are selected for their diversity on a number of fronts. They include three committees traditionally considered to be distributively oriented that are also (see chapter 3) populated to some degree by legislators from high-demand districts (Agriculture; Interior; and Public Works). However, these three committees exhibit significant differences in the character of their clientele groups. The Agriculture Committee addresses the policy issues of a well-organized and politically active constituency (Hansen 1991; Browne 1995). Interior and Insular Affairs, while serving districts with distinctive geographic and demographic characteristics, does so without much in the way of sizable district-based, politically self-actualized interest groups.[10] The third committee, Public Works, is not often thought to be oriented to the needs of a particular clientele group or district type, but has evolved into a panel often considered one of the main providers of federal project grants to localities. A fourth panel, Veterans' Affairs, addresses the policy issues of a unique clientele group, but because its constituency is so evenly distributed across the country, we found no evidence in chapter 3 that it was composed of a disproportionate number of representatives from high-demand districts (see also Cox and McCubbins 1993, 193). The fifth panel, Banking, is more commonly deemed a "policy" committee—a legislative panel that attracts members because of the opportunity it affords to work on particular issues of national importance (Deering and Smith 1997, 72)—yet evidence in chapter 3 shows that more than a few times it has drawn members with similar district characteristics. The sixth panel, Science, is a slightly newer one (formed in 1958 as the Science and Astronautics Committee and thus not examined in chapter 3) and manages policy regarding science and space research and development. Because much of this committee's legislative purview has obvious distributive spin-offs (funding for NASA programs, grants through the National Science Foundation, etc.) this panel is sometimes considered constituency-oriented (Deering and Smith 1997; Cohen and Noll 1991). However, Chairman Robert Walker claims that when he assumed control of the panel at the start of the 104th Congress, he endeavored to "eliminate pork from every bill [the committee] considered."[11]

Furthermore, analysis of outlays across these four congressional terms allows for at least a partial natural experiment in the effect of parties on the distributive character of committees. From a theoretical perspective, we might expect the process of budgetary decisions to change when control of Congress shifts from Democratic to Republican. The budgetary priorities of Democratic and Republican members may be different, and thus the distributive effectiveness of certain committees may change as a result of the majority transition. I am, therefore, able to contrast trends in the distribution of federal benefits during Democratic congresses (the 99th, 100th, and 101st Congresses) with those of one Republican-controlled congress (the 104th Congress).

As with questions about units of analysis and levels of aggregation, the methodology by which to analyze the influence of committee membership on the distribution of federal outlays is also an unresolved issue. One straightforward technique might simply entail comparisons of the central tendencies of committee members and non–committee members as to the level of funding directed to their home districts by programs under the jurisdiction of that panel. While these tests often show sizable and statistically significant differences in the level of benefits to the two populations—whether one examines means or medians—such analysis ignores significant problems in the interpretation of the findings. Not the least of these problems is that district characteristics, along with several other potential factors, may substantially affect the level of federal funds to a district. Since my specific interest is to pick out the effect of committee membership on disproportionate benefits to legislators' districts aside from other factors, I turn to a more sophisticated method involving regression analysis adjusted for data that are highly susceptible to extreme outliers, as federal outlays data can be.

The specification of models for this study is slightly different than for previous analyses. Besides the outlays aggregated by committee of jurisdiction, I take note of membership on both the relevant authorizing committee and its Appropriations subcommittee counterpart, include a more comprehensive measure of district demand, and provide for an interaction between constituency demand and committee membership. In addition, I incorporate standard control measures for such models—variables like seniority, party, electoral vulnerability, and so on. Below I explain several of the important variables. Table 4 provides a list of independent variables and their sources.

Committee Membership

I model a more realistic budgetary process than is customary in studies of the distribution of federal outlays, including membership not only of authorizing committees but also of Appropriations subcommittees (Kingdon 1966).[12] Federal outlays are determined through a combination of authorizing and appropriating legislation. Authorizing committees formulate policies and programs and determine "authorization" amounts or, more accurately, the authority by which Congress can appropriate funds at a certain level. Appropriations subcommittees (under the sanction of the full Appropriations Committee) construct legislation that permits agencies to incur obligations and the Treasury to make payments for designated purposes at a level specified in the statute.[13]

Evidence presented in chapter 3 dispelled the belief that Appropriations Committee members are fiscally disinterested "guardians of the federal treasury." Therefore, I expect Appropriations members to be just as likely to seek particularized benefits for their districts as authorizing com-

Table 4   Independent Variables for Tests of the Distribution of Federal Outlays

Variable	Description (Source)
Authorizing committee	Member = 1; otherwise = 0 *Examples*: Agriculture; Banking, Finance, and Urban Affairs; etc. (Nelson 1994)
Appropriations subcommittee	Member = 1; otherwise = 0 *Examples*: VA, HUD, and Independent Agencies; Energy and Water Development; etc. (LEGI-SLATE, Inc.)
District demand	Committee "demand" score (see text)
Party affiliation	Republican =1; Democratic = 0 (Nelson 1994)
Tenure	Number of terms served (Nelson 1994)
Electoral margin	Winners' percentage of the two-party vote (Ehrenhalt, various years)
State capital	Congressional district contains all or part of state capital = 1; otherwise = 0 (Bickers and Stein 1991, and author)

mittee members and to exhibit similar behavior. The emergency Kosovo measure described in chapter 2 is an excellent example of the distributive behavior of the Appropriations Committee, and interviews with former members of Congress (including a previous member of the Appropriations Committee) confirmed that such behavior is more or less standard on the Appropriations panel.[14]

Measuring District "Demand"

The relationship between the economic and social demands of districts and spending for specific federal programs should be easy to identify (Stein 1981). For instance, low-income housing grants should flow to districts with high levels of poverty and unemployment. Similarly, cotton production stabilization benefits should go to districts heavily dependent upon cotton farming. However, properly capturing the notion of district demand for financial benefits can be complicated by the endogeniety problem created through previous expenditures on the same or similar programs in the district. Prior federal expenditures may reduce certain types of constituency need, or at least alter that need in some way (Carsey and Rundquist 2001; Rundquist and Carsey 1998). To partially account for this problem in variable identification, I employ measures that capture

Table 5　Authorizing Committees and Their Measures of District Demand

Committee	Measures of District Demand	
Agriculture	Percentage employed in farming, fishing, and wildlife	Percentage living rural farming areas
Banking, Finance, and Urban Affairs	Percentage living urban areas District contains one of the fifty largest cities (dummy)	Percentage African-American Percentage employed in finance, insurance, and real estate
Interior and Insular Affairs	Population density Percentage Native American	State acreage owned by the National Park Service and Bureau of Land Management
Science, Space, and Technology	Location of the top 100 research universities	Percentage employed in educational services
Public Works and Transportation	Percentage commuting to work	Percentage unemployed
Veterans' Affairs	Percentage veterans	Number of beds in district VA hospitals

a relevant set of district characteristics that are least likely to be affected by prior governmental expenditures (e.g., coastal areas, percent African-American, etc.).

To estimate the extent to which congressional districts "require" the specific policy benefits under the control of each authorizing committee, I create a profile for each one similar to those used for the study of committee composition in chapter 3. Again, the profiles describe certain key economic, social, or geographic characteristics that indicate a particular constituency's level of interest in the issues under a committee's jurisdiction, but they vary slightly from those used earlier due to availability of different or better information for the shorter period of study. Table 5 lists the committees and their measures of "demand."

Like the measures of district interest in specific committee jurisdictions used in the previous chapter, I create a single combined score for district "demand" from standardized component variables (mean of zero, standard deviation of one). For example, the measure of district demand for the Agriculture Committee is an additive scale of standardized measures of both the percentage in each district employed in farming and the percentage living in rural-farm areas. The partial aim of this measure is to differentiate members that rank high on both components of the two-component demand score, whose constituencies should have a greater demand for the policy benefits provided by that committee, from members who rank high on only one component, whose districts would have less demand. Returning to the agriculture example, the measure of "demand" for the benefits under the jurisdiction of the Agriculture Committee takes into account both the percentage in each district employed in farming and the percentage living in rural farming areas. Members who rank high on both components have a greater "demand" for the policy benefits provided by the Agriculture Committee than those who rank high on only one of the two components.[15] An additional reason for the aggregate score is provided below.

The Interaction of Committee Membership and District Demand

One major distinction between earlier studies and my specification of committee membership is the treatment of its relationship with district characteristics. Previous researchers conceptualized a relatively simple effect of committee membership and district "demand" on the distribution of particularized benefits. That is, district demand and committee membership are thought to be related in their influence on procuring increased federal outlays, but the relationship usually appears in one of two ways (see figure 1). Studies of distributive theory that concentrate on committee composition often conceptualize the relationship as linear (figure 1a); that is, district characteristics influence the assignment choices of representatives and subsequently panel membership results in the ability to bring home more federal projects. In this case, constituency demand is thought to be causally prior to any effect of committee membership on securing increased district outlays. Alternatively, research on distributive politics that explores the allocation of outlays has frequently conceived of district need and committee membership as relatively separate (figure 1b). Need can influence both the choice of representatives' committee assignments and the distribution of outlays, but this is distinct from the effect of panel membership on funds to the constituency.

Neither perspective is particularly accurate, and therefore I explore a slightly more complex relationship between these two factors that are so important to the allocation of federal funds. While I examine the *direct* effect of constituency demand and committee membership as described above, I also hypothesize an interaction effect of the two *combined* for the pursuit of targeted benefits (figure 1c). The interaction variable accounts for a presumed positive effect of the combination of committee membership and high levels of district demand on the pursuit of federal benefits. That is, given the hypothesized distributive relationship, district demand should influence a legislator's choice of committee assignments as well as outlays, while at the same time just being a member of a committee should have an independent effect on a legislator's ability to secure more funds from programs under its jurisdiction. However, I contend that their special position of policy influence should make members from high-demand

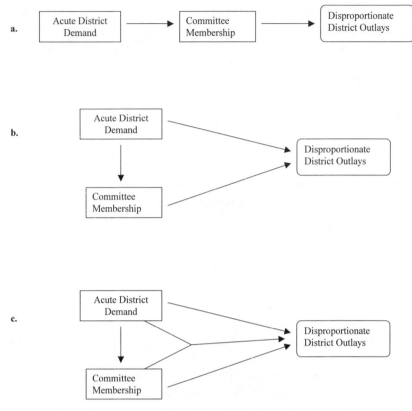

Figure 1   Congressional district demand, committee membership, and the relationship with federal outlays

constituencies even more aggressive and, ultimately, more successful in directing particularized federal funds to their home districts than low-demand committee members. Often legislators have more than one committee assignment, and these multiple memberships can serve varied purposes—district needs, individual policy agendas, party policy programs, and so on. For representatives with acute district interests in the programs of a particular committee, the distributive theory presumes that they are likely to be strongly motivated to use their membership to help meet the needs of constituents and thus maximize their reelection prospects. Therefore, an additional reason for *one* measure of constituency characteristics is that it allows me to gauge the effect of interaction between committee members and district need on the distribution of federal benefits through the use of a single multiplicative demand term (Jaccard, Turrisi, and Wan 1990).

Other Important Factors

Like many authors of previous studies of distributive politics, I include a number of institutional and political variables that are normally anticipated to have some relationship to congressional decisions concerning funding for federal programs.

Seniority/Tenure	Scholars have assumed that senior members are likely to be closer to the nucleus of policy decision making in Congress and thus better able to extract benefits for their districts. These individuals often have more committee and subcommittee seniority and are practiced in the construction of policy language, the use of chamber procedures (Hibbing 1991), or the ability to pressure implementing agencies (Fiorina 1989) in ways that can benefit their constituencies. Seniority is also valuable in assuring vote-trade reciprocity— senior members have better-established reputations, and their increased likelihood of reelection makes them less of a risk in repaying their voting debts in the future (see, for example, Moore and Hibbing 1996; Svorny 1996).
Electoral Uncertainty	As they do in theories about constituent contact and service (e.g., Fenno 1978), scholars hypothesize that members who face more electoral uncertainty will turn to federal programs that allocate money to constituents as a way to boost their local economy and increase their ability to credit-claim with voters (Anagnoson 1982; Stein and Bickers 1994a). The transportation bill discussed at the opening of this chapter is a good illustration of such behavior. If bringing home federal money and programs is a means of improving reelection prospects, then those legislators in electoral trouble are even more likely to pursue this aim as a campaign tactic. Therefore, under this belief, there should be evidence of a systematic link between electoral vulnerability and greater federal outlays. Though scholars have utilized numerous measures of district marginality (see Mayhew 1974b; and Jacobson 1987

for a few examples), I employ a standard variable of vote margin in the previous election for an indication of future electoral uncertainty.

Majority Party | Similarly, if parties seek ways to bolster their members' electoral prospects, outlays to their individual districts may be one effective method. Specifically, the majority party has an institutional upper hand in that it dominates agenda setting, committee organization, and floor consideration of legislation. Furthermore, through its sheer size (in terms of membership) in a largely majority-rule institution, the majority party should be in a position to give its members an advantage in directing benefits to their districts as opposed to those of the opposition party (Alvarez and Saving 1997a).

State Capital | Some of the programs examined here allocate their money first to state governments, which are then responsible for reallocating the money to the individuals, organizations, or institutions that qualify. Distribution of federal aid for such programs is recorded by the database as having been entirely directed at districts that include state capitals (Levitt and Snyder 1995). I attempted, therefore, to remove as many of these programs as I could identify;[16] however, it was not possible to account for every affected program, so I included a control for state capitals.[17]

Measuring Outlays

In determining the capacity of committees to disproportionately favor panel members by delivering particularized benefits, we must aggregate data regarding the amount each district received from the federal programs within each panel's jurisdiction. This yields a total level of funding received by each district from *all* programs authorized by individual standing House committees. Of course, as discussed in chapter 3, committee jurisdictions are not always straightforward; they are frequently much broader than the formal boundaries written into the chamber rules. To establish which committee had jurisdiction over each program, I examined the subject matter of authorizing committee and Appropriations subcommittee hearings (for a similar use of hearings, see Baumgartner, Jones, Rosenstiehl, and Lorenzo 1994). I determined which committee had jurisdiction over a program by counting the number of times the panel held a hearing on the federal agency that administers each program over a seven-year period (1983–90). For purposes of accuracy, I narrowed my focus to the "subagency," like the Agriculture Stabilization and Conservation Service, rather than the Cabinet-level department, like the Department of Agriculture.[18]

For most programs, identifying the committee of jurisdiction was relatively uncomplicated: one authorizing committee and one Appropriations subcommittee held the preponderance of hearings concerning an agency. Occasionally, hearings on a specific agency's programs were spread across several committees. In such cases I repeated the analysis using specific program names (e.g., Rural Housing Preservation Grants) rather than the agency to determine the committee most actively involved in the program's formulation and oversight.

Since outlays are aggregated into authorizing committees of jurisdiction, and the jurisdictions of authorizing committees and Appropriations subcommittees are not parallel,[19] I match the authorizing committee with one *primary* Appropriations subcommittee. That is, the Appropriations subcommittee that had authority over the largest dollar amount of programs within the authorizing committee's jurisdiction was considered the authorizing committee's companion Appropriations panel.

After programmatic jurisdictions were resolved, I simply aggregated the dollar amounts for all programs under the purview of a specific committee for each district for a two-year period. Rather than using individual years, I grouped years into congressional terms, since major program budgetary decisions (often contained in large reauthorization measures) frequently take an entire term to complete. For accuracy, I include a one-year lag in the implementation of budgetary decisions to account for the delay between when a program is authorized or appropriated in Congress and when the funds are actually spent. Therefore, I correlate FY1986 and FY1987 outlays with congressional variables for 1985 and 1986 (the 99th Congress), FY1988 and FY1989 outlays with variables for 1987 and 1988 (the 100th Congress), and so forth.

The Models

To account for the inefficient estimates that result from heavily tailed, outlier-prone error distributions, I employ a robust regression technique that involves an iteratively reweighted, least squares procedure.[20] Where a small number of cases apply a significant amount of leverage to the parameter estimates, the robust regression model reduces their influence and provides more efficient estimates.

The model for this analysis is

Benefits$_{it}$ = α_1 + β_1(authorizing committee membership$_{it}$) + β_2(appropriations
        subcommittee membership$_{it}$) + β_3(district demand$_{it}$) + β_4(authorizing
        committee membership/demand interaction$_{it}$) + β_5(appropriations
        subcommittee membership/demand interaction$_{it}$) + β_6(tenure$_{it}$) +
        β_7(majority party affiliation$_{it}$) + β_8(electoral uncertainty$_{it}$) + β_9(state
        capitol$_{it}$) + e_{1it},

where i is a specific congressional district, and t is one congressional term (or its associated outlay years).

To test my hypotheses of the influence of committee membership, I focus on the effect that the committee membership variables (β_1 and β_2) and the interaction of committee membership and district demand (β_4 and β_5) have on district outlays. In the discussion that follows, I report only the effect of committee membership (and membership combined with district demand), leaving all other significant variables at their mean or mode (depending on whether or not the variable is binary). Using the parameter estimates from the above model, I report for each committee the expected funds from programs under its jurisdiction going to the district of a committee member at the average level of district demand for all committee members. This is contrasted with the expected funds directed to the district of a legislator with the same level of constituency demand who is not a member of the committee. Therefore, given a constant level of constituency interest in a committee's benefits, the results show the extra "kick" in dollar terms a legislator might bring home to the district because she has a seat on that panel. I repeat this analysis using the associated Appropriations subcommittee and its members' average levels of district demand.

The only parameter estimates accounted for in the following bar charts are those where the F-tests reveal that the system of committee variables (β_1 and β_4 for the authorizing committee, or β_2 and β_5 for the Appropriations subcommittee) along with the demand score are significantly different from zero.[21] In instances where no data are reported (no bars), the statistical tests did not indicate that we should expect committee membership in that congressional term to have had a significant effect on the committee-controlled outlays directed to legislators' districts. Hence, the indicators of statistical significance are implicit in the findings reported in the figures, but I discuss more thoroughly (and in some ways leave to the discretion of the reader) the substantive significance of these differences.

Findings

Agriculture Committee

The impact on district benefits of membership on a committee with authority over agriculture policy can only be described in the starkest terms (see figure 2). Not unexpectedly, a seat on either the Agriculture Committee or the Appropriations Subcommittee on Agriculture and Rural Development consistently results in extremely large disparities in the level of federal agriculture benefits directed at a legislator's constituency, even when holding all other effects constant—*including district characteristics*. For instance, an assignment on the standing Agriculture Committee in the four congressional terms of figure 2 results in a minimum difference in agriculture outlays of $52 million over what the equivalent district would receive if its representative was not on the panel in the 104th Congress. In the 99th Congress this difference was a substantial $130 million—committee members could expect almost six times the level of federal agriculture funding. A similar trend obtains for membership on the Appropriations subcommittee. At a minimum, the difference between the districts of panel members and nonmembers (with a level of district demand equivalent to the subcommittee average) is $29 million in the 104th Congress and at a maximum, this disparity jumps to a staggering $137 million in the 100th Congress. In the latter example, Appropriations subcommittee members could look forward to nearly four times the level of agriculture outlays.

Banking, Finance, and Urban Affairs Committee

The results for Banking Committee outlays are not nearly as dramatic as those for agriculture programs (see figure 3). The effect of Banking panel membership on constituency benefits ranged from no significant difference in the 104th Congress, to a more sizable but still modest boost of approximately $6 million for legislators in the 100th Congress. Examining committee outlays for members of the related Appropriations subcommittee—VA, HUD, and Independent Agencies—we see a much larger variance in the effect of panel membership. While again there is no meaningful effect of a committee seat in the 104th Congress, there is a considerable difference in outlays for HUD subcommittee members in the 100th Congress: a subcommittee assignment with equivalent levels of district demand garners almost $20 million in additional banking and urban housing monies. One further note: the cause of the sea change in the level of funding for programs under the authority of the Banking Committee between the 99th and 100th Congresses cannot be pinpointed to the introduction or expansion of a single program. While a number of categories

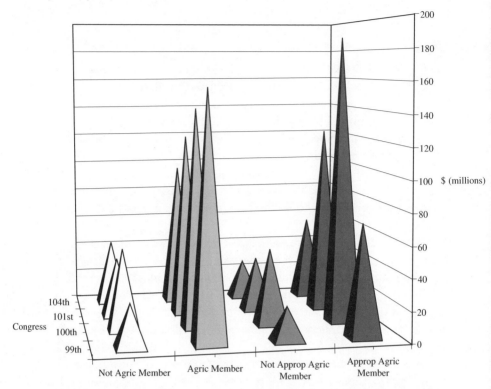

Figure 2 Expected Agriculture outlays for legislators with seats on (and off) related committees

of Banking outlays experienced significant growth over the two congressional terms, perhaps the most dramatic was a tenfold increase in spending on low-income housing assistance.

Interior and Insular Affairs Committee

The results of tests on Interior Committee programs are in some ways similar to those for its complement panel that controls agriculture outlays, but at a considerably different level of spending: instead of tens or even hundreds of millions of dollars, committee membership may only bring the difference of a few hundred thousand or perhaps a million dollars in Interior funds to a congressional district (see figure 4).[22] For membership on the Interior panel itself, the difference in federal interior funds for a committee seat ranged from zero in the 99th Congress to about $600,000 in the 101st Congress. This latter disparity represents about two-and-a-half times the level of outlays that the same district would receive if it did not have representation on the committee. There were

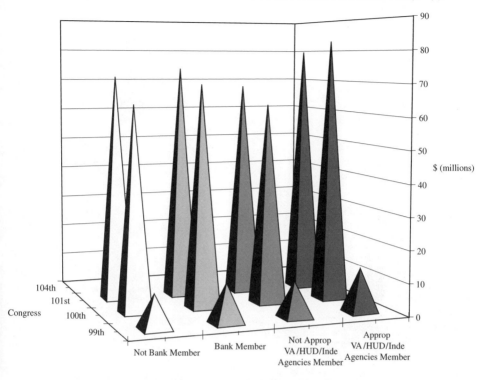

Figure 3 Expected Banking outlays for legislators with seats on (and off) related committees

similar findings for membership on the Appropriations Interior subcommittee—the advantage of a committee seat in the 99th Congress made no difference at all, but two terms later might have resulted in additional Interior funds equivalent to approximately a half-million dollars.

Public Works and Transportation Committee

Outlays for programs under the authority of the Public Works and Transportation Committee provide the most surprising contrast with other panels that are often considered distributively oriented, like the Agriculture or Interior panels. Despite the example offered at the beginning of this chapter, in no congressional term did membership on either the standing Public Works and Transportation Committee or its Appropriations counterpart, the Transportation and Related Agencies Subcommittee, result in significantly higher outlays for legislators (no figure provided). Committee members could expect $10–$20 million in public works spending each congressional term, but so could legislators not belonging to the committee. Ironically, for a committee so frequently asso-

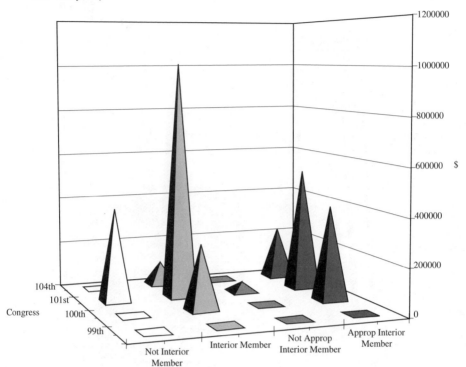

Figure 4   Expected Interior outlays for legislators with seats on (and off) related committees

ciated with providing particularized benefits to members' districts, no advantage is apparent in outlays going to members' constituencies.

Science, Space, and Technology Committee

The effect of Science Committee membership on the receipt of funds from science-oriented federal programs varied considerably depending on whether we examined the standing committee or the Appropriations subcommittee (see figure 5). Although members of the standing Science Committee can expect to receive about twice the outlays that legislators from similar congressional districts would reap in the first two congressional terms explored, this difference translates into only around $1.5 million. Additionally, by the last congressional term examined, the difference in expected funds to committee members' districts is almost imperceptible (more on this change below). However, this trend does not hold for representatives on the relevant Appropriations subcommittee—the

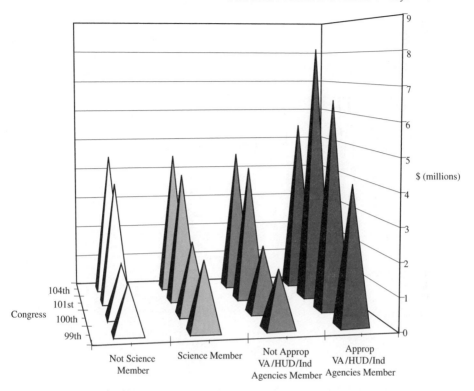

Figure 5   Expected Science outlays for legislators with seats on (and off) related
committees

VA, HUD, and Independent Agencies panel. By contrast, Appropriations
subcommittee members could expect to receive at least an additional
$1 million in science funding in the 104th Congress, and in one term (the
100th Congress) the extra "kick" of committee work was likely to result
in more than $4 million in science outlays. The latter case represented a
level of funding for Appropriations subcommittee members that was three
times the amount given to an equivalent district of a non–committee
member.

Veterans' Affairs Committee

Whereas for science outlays it was the Appropriations subcommittee that
offered a real boost to the level of committee-controlled funds directed
at legislators' districts, the opposite holds for federal veterans' programs:
the standing Veterans' Affairs Committee, not the Appropriations subcommittee, provides the best opportunity for boosts in the outlays to

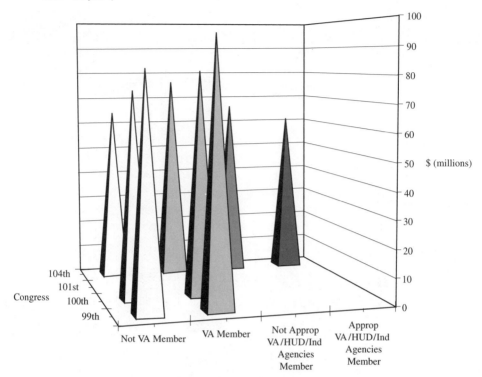

Figure 6   Expected Veterans' Affairs outlays for legislators with seats on (and off) related committees

committee members' districts (figure 6). With the exception of one congressional term, the 101st Congress, a seat on the Veterans' Affairs panel was likely to result in somewhere between $6.5 million and $12 million in additional veterans outlays while holding the effect of district demand levels constant. In the 101st Congress, however, the expected difference in the veterans spending between committee members and nonmembers is undetectable. On the other hand, a seat on the VA, HUD, and Independent Agencies Appropriations Subcommittee is not as lucrative for representatives. In fact, not only is there no discernible difference between committee members and other legislators with respect to veterans' outlays, but in one term, the 104th Congress, subcommittee members could expect to receive significantly less in veterans spending, by about $5 million. Ironically, the same Appropriations subcommittee that controls the bulk of funding for programs within the jurisdiction of the Banking and Science committees and frequently provides members a greater advantage with respect to outlays than does the authorizing committee, offers no advantage at all for members when it comes to veterans spending.

Additional Factors

Two control variables had a consistent effect on the level of spending in members' districts: party membership and the location of state capitols. This is not to say that these variables always produced significant parameter estimates, but they were found to have statistically significant effects more often than not. Unsurprisingly, in the 99th through 101st Congresses, the majority party Democrats were likely to receive significantly higher spending in their districts from programs studied here. However, what was very surprising was that even in the Republican-controlled 104th Congress, it was *still* the Democrats who received significantly higher outlays for programs under the control of the Agriculture, Banking, Interior, and Science committees (more on this below).

Regarding the latter variable—whether or not the district contains a state capitol—the significance of its influence in all likelihood simply reveals that my effort to eliminate all programs whose spending is mainly coordinated through state governments (described above) was not entirely successful. I find it unlikely that members who represent these areas have special abilities to garner disproportionate outlays, since this variable was found to be significant across a number of different types of programs (agriculture, science, veterans, etc.).

Discussion

The analysis of the distribution of outlays for federal programs under the authority of six standing House committees reveals several notable trends. First and foremost, there does seem to be a relationship between committee membership and the distribution of federal funds from programs sorted by their committees of jurisdiction. Controlling for many characteristics of congressional districts, I still find effects of committee membership on the provision of government dollars to constituencies. This trend does not occur consistently with programs under the purview of every committee examined here, but it does occur quite often and frequently results in a difference for committee members of a few million to several tens of millions of dollars in needed federal funds. Moreover, this phenomenon is not simply confined to panels usually considered constituency-oriented. For instance, federal programs under the authority of the Banking Committee, often thought of as a "policy-oriented" panel, provided disproportionate benefits to the districts of members on the two committees (the standing committee and the Appropriations Committee) primarily responsible for setting their budget levels.

Perhaps more significantly, I find that the Appropriations subcommittees that maintain shared control over the budgets of important programs under the authority of these six standing committees are even more likely to provide federal benefits to members' home districts than the authorizing panels. In retrospect, this should not be completely unexpected. Appropriations subcommittees have a more direct link to the dollar amount of outlays recorded in the Bickers and Stein (1990) data. As stated earlier, the data originate with the FAADS system, which records "obligations"— that is, spending commitments by the federal government. This budget level requires the legal authority for federal agencies to incur the obligation and make payments, which is done in the appropriations legislation. The statute that establishes or continues a federal program or agency is the authorization, which is the responsibility of the standing legislative committee. But this authorization occurs prior to the appropriation, which, of course is the duty of the Appropriations Committee. Given the structure of the budgetary process, it might be more fitting that authorizing committees would have a larger effect on the *number* of grants to congressional districts (Stein and Bickers 1995), but Appropriations subcommittees would be more directly linked to the dollar outlays.

Additionally, it was not necessarily the case that committees composed of a large numbers of high-demand legislators were the only ones providing disproportionate outlays to their members' districts. Certainly, the panels with authority over agriculture programs were both composed of representatives from farm-oriented districts and prodigious providers of disproportionate agriculture-oriented benefits to their members. But similarly, the Veterans' Affairs Committee, which does not offer much evidence of being an outlier panel at any point in the period examined, also does a very good job of supplying increased funding to its members. In contrast, the Public Works panel, which is quite often composed of members from high-demand districts, shows no signs of disproportionately supplying committee-controlled federal funds.

Finally, there are interesting results regarding party effects. First, as noted above, the variable for party affiliation shows that majority party status does not necessarily result in increased outlays for committee members; rather, we find that Democratic Party membership is critical. Even when the Republicans take control of the House in the 104th Congress, Democrats are still able to provide themselves with a heightened level of funding from programs under the authority of several committees, apart from any committee effect. This seemingly strange finding actually corresponds quite comfortably with Alvarez and Saving's (1997b) discovery that the electoral payoff of providing distributive benefits to one's district can be conditional on the party affiliation of the legislator. Specifically, they find that Democrats are significantly more likely than Republicans to reap rewards at the ballot box from bringing home federal largesse.

Second, there are also indications that Republicans were at least partially successful in imposing their fiscal conservatism with regard to using the federal budget for disproportionate gain by committee members. One of the more extreme examples of this occurs with outlays controlled by the Banking panel, which in the congresses under the control of a Democratic majority were supplied to the districts of committee members at a significantly higher level than those of nonmembers. However, under the Republican 104th Congress, there is no evidence of any difference in Banking-controlled outlays to committee members. In another example, I find that membership on the Science Committee proves to be somewhat valuable in securing greater federal benefits for one's district in the 99th through 101st Congresses. However, there is almost no difference in science spending once the Republicans take control of the House in the 104th Congress. The phenomenon captured in the data comports closely with former Science Committee Chair Robert Walker's (R-PA) claims that he went out of his way to ensure that panel members did not insert special projects directed at their own districts in science-authorizing legislation.

Conclusion

The findings of this analysis correspond with those of several other recent studies of distributive theory (Alvarez and Saving 1997a; Carsey and Rundquist 1999, 2001; Rundquist, Lee, and Rhee 1996). Convincing evidence exists that several of the committees examined here were frequently able to provide disproportionate benefits to the districts of panel members. Although this result is not completely consistent across all committees or all years, there is enough data to support the distributive contention that in many instances members of Congress can rely on their coveted committee assignments to supply their districts with a much higher level of federal benefits than they would receive otherwise, usually for programs important to their constituencies.

Several theoretical and methodological questions remain to be answered in such a study of committee effects on the distribution of federal funds. The questions run the gamut from whether or not I have adequately or accurately measured district demand to the appropriate specification of the statistical model. Thus, I see the research presented here as a promising step in the correct direction for the examination of distributive policy making.

Perhaps the most glaring hitch for a distributive theory of committee output is that very inconsistency with which committee membership is shown to disproportionately influence panel outlays. Why is there so much variability in the capacity of committee members to attain significantly more federal funds than other legislators *consistently* across all four congressional terms? Put another way, why aren't there more committees like Agriculture, where members consistently receive benefits at a considerably higher level than non–committee members? One possible answer lies where this chapter began—the massive, six-year transportation reauthorization. Major opportunities to provide for the special needs of one's constituency may not come around every year or even every congressional term. Though appropriations bills must pass annually, the statutory language that specifies the size and features of federal programs is often considered every four, five, or six years. Just a few examples of such multiyear authorizing legislation, aside from transportation, include the Small Business Administration reauthorization, the Department of Agriculture reauthorization, and the Elementary and Secondary Education Act reauthorization.

Moreover, individual legislators may not require disproportionate outlays over the entire authorization period in order to successfully creditclaim with constituents. In this manner special consideration for the district provided through huge authorization bills can yield federal benefits "that keep on giving." Immediately following the bill's passage, it may be enough for a politician to point to the statute and say, "Look what I have done for the district." Three or four years may pass before the outlays actually appear, at which time the legislator may point to the material benefit and claim again, "Remember what I did for the district."

This study is clearly not the last word in understanding the complicated relationship among district characteristics, federal outlays, and committee membership. Nonetheless, exploring a broad array of committees over several congressional terms reveals evidence to further support, at least in part, a distributive notion of House committee organization and output. What remains is to understand how the gains-from-exchange basis of parts of the legislative structure influences representative's preferences on proposals for reforms in committee arrangements.

In the following three chapters I move on to the reforms part of the analysis. I study three major institutional junctures in the development of the modern House of Representatives. Specifically, I examine the extent to which the reaction of legislators to efforts at jurisdictional restructuring of House committees is based on their reelection goals and the pursuit of district benefits through committee assignments. I explore both the individual committee hypothesis, that members of Congress will oppose alterations to the authority and jurisdictions of committees that control programs important to their district's well-being, and the system-wide hypothesis, that broad reorganization proposals will provoke widespread opposition developing from the same collective motivation. As before, I also study whether increasing party polarization and caucus influence on congressional structure have meaningful effects on the reelection motivations of members faced with radical committee reorganization.

Chapter 5

The Postwar Failure of Congressional Reform:
The Legislative Reorganization Act of 1946

THE FIRST EFFORT AT SYSTEM-WIDE RESTRUCTURING OF HOUSE committee jurisdictions and the policymaking process in the postwar period occurred during the 79th Congress (1945–46). This process was the culmination of several years of protests both among the general public and on Capitol Hill over the state of congressional politics and the combative relationship between Congress and the White House. After more than a year of consideration and a reform process that proceeded sporadically, the House and Senate enacted a package of reforms that, it was hoped, would radically reshape an apparently outdated committee structure. Furthermore, reform advocates wished to unify policy agenda-setting and enable Congress to control a rapidly growing federal budget as well as present a united front in its bargaining with the president.

Ultimately, however, the Legislative Reorganization Act of 1946 (hereafter, LRA) accomplished little of what the reformers sought. Changes in fiscal decision making never curbed the rapid rise in federal spending, and soon the modifications were abandoned. Control over the direction of policy decision making remained fragmented among an even smaller number of committees and their increasingly powerful chairs. If anything, the changes resulted in House leadership abdicating ever more authority over the legislative agenda (Deering and Smith 1997; Davidson 1990). And, most important for the rank-and-file, the rearrangement of committee jurisdictions simply served to update a collection of decision-making bodies that in many ways quite satisfactorily served the needs of career-oriented politicians. The reforms eliminated largely inactive and useless panels, and concentrated similar issues and jurisdictions into panels that would just as adequately allow members to provide for their constituent's economic and social needs. In the face of widespread and radical reforms, particularly for the House, members rejected a number of the most extreme measures (some important points of contention seemed not even to be up for negotiation) and crafted a package of changes that would help to perpetuate the distributive and electoral status quo.

This chapter begins the examination of the effect of distributive and electoral politics on the process of congressional reform. I specifically explore how the electoral connection shapes the preferences and behavior of legislators faced with important decisions as to how they would or would not restructure the institution. I investigate how the career aspirations of members of Congress influence the success and failure of several reform proposals considered during the 79th Congress. I use data on the alteration and composition of several House committees, both before and after the reforms, and I examine legislators' objectives and their ability to shape a favorable congressional structure in this period of organizational uncertainty.

The following section lays out the development of congressional careers and describes changes in the committee system during the eighty years preceding the 1946 reforms. This important history offers insights into the ways that electoral changes and House institutional arrangements contributed to the career strategies of legislators and, ultimately, how these structural forms were themselves molded to help members provide for the needs of their districts and to maximize their own electoral prospects. Following this, I provide a brief history of the passage of the Legislative Reorganization Act in 1945–46. I then analyze four prominent reform proposals that I see as critical opportunities for members of Congress to decide how the institution was going to operate. Ultimately the suggestions for changes—jurisdictional restructuring, limitations on the agenda powers of committees, budgetary reforms, and the elimination of several forms of private legislation—either went unrealized or were implemented in ways that perpetuated existing distributive arrangements and reelection incentives.

Prelude to Reform: The Development of Standing Committees in the House and the Electoral Connection

In many ways the failure of the LRA to substantially alter the nature of congressional committee jurisdictions and powers is best understood in the context of the development of legislative careers and House institutional structures in the years between 1865 and 1945. From Reconstruction to the end of World War II, legislators not only cultivated a career orientation to their positions, but also established a system of legislative panels that were ideally suited to serve their reelection requirements. Recounting a number of important events and institutional changes since the mid-1860s can be instructive for an understanding of what led up to the reform act in 1946.

The Growth of Careerism in the House

Members of the House of Representatives at the end of the Civil War barely resemble the career politicians that we have known for most of the twentieth century. In 1865, most members served no more than two congressional terms. Election to many House seats was controlled by local party machines and was frequently rotated to different politicians according to the geopolitical needs of the area. However, as the nineteenth century wound down, House members began to see their elective positions more as career posts. By the turn of the century, the mean House member had served just over three terms and less than a quarter of the members were in their first congress (Abram and Cooper 1968; Polsby 1968; Brady, Buckley, and Rivers 1999).

The reason for this transformation to more career-oriented politicians is not entirely clear, but one plausible explanation is that the federal government was becoming more significant in important political decisions of the day, and politicians began to see election to federal office as more influential and professionally rewarding (Kernell 1977). For a variety of reasons, the federal government was taking on a much larger administrative role in the late 1880s than it had previously (Dodd and Schott 1979; Higgs 1987; Skowronek 1982). This growth included the creation of a professional civil service and a number of measures regulating or promoting various industries, including the creation of the Interstate Commerce Commission in 1887 and the Department of Labor in 1888, elevation to cabinet status for the Department of Agriculture in 1889, and institution of public works grants for road construction after the turn of the century (Dodd and Schott 1979). Furthermore, adoption of tariff barriers for many industries and commodities prior to the turn of the century, "meant that the economic welfare of communities throughout the country became tied to national policies" (Kernell 1977, 674). Several protectionist measures were enacted after the end of the Civil War (Tarbell 1912; Stanwood 1903), and Chamberlain argues that tariff legislation was among the most important responsibilities of the federal government in the 1890s. Protectionist legislation included a number of enactments spurred on by the economic depression and demands by local business interests—the Tariff Act of 1890, the Wilson Act of 1894, and the Dingley Act of 1897 (Chamberlain 1967, chap. 3). By the turn of the century, federal office was becoming a substantially more influential elected position, able to provide for local economic needs.

Regardless of the reason why politicians began to seek longer tenure in Washington, to ensure their political survival, members had to devise new strategies to maximize their probability of reelection. Two developments in the latter part of the nineteenth century significantly altered House elections and strengthened the electoral link between representatives and their constituents. The first change was the widespread abandonment of the local party caucuses and the process of rotating individuals for House seats. This was replaced by a system of direct primaries for federal office. After the Civil War a small number of states began to regulate the process of nominating candidates for public office in order diminish the prevalence of bribery, fraud, and intimidation in elections. However, not until the late 1880s and early 1890s did most states establish laws requiring formal primaries for many local, state, and federal elections (Merriam and Overacker 1928). Kernell argues that the establishment of "[d]irect primaries liberated the congressman from the caucus and allowed him to employ proven campaign skills and the resources of office to maximum advantage" (1977, 677).

The second development that altered the process of House elections was the introduction of the Australian ballot.[1] Again intended to reduce negative influences on the electoral process, the use of more secret forms of balloting was instituted in thirty-two states (235 House seats) between 1889 and 1892, and in another seven states (70 seats) over the next four years. Katz and Sala assert that this electoral change further diminished the power of local party machines and encouraged representatives "to define and expand their personal reputations with voters. Reelection-seeking members thenceforth had incentives to blow their own credit-claiming horns as often as possible" (1996, 23).

Development of the Congressional Committee System

The expansion of careerism in the House in the latter half of the nineteenth century was accompanied by the development of the congressional committee system more along the lines that we know it today. Around the time of the Civil War, in the 38th Congress (1863–64), the House had thirty-nine standing committees with 313 committee seats for 243 representatives. This arrangement rapidly changed as members sought longer terms of service and a greater career investment in the institution of the House. By the 57th Congress (1901–02), the number of standing House

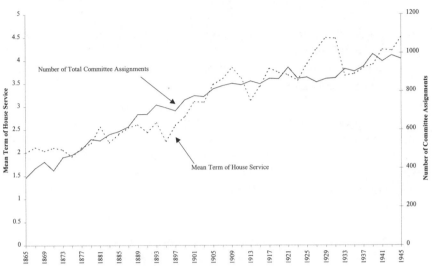

Figure 7   Committee and career development in the House of Representatives,
1865–1945

committees jumped to sixty, with 778 seats for 391 members. Figure 7
traces the development of committee assignments along with the mean
number of terms of service for House members from 1865 to 1945. The
figure shows the concurrent growth of careerism and the size of the House
committee system.

During this transformation the House experienced specific growth in
the number and type of committees that created and authorized programs
for federal spending in congressional districts and had the potential to assist members in serving the particular needs of their constituents: Appropriations, Banking and Currency, Mines and Mining, Pacific Railroads
(all created in 1865); Education and Labor (1867); War Claims (1873);
Levees and Improvements of the Mississippi River (1875); Rivers and
Harbors (1883); Merchant Marine and Fisheries (1887); Irrigation and
Reclamation, Civil Service (1893); Roads (1913); and Flood Control
(1916; see Galloway and Wise 1976, 72–73). Many of these panels were
also considered very popular with legislators. In examining assignment
transfers, Stewart (1995) finds that among the most attractive committees
between 1859 and 1911 were Rivers and Harbors (ranking first), Agriculture (third), Banking and Currency (tied for seventh), Post Office and
Post Roads (tied for seventh), Mines and Mining (twelfth), and Indian Affairs (thirteenth). Several scholars note that the attractiveness of such assignments is understandable, since government outlays for such things as

post offices, public roads, and river and harbor projects were an important source of federal funds to local communities (Kernell and McDonald
1999; Moulton 1912; Stewart 1995, 19; Wilson 1986).

As the form of the committee system was changing, so were its internal
dynamics. To some extent the growth in committees, or at least committee assignments, is related to the growth in the size of the House. Nevertheless, Stewart (1992) argues that there is more to this explanation of
committee expansion, since the growth in number of assignments far out-
paced the growth in chamber size. He subsequently finds that between
1896 and 1910 there was a change from transitory committee assignments to a norm of committee seat "property rights" (Stewart 1995).
Stewart shows that in the 45th Congress (1877–78), 36 percent of re-
elected legislators returned to their committee appointments in the next
congress. However, by the 65th Congress (1917–18), 56 percent of incumbent committee assignees served in the same position the following
term (Stewart 1992, 176–77). Katz and Sala (1996) similarly find that,
after the electoral reforms that strengthened ties between politicians and
their electorate, representatives were more likely to exercise their right to
retain their committee seats. Growth in terms of committee seats in the
period Stewart examines (1875–1921) was most rapid for panels categorized as having appropriating authority over the federal budget. Among
these eight committees were such constituency-oriented panels as Agriculture, Post Office, and Indian Affairs.

The transition to a committee system that could better serve the electoral needs of members was further aided in 1910 by the revolt against
Speaker Joe Cannon. The conventional wisdom is that, prior to the institutional changes imposed on the leadership that year, most control over
committee assignments and operations was in the hands of the speaker
(e.g., see Price 1977). Stewart (1992), however, disputes the claim as to
complete Speaker autonomy and demonstrates that leadership had to be
responsive to members' demands for expanded access to seats on specific
committees (see also Follett 1896; Lawrence, Maltzman, and Wahlbeck
1999). Either way, by 1910 widespread dissatisfaction with the more or
less autocratic reign of the Speaker led to a revolt that brought about the
removal of the speaker's seat on the Rules Committee, as well as a transfer of his authority over committee assignments to party committees on
committees. One of the major complaints against Cannon, and possibly
the largest factor in his demise, was this abuse of the power to appoint
members to committees. Jones (1968) indicates that Cannon frequently
moved people from committee to committee in retaliation for their lack
of support for his legislative agenda.

Growth of Government and the Federal Budget

Once career politicians fashioned a committee structure over which they had greater control, they needed only one more ingredient to secure the role of these decision-making bodies in providing for constituent needs and, hence, members' reelection prospects—government money. The flow of federal funds began with governmental expansion in the late nineteenth century and grew to a gush with the introduction of Roosevelt's New Deal programs in the 1930s. Between 1917 and 1945, such nonmilitary federal spending increased nearly tenfold. In order to provide for the economic needs of constituents, Congress, mostly under FDR's New Deal agenda, initiated the expansion of the federal role in public works programs with such measures as the Federal Employment Stabilization Act of 1931, the National Industrial Recovery Act of 1933, and the creation of agencies like the Civilian Conservation Corps and the Works Progress Administration.

By the early 1940s, a resurgent and more career-oriented Congress was chafing under unrestrained executive control of federal programs and public works projects. To reassert its authority over the distribution of government funds and budgetary decision making, Congress acted to dismantle some of the executive apparatus for central planning of such projects. The most profound action was the termination of the National Resources Planning Board in 1943 (Bailey and Samuel 1952, 167). Sundquist maintains that several legislators stated publicly that they cut the agency because they felt this type of economic planning should be centered in Congress, not the executive branch (1981, 143–44). One of the more outspoken legislators on this point was reform advocate and later reform committee member Representative Everett Dirksen (R-IL). Of course, public works projects were not the only means of providing for home districts. The New Deal era was replete with subsidy programs and financial assistance for specialized segments of the economy and social groups.

A Joint Committee and a Reorganization Plan

By 1945, the war was coming to a close, and Congress was beginning to consider the transition back to a peacetime economy and rebuilding war-torn Europe. At the same time, however, widespread demands to alter the rules governing the policy process and the system of legislative committees were reaching their peak, both from outside the Capitol and from within the halls of Congress.[2] The weakened policy position of Congress had led not only to direct attacks on the presidential administration (as in the case of economic planning), but also to calls for reforms in the way the body made its policy decisions. Any serious consideration of radical restructuring in Congress had been put on hold until the end of the war. Nevertheless, wartime cutbacks heightened public sensitivities to the perquisites of legislators. An ill-fated attempt to extend civil service pensions to the legislative branch along with the distribution of X-cards (exemptions from emergency gasoline rationing) to members of Congress in 1942 ignited public outcry that change was needed on Capitol Hill. Further concern for the policy influence of the legislative branch vis-à-vis the president was also raised that year in Washington, as Roosevelt seemingly bullied Congress into passage of farm price-support legislation by simply threatening to act unilaterally if the legislature was unwilling to go along (Byrd 1988, 540; Maney 1978).

Over the next few years numerous magazine and academic articles and books were published recounting the failings of Congress and blaming its inadequacies primarily on an obsolete committee structure and outmoded leadership arrangements (e.g., see Gore 1943; La Follette 1943; Outland 1945; Perkins 1944). Included in the reform chorus were two influential reports, one published by the American Political Science Association (APSA; a report that had been under development since 1942; see APSA 1945) and the other by the National Planning Association (NPA), spelling out specific failings and remedies for the institution (Heller 1945).

George Galloway, former assistant research director of the Twentieth Century Fund, and chair of the APSA Committee on Congress, identified the major problems facing Congress as being (1) a committee system that was antiquated and suffered from overlapping jurisdictions; (2) a lack of adequate information and oversight resources; (3) no unity of command (power scattered among eighty "little ministries"); (4) undue pressures from constituents and pressure groups; and (5) artificial separation of powers making teamwork between Congress and the administration difficult (Galloway n.d.).

A considerable amount of pressure for congressional restructuring originated from members of Congress themselves and their actions did not end with mere grandstanding. In the 78th Congress (1943–44), thirty different congressional restructuring bills were introduced by twenty-two different House members.[3] These bills ranged from grants of subpoena power for specific committees to the establishment of joint committees for consideration of numerous policy issues and provisions for expert committee staff. The pace of reform picked up even more at the start of the 79th Congress in 1945. In the month of January alone, twenty-three different reform measures were introduced in the House by many of the same legislators.[4] These proposals were not only suggestions for institutional rearrangements, but also meant to foster public support and pressure on legislators to generate substantial congressional reforms.

Movement toward formal consideration of reform proposals had already begun at the end of the 1944 legislative session, when the House and Senate finally approved a resolution introduced by Senator Francis Maloney (D-CT) and Representative A. S. "Mike" Monroney (D-OK) to establish a joint committee for consideration of congressional reorganization.[5] At the start of the next congressional term in 1945, Maloney died, and long-time reform advocate, Senator Robert La Follette Jr. (Progressive-WI), was named to replace him as chair of the Joint Committee on the Organization of Congress (hereafter, the La Follette-Monroney Committee). The committee quickly named George Galloway as its staff director (essentially its only staff member), and ten other legislators were appointed to the panel.[6] Beginning in mid-March and running through the end of June of that year, the committee held thirty-nine days of hearings with 102 witnesses, including more than 60 members of Congress (Rundquist 1985).

On March 4, 1946, the La Follette-Monroney Committee submitted thirty-seven reform recommendations to Congress in the form of Senate Report 1011.[7] The recommendations ranged from substantial consolidation of the number of standing committees in both chambers to increases in administrative staff and pay raises for members of Congress. Senator La Follette subsequently introduced the panel's proposals in the form of a bill (S. 2177), and the Senate began deliberations on the plan in early June 1946. After five days of debate and a handful of amendments, the bill passed the Senate on a 49–16 vote. The reorganization plan then headed for the House, where, after deep divisions in the chamber about the restructuring proposals, it lay on the Speaker's desk for nearly six weeks. With the congressional term winding down, reform advocates felt it was imperative that they secure a rule for floor consideration of the bill, or else any effort at congressional restructuring would die in that legislative term. In order to win approval of a rule, Monroney had to agree to a number of substantial revisions, including the removal of provisions for party policy committees and a legislative-executive policy council.

After one day of debate and a hailstorm of floor amendments, Monroney and Dirksen won House passage of the bill by a vote of 229–61 on July 25, 1946. With members beginning to leave Washington to campaign at home, Senator La Follette was faced with the dilemma of either attempting to reconcile the two versions with a conference committee— the amount of time that would take spelled certain death for any effort at substantial reform in that Congress—or acceding to the House alterations and passing the amended version in the Senate. La Follette opted for the latter, and the next day the Senate agreed to the tremendously weakened version of the bill. President Harry Truman signed the measure into law on August 2, 1946.[8]

Rejection of Substantial Alterations in Committee Powers over Policy Determination

The debate surrounding congressional reform in the 79th Congress involved a number of proposals that would have substantially restructured the legislative process in both chambers along with the authority of standing committees to determine the direction of policy matters under their purview. In many ways the proposals represented critical junctures for legislators to decide how they wanted to structure policy decision making in the House. Legislators were faced with decisions regarding extensive consolidation of committee jurisdictions, the imposition of budgetary controls, the institution of party policy committees, the introduction of committee "docket days," and the reduction of private legislation (among others). All of these choices, however, had profound implications for the autonomy of legislative committees and the means by which representatives provided for district needs and consequently helped to secure their own political survival. For instance, rearrangement of committee policy property rights was a decision about increasing informational and policymaking efficiency while at the same time reducing the constituency bias in committee membership. Imposing fiscal controls through a joint budget committee would have the effect of increasing chamber influence (or, moreover, the influence of the collection of both chambers) on the legislative output of individual committees at the expense of their autonomy in policy areas of special interest to their membership. In a similar fashion, allowing the general membership of the chamber to plead for their policy proposals in the open forum of committee hearings would additionally erode the exclusive control of committees over their legislative agenda. Introduction of party policy committees was meant to have the same effect of reducing the authority of committees to control their own agendas and determine policy outcomes, but this power would be surrendered to party rather than chamber structures. Finally, altering the process of considering private claims by constituents was not so much a decision about dropping this form of constituency service as it was about updating this legislative function to accord with the modern resources and demands on members of Congress. I will argue that the outcome legislators chose in each of these instances—whether acceptance or rejection of a reform proposal—was motivated by their drive to provide for constituency demands and their own reelection prospects. The organization of the House in the ensuing years after the Legislative Reorganization Act did not change this character in any meaningful way.

Consolidation of Congressional Committees: A Ripple Rather Than a Tidal Wave

If there is one change that the Legislative Reorganization Act of 1946 is known for among political scientists, it is the consolidation of 48 standing House committees into 19 panels and 33 standing Senate committees into 15 panels. In rearranging committees and jurisdictions, the intent of reformers was to create a system of panels that better met the informational needs of the chamber. La Follette, the reform committee co-chair, stated that the existing committee structure and configuration of jurisdictions was "not conducive to the formulation of coherent and continuous legislative policy" (1943, 94), and that "[s]implification of the committee structure would afford a greater opportunity for each individual Senator or Congressman to concentrate his energies on one or, at the most, two committees. He would become more expert in his chosen field, and the service and effectiveness of the committees would improve accordingly" (La Follette 1943, 95). Monroney, the other co-chair, agreed on the informational aim of the reforms, asserting that "[b]y improving the importance of the consolidated committees and defining their jurisdiction more closely, members of these committees could become specialists in their particular line" (Monroney 1945, 9). Reform committee member Senator Wallace White (R-ME), suggested that one method of achieving panels with greater informational utility for the legislature was to end the "geographical principle" of district advocates dominating committees and to constitute them so that representatives of related economic interests would be balanced by members from noninterested constituencies (e.g., balancing legislators from farm districts on the Agriculture Committee with those from urban districts).[9]

Many of the committees whose policy purviews were merged into larger committees with broader jurisdictions were almost completely inactive and frequently described in such terms as "hangovers of lively legislative issues long since settled"[10] or "ornamental barnacles on the ship of state" (Galloway 1946, 64). Both Monroney and Galloway later hailed the consolidation of committee jurisdictions as "the keystone in the arch of congressional reform" (Galloway 1953, 276; Monroney 1949). Despite the generous recollection of the significance of this alteration in committee structure, the jurisdictional consolidation scarcely reduced the attraction of these committees to members seeking to serve narrow constituency needs.

Committee Composition Before the Legislative Reorganization Act

There is little disagreement that by the end of World War II congressional committees were the locus of power in both chambers (Deering and Smith 1997). In the 1920s, "[t]he party caucus disintegrated, party discipline declined, and party government was replaced by loose coalitions of voting blocs with shifting leadership" (Galloway and Wise 1976, 174; see also Cooper and Brady 1981). By the early 1940s, about the only significant duty the party performed in Congress was to assemble at the start of each term to elect its chamber leaders (Speaker, Majority Leader, etc.). Enactment of important legislation no longer required the support of party leaders to steer bills through committees and on to floor approval; instead the critical components were support of the mighty committee chiefs and an almost institutionalized deference to their authority and expertise (Huntington 1965, 19–20; Sundquist 1981, 177–78). In effect, there was no active partisan check over the actions of committees.

As demonstrated above, all the factors were in place by the 1940s that allowed legislators to take advantage of the existing structure for their own reelection prospects—the federal budget was eight times what it was just twenty years prior, 90 percent of House members were seeking reelection each term, and there were well-established norms of seniority and property rights to committee assignments. These factors had been emerging for many years in Congress, and members had skillfully adapted the committee system to better serve their most critical political objective—reelection.

Among the forty-eight committees in the House in 1945–46, several had jurisdictional boundaries that were attractive to members seeking to attend to district needs.[11] They ranged from maritime-oriented panels (Merchant Marine and Fisheries; Rivers and Harbors) to panels focused on the operations and employees of the federal bureaucracy (Expenditures in the Executive Departments and Civil Service). Political scientist James McGregor Burns, drawing on examples such as the House Agriculture Committee, argued in the late 1940s that panels had for decades been composed of high-demand members. He declared that "[i]t is only natural for Congressmen to seek membership on the committees that affect the major interests of their constituents" (Burns 1949, 55). In his study of the Rivers and Harbors Committee from 1889 to 1913, Wilson notes that, even in historically distant periods, representatives understood "that they [had] an important obligation to represent their district" and, at least in the case of this panel, sought assignment to a committee of specific interest to their district needs (Wilson 1985).[12]

Will an analysis of committee composition similar to the tests conducted in chapter 3 bear out Burns's contention that many panels were dominated by members representing high-demand districts? As in the earlier analysis, I consider the extent to which, if at all, members with intense constituency interests were occupying seats on committees of notable importance to their districts. Instead of focusing on the temporal dimension of changes in composition over the years, I survey only committees in the pre-reform Congress, 1945–46, to analyze evidence of a disproportionately large number of high-demand members. I concentrate on thirteen committees whose policy jurisdictions were most likely to lend themselves to serving the specific needs of individual localities. The tests are identical to those used in chapter 3, in that I use data on the geographical, social, and economic characteristics of all members' congressional districts. As before, I test whether Agriculture is dominated by representatives from farming districts or Merchant Marine and Fisheries by maritime-oriented legislators, but I add to the previous analysis several committees with more narrow jurisdictions, like Flood Control; Rivers and Harbors; Indian Affairs; and Mines and Mining.[13]

To roughly determine the appropriate jurisdiction and constituency characteristics related to each panel's work, I examine the policy issues considered during their committee hearings in the 78th (1943–44) and 79th (1945–46) Congresses, using the CIS Congressional Committee Hearings Index. As before, some committees had relatively narrow jurisdictions and, hence, have one measure of district characteristics (e.g., percent of population employed in mining for the Mines and Mining Committee). Other committees had multiple issue dimensions and thus warranted an equivalent number of measures of constituency attributes (e.g., the Rivers and Harbors Committee). Those with multiple component measures required a demand "index" that was calculated by standardizing the components (using a mean of zero and standard deviation of one) and summing them. Again, the justification for this score is that a district which ranked high on both components of a two-component demand "score" should record a higher score than a district which ranks high on only one component. Since these tests were for congressional districts during the 1940s, it was not always possible to find or aggregate data to the district level for each committee,[14] so in some instances state-level data were substituted. The measures employed for each committee are listed in table 6.

Like the earlier tests, this one relies on a modified difference-in-medians

Table 6 Tests of Distributive Outliers for Constituency Committees, 79th Congress (1945–46)

Committee	Significance Level
Agriculture (percentage employed in farming and percentage living in rural farming areas)	.00
Banking and Currency (percentage employed in finance, insurance, and real estate and in central city [dummy])	.71
Civil Service (percentage employed in government and district within 100 miles of D.C. [dummy])	.42
Expenditures in the Executive Departments (percentage employed in government and district within 100 miles of D.C. [dummy])	.54
Flood Control (relative flood-potential level)	(.37)[a]
Indian Affairs (percentage state population Native-American)	(.00)
Irrigation and Reclamation (percentage employed in farming)	.06
Labor (percentage employed in blue-collar industries and percentage of state work force unionized)	.48
Merchant Marine and Fisheries (district is coastal, contains a maritime academy or includes one of the twenty-five most active ports)	.00
Mines and Mining (percentage of state population employed in mining)	(.00)
Public Lands (population density and state acreage owned by NPS and BLM)	.00
Rivers and Harbors (relative flood-potential level and district contains one of the twenty-five most active ports)	.03
Roads (percentage employed in construction)	.05

[a] Figures in parentheses represent significance levels for Wilcoxon rank sum tests for difference in variance.

test using a Monte Carlo simulation technique to create a distribution of medians from ten thousand randomly drawn sample committees. Again, a committee whose actual median demand score is greater than 95 percent of the random committee medians is considered to be a significant outlier with respect to constituent needs. When narrow committee jurisdictions dictated that I rely on only a single, state-level measure of characteristics, it was nearly impossible to adequately conduct such a difference-in-medians test.[15] Since these were still very relevant measures for the jurisdictions of the committees being examined (e.g., percentage employed in mining for the Mines and Mining Committee; percentage of Native American population for the Indian Affairs Committee; and relative flood potential level for the Flood Control Committee),[16] I conducted a somewhat less stringent test of the equality in the distributions of the committee versus the rest of the chamber—the Wilcoxon rank sums test (Hogg and Craig 1995).[17]

Table 6 reports the results of the composition tests of constituency-oriented committees in the 79th Congress (1945–46). The tests indicate that several panels in this pre-reform era were dominated by representatives with acute constituency interests in the matters considered by their panels. As reported earlier, the Agriculture Committee was dominated by farming interests, and the Merchant Marine and Fisheries panel was overrun by members from maritime-oriented areas. In addition, the Indian Affairs Committee had a disproportionate concentration of members from states with large Native American populations; the Mines Committee had an excessive number of representatives from states with high mining employment; the Public Lands Committee was composed of a disproportionate percentage of legislators from districts with large acreage administered by the Interior Department; the Rivers and Harbors Committee had an excessive number of members representing areas with flood and port concerns; and the Roads Committee had a disproportionate membership with high construction employment at home.[18] Although not quite at the level of significance set earlier, the Irrigation and Reclamation Committee was composed of a large percentage of members with extreme farming interests in their districts.

Interesting patterns also emerge in committees that were not extreme with regard to the constituency needs of their members. For example, neither committee concerned with the federal bureaucracy—Civil Service, and Expenditures in the Executive Departments—was an outlier with respect to district characteristics. Also, panels whose successors are frequently outliers in subsequent years (as shown in the analysis from chapter 3), do not seem to be so in this period, including the Banking and Currency, and Labor committees (eventually half of the Education and Labor Committee). The analysis establishes that before the House considered serious restructuring of committee jurisdictions and the policy process, members had firmly entrenched themselves in a number of panels that were beneficial to the needs of their districts.

The Effect of Reforms on Committee Composition

Despite the importance of many committees in this period, both from a policy and constituency standpoint, the common complaint among reform advocates was that there were simply too many committees. Monroney's often repeated expression was that the number of committees "just grew like Topsy from the beginning of this Nation." [19] Consideration of committee consolidation in 1945 and 1946 was surprisingly restrained. Little opposition was raised to most jurisdictional changes, and beyond the budgetary reforms which were to substantially alter the role of the Appropriations Committee, only one specific committee alteration—consolidation of the Post Office and Post Roads panel within a larger panel that also included civil service matters—produced any kind of organized opposition either in committee testimony, internal congressional memoranda, or floor debate. As stated earlier, many committees were merged into panels with wider jurisdictions because they were largely inactive. Table 7 offers the consolidation pattern of committees in the House along with the number of hearings and bills reported by each standing committee in the 79th Congress. The data demonstrate that many eliminated committees were practically dormant or had no conceivable positive effect on members' reelection needs or institutional advancement (Davidson and Oleszek 1977).

To most members, the consolidation of inactive committees and committees with similar (if not overlapping) jurisdictions into a smaller number of panels with more seats and broader policy jurisdictions was a welcome change. They saw this restructuring as a means of reducing the likelihood of being assigned to inactive and irrelevant panels, and increasing the probability that their assignments would help to ensure their effectiveness in managing policy development. James Wadsworth (R-NY), a reform architect and member of the Republican Committee on Committees,[20] stated during floor deliberation that consolidating committees would keep members from being assigned to committees that seldom met or did anything, and would help legislators avoid having to wait for seats on panels that appealed to them.[21] Fewer committees with broader jurisdictions would give more junior members an opportunity to participate in policymaking and allow them to serve the needs of their constituents.

In the end, the elections of 1946 smoothed the way for the restructuring of committee jurisdictions. A surprisingly high proportion of the House, 102 members, did not return at the start of the 80th Congress, including a moderate number who voluntarily retired (32 members). Among the 70 members who lost their reelection bids, most were Demo-

Table 7 Committee Changes Resulting from the Legislative Reorganization
Act of 1946

Pre-LRA Committees	Number of Hearings, 78th Congress	Number of Bills Reported, 78th Congress	Post-LRA Committees
Agriculture	138	34	} Agriculture
Appropriations	509	45	} Appropriations
Military Affairs	181	68	} Armed Services
Naval Affairs	178	75	
Banking and Currency	119	14	} Banking and Currency
Coinage, Weights, and Measures	6	2	
District of Columbia	35	42	} District of Columbia
Education	21	2	} Education and Labor
Labor	55	3	
Foreign Affairs	93	12	} Foreign Affairs
Expenditures in the Executive Departments	19	8	} Expenditures in the Exec Depts
Accounts	1	64	
Disposition of Executive Papers	0	0	
Election of Pres, VP and Reps	0	0	
Elections #1	12	1	} House Administration
Elections #2	1	1	
Elections #3	2	3	
Enrolled Bills	0	0	
Library	3	5	
Memorials	0	0	
Printing	0	40	
Indian Affairs	25	30	
Insular Affairs	39	4	
Irrigation and Reclamation	31	14	} Public Lands
Mines and Mining	0	6	
Public Lands	64	46	
Territories	0	9	

crats. As a result, Republicans assumed a majority in both chambers
and consequently controlled the implementation of the new committee structure. This meant that there would be little concern about Democrats whose committee chairs were going to be lost due to jurisdictional
restructuring, since they were to lose their chairs to the Republicans
anyway.

Table 8 gives some insight into how the jurisdictional restructuring
affected members of exclusive and distributive committees. The table

Table 7   (continued)

Pre-LRA Committees	Number of Hearings, 78th Congress	Number of Bills Reported, 78th Congress	Post-LRA Committees
Interstate and Foreign Commerce	172	46	} Interstate and Foreign Commerce
Immigration and Naturalization	33	74	
Judiciary	124	60	Judiciary
Patents	8	4	
Revision of the Law	1	4	
Merchant Marine and Fisheries	137	30	} Merchant Marines and Fisheries
Census	2	0	
Civil Service	57	19	Post Office and Civil Service
Post Office and Post Roads	61	27	
Flood Control	33	5	
Public Buildings and Grounds	68	11	Public Works
Rivers and Harbors	34	2	
Roads	45	4	
Rules	89	142	} Rules
Un-American Activities	n.a.	n.a.	} Un-American Activities
Invalid Pensions	9	6	
Pensions	1	1	Veterans' Affairs
World War Veteran's Legislation	36	16	
Ways and Means	173	31	} Ways and Means
Claims	0	737	(Abolished)
War Claims	0	1	(Abolished)

SOURCE: Galloway 1946.

identifies the percentages of 79th Congress Democrats and Republicans who returned to a committee or its successor, did not return to the House, or were compensated for their loss with either a leadership post, a transfer to an exclusive committee, or a committee or subcommittee chair position. These assignments are juxtaposed with transfers that might be considered to have been uncompensated (i.e., none of the above occurred).[22] For the exclusive committees, almost all members, regardless of party, either returned to their original assignments, lost their congressional seats, or were properly compensated in some way. Only three Democrats were forced to take significantly worse committee assignments.

Table 8   Compensation Patterns for Committee Alterations as a Result of the LRA of 1946

	Returned to Committee	Did Not Return to House	Transferred to Exclusive Committee or Leadership Post	Granted Other Committee or Subcommittee Chair	Uncompensated (Transferred to Other Committee)
Exclusive Committees					
Appropriations					
Republicans	83% (*n* = 5)	17 (3)	—	—	—
Democrats	60 (15)	40 (10)	—	—	—
Rules					
Republicans	50 (2)	—	25 (1)	25 (1)	—
Democrats	50 (4)	13 (1)	13 (1)	—	25 (2)
Ways and Means					
Republicans	90 (9)	10 (1)	—	—	—
Democrats	71 (10)	21 (3)	—	—	7 (1)
Distributive Committees					
Agriculture					
Republicans	67 (8)	8 (1)	25 (3)	—	—
Democrats	69 (11)	25 (4)	—	—	6 (1)
Banking and Currency					
Republicans	70 (7)	20 (2)	—	—	10 (1)
Democrats	53 (8)	47 (7)	—	—	—
Civil Service					
Republicans	25 (2)	25 (2)	13 (1)	—	38 (3)
Democrats	23 (3)	31 (4)	—	—	46 (6)
Expenditures in the Executive Departments					
Republicans	50 (4)	25 (2)	25 (2)	—	—
Democrats	14 (2)	43 (6)	—	—	43 (6)

On the constituency-oriented panels, Republicans only occasionally were compelled to take other committee assignments. This was frequently limited to one or two members (with the exception of Roads), who were often granted what would be widely considered better assignments, like Interstate and Foreign Commerce or Armed Services. Democrats were much more likely to experience uncompensated loss of seats, but their removal came with little hardship, and often, to the contrary, the loss was a welcome change. For the most part, incumbents were able to retain at least one of their many previous committee assignments in the newly restructured House—mostly owing to the large turnover of Democrats in the 1946 election. Moreover, many legislators were able to dump committee positions with little relevance to their electoral needs or political ambitions. For example, four of the six Democrats who would potentially

Table 8 (continued)

	Returned to Committee	Did Not Return to House	Transferred to Exclusive Committee or Leadership Post	Granted Other Committee or Subcommittee Chair	Uncompensated (Transferred to Other Committee)
Flood Control					
Republicans	22 (2)	11 (1)	33 (3)	33 (3)	—
Democrats	33 (4)	17 (2)	—	—	50 (6)
Indian Affairs					
Republicans	25 (2)	25 (2)	25 (2)	13 (1)	13 (1)
Democrats	15 (2)	54 (7)	—	—	31 (4)
Irrigation and Reclamation					
Republicans	50 (5)	—	30 (3)	10 (1)	10 (1)
Democrats	27 (3)	27 (3)	—	—	45 (5)
Labor					
Republicans	57 (4)	28 (2)	—	14 (1)	—
Democrats	38 (5)	46 (6)	—	—	15 (2)
Merchant Marine and Fisheries					
Republicans	22 (2)	—	33 (3)	33 (3)	11 (1)
Democrats	42 (5)	33 (4)	—	—	25 (3)
Public Lands					
Republicans	56 (5)	—	33 (3)	—	11 (1)
Democrats	33 (4)	50 (6)	—	—	17 (2)
Rivers and Harbors					
Republicans	45 (5)	18 (2)	—	18 (2)	18 (2)
Democrats	20 (3)	40 (6)	—	—	40 (6)
Roads					
Republicans	33 (3)	11 (1)	—	11 (1)	44 (4)
Democrats	33 (4)	33 (4)	—	—	33 (4)

lose their assignments after the merging of the Flood Control panel into Public Works represented regions with quite low actual flood potential (north central Washington, northwest Alabama, western Montana, and central Texas). These four members were four of the five lowest demanders with respect to district flood potential on the committee in the 79th Congress. Similarly, some members were relieved of duties on less important committees so that they could concentrate on issues of acute significance to their districts. For example, after the implementation of the LRA, James Domengeaux, from New Orleans, relinquished assignments on Elections No. 1, Insular Affairs, Irrigation and Reclamation, and World War Veterans' Legislation so that he could focus his efforts on the Merchant Marine and Fisheries Committee. New Orleans was one of the busiest ports in the country.

Similarly, King finds that the membership of the panels that were merged more often than not had overlapped considerably. Looking at a number of panels that were eventually combined to become the Interior and Insular Affairs Committee, for example, 60 percent of the Public Lands Committee membership also served on the Irrigation and Reclamation Committee, 39 percent of Public Lands members served on Mines and Mining, 37 percent of Mines and Mining members served on Indian Affairs, and 30 percent of Indian Affairs members served on Irrigation and Reclamation. King uncovers similar overlap among the major committees that eventually made up Public Works, Judiciary, and Post Office and Civil Service. He states, "It is no surprise that these committees were bundled together. The postreform committees embraced membership patterns found before the reforms, thereby reinforcing coalitions rather than forging new ones" (King 1997, 61–62).

Therefore, the effects of committee restructuring beg the question: Did jurisdictional consolidation and reduction in the number of committees affect the ability of the newly created panels to attract members with disproportionate constituency needs? Two hypotheses suggest what one might find.

> **Hypothesis A—Few Issue Outliers:** *Since some of the new committees merged a number of different panels with differing constituency interests and since committees were going to grow in size (for the critical committees, the increase was about 25 percent), they will attract a more diverse group of legislators with a wide range of constituency needs. Therefore, there will be few committees composed of high-demand legislators when examining narrow constituency characteristics.*

> **Hypothesis B—Many Issue Outliers:** *Merging of related policy issues into a single committee jurisdiction increased the concentration of members with similar constituency needs. With greater opportunities for committee transfers, due to electoral volatility in the 1946 and 1948 elections, and increased size that would allow more members from "interested" districts to get seats on relevant panels, there will be just as many committees with high-demand membership.*

The anecdotal evidence concerning the composition of committees from the period is not entirely conclusive. James McGregor Burns contends that both hypotheses are partially correct as a result of the 1946 reforms. "As a result of being reshuffled and 'streamlined' in the 1946 reorganization of Congress, some committees became more representative but others remained out of focus" (Burns 1949, 55). Galloway also conceded after the reforms that a number of panels were "dominated by members from particular regions or economic interests . . . [because] congressmen naturally seek assignment to committees having jurisdiction over matters of major concern to their districts and states" (Galloway 1953, 281). Both scholars point to the House Agriculture, Interior, and Merchant Marine and Fisheries committees as examples of panels that remained dominated by high-demand members after the institution of committee restructuring at the start of the 80th Congress.

Using the same kinds of tests conducted earlier, I examine the extent to which committees created as a result of the LRA remained overrepresentative of the narrow constituency interests prevalent in the pre-reform House. Table 9 presents similar medians tests, but for the newly created committees in the following congressional terms (the 80th–82nd Congresses). I employ the same measures of constituency characteristics to see if the successors to the pre-reform committees remained attractive to a disproportionate number of members with narrow district needs. By using the original measures of district demand on the new committees, I have in part biased the tests against finding outliers or in favor of accepting Hypothesis A. That is, even if the newly expanded committees appeal to members for constituency reasons, because of the broader jurisdictions a committee composed of high demanders may not appear as such under this test. A variety of high-demand representatives may be on the committee, but by testing for only one kind of high-demand district at a time, I may not capture the distributive character of the panel membership. (See chapter 3 for similar tests of committee outliers using more combined measures of district demand.)

The table shows, not unexpectedly, that committees that were not subject to jurisdictional changes remained about as attractive to members with similar district interests after the reforms as they had been before the reforms—Agriculture and Merchant Marine remained outliers, while Expenditures in the Executive Departments was generally representative of the entire chamber. However, several panels that were merged with others also remained exceptionally attractive to members with related constituency needs—Public Lands still disproportionately drew legislators with Native American and mining concerns in their districts, and Public Works still attracted members representing areas with rivers and harbors or road construction interests. Returning to the demand scores used in chapter 3, we see that even using multiple measures of district interest in a combined score the committees are found to be outliers in this post-reform period. Interestingly, after a few congressional terms, in the

Table 9   Tests of Distributive Outliers for Constituency Committees, 80th–82nd Congresses (1947–1952)

Committee	Signif. Level, 80th Congress	Signif. Level, 81st Congress	Signif. Level, 82nd Congress
Agriculture			
Agriculture measures	.00	.00	.00
Banking and Currency			
Banking and Currency measures	.60	.09	.01
Education and Labor			
Labor measures	.46	.14	.60
Expenditures in the Executive Departments			
Expenditures measures	.30	.21	.13
Merchant Marine and Fisheries			
Merchant Marine measures	.00	.00	.00
Post Office and Civil Service			
Civil Service measures	.97	.33	.42
Public Lands			
Indian Affairs measures	(.00)[a]	(.00)	(.00)
Irrigation and Rec. measures	.52	.14	.66
Mines and Mining measures	(.12)	(.02)	(.05)
Public Lands measures	.53	.14	.66
Public Works			
Flood Control measures	(.17)	(.36)	(.43)
Rivers and Harbors measures	.02	.02	.02
Roads measures	.12	.03	.07

[a] Figures in parentheses represent significance levels for Wilcoxon rank sum tests for difference in variance.

82nd Congress (1951–52), the Banking Committee began to disproportionately attract members with financial concerns in their home districts—something it had not done prior to the reforms. Although Public Works seems to lose its attractiveness to members with road construction interests, a study of the Public Works Committee from the 1960s to 1990s shows that, once construction of the Interstate Highway System began to gain momentum (and federal dollars), this committee regained its attractiveness to such representatives (Adler 2002).

Altogether, the jurisdictional reshuffling had little effect on the constituency orientation of many committees in the House. A fair number of panels were dominated by high-demand members before the institution of the LRA in 1947, and most remained so after the changes. Either a panel experienced no significant jurisdictional changes, or the changes it underwent did not affect its attractiveness to members seeking to provide for narrow district needs. House panels after the reforms, although they could still be composed of policy experts—easy to imagine in the case of an Agriculture Committee dominated by members from farm areas—were hardly different in terms of the district interests of members than they had been before the changes, and they certainly had not lost the "geographic principle" that reformers had intended to bring to an end.

Regaining Policy Control from Committees: A Doomed Idea from the Start

Efforts to curb the powers of committees and their influential chairs in this period were based on the belief that coordinated congressional decision making would make Congress a more effective policy player in its dealings with the president. Of course, all of these changes intended to enhance the policy process would increase the powers of either chamber-wide or party-controlled bodies at the expense of the committees' autonomous domination of policies under their existing authority.

Imposition of Budgetary Limitations: The "Most Complete and Dismal Failure of Reorganization"

The budgetary reforms proposed and instituted in the LRA exemplify how well-meaning reforms, intended to improve congressional oversight of federal spending, are often opposed and quickly abandoned when they interfere with the ability of independent committees to allocate federal funds with impunity.[23]

As a result of growing public debt after the war (nearly \$275 billion), an increasingly complicated process of appropriations decision making and oversight, and concern that Congress was becoming marginalized with respect to fiscal matters involving executive departments,[24] there emerged a "widespread public demand that Congress strengthen its control over the public purse" (Galloway 1946, 249–54). The most common perception among reformers was that the lack of coordination in appropriations and taxation decisions was the core of the Congress's deficiencies in budgetary decision making. For example, the National Planning Association stated that, among the major problem areas, "there is little effort made (a) to relate total revenue and total appropriations so that they are balanced or designedly unbalanced, (b) to analyze specific revenue measures in terms of total revenue requirements, (c) to align specific appropriations measures with a predetermined level for total appropriations" (Heller 1945, 15).

In response to fears of Congress's increasing marginalization on fiscal matters, the La Follette-Monroney Committee prescribed that the congressional budget process include a new Joint Committee on the Legislative Budget, composed of members of the House Ways and Means and Appropriations committees and the Senate Finance and Appropriations committees. The obvious intent of the planned change would be to coordinate and manage fiscal decisions on a chamber-wide basis. The proposed committee was to meet at the start of each session and, through a concurrent resolution, set an overall spending limit (as well as targets for fiscal receipts) for the coming fiscal year by February 15 of each year.[25] If this sum was exceeded, all appropriations would be cut back pro-rata to bring them within the agreed total, or Congress would be required to pass a new resolution authorizing an increase in the national debt.

This radical restructuring of the budgetary process, which effectively encumbered the attempts of authorizing and appropriations committees to control the distribution of federal funds, was not well received in the House. The day prior to floor consideration of the La Follette-Monroney proposal, twenty House Appropriations Committee members went on record as opposing the budgetary provisions in the bill and authorized Appropriations Chair Cannon to offer a floor amendment to remove the proposal (Rundquist 1985, 15). On the floor a number of members engaged in a lengthy and somewhat heated debate as to the implications of this provision for governmental spending and the process of appropriating funds for specific programs. Foreshadowing the ultimate failure of this reform, Appropriations Committee member Representative Francis Case (R-SD) pointed out that the bill "makes no requirement that the Congress shall adopt the report of the Budget [the annual budget resolution]," to which Appropriations ranking minority member Representative John Taber (R-NY) somewhat smugly responded, "No; that is true. It could make no such requirement."[26]

The plan was ill-conceived from the start. It created a committee that was enormous and unmanageable. The panel had no staff and no means of compelling agreements among members from different committees and chambers or enforcing agreed-upon limits during subsequent appropriations deliberations. In 1947 the House approved a resolution to cut President Truman's budget by $6 billion. However, a highly partisan controversy developed in the conference committee, and legislators were unable to agree on a final figure, resulting in no budgetary agreement for FY1948. Although the next year legislators did agree to an expenditure ceiling calling for a $2.5 billion cut in the president's request, without any enforcement mechanism the resolution was ineffective. Congress eventually approved outlays approximately $6 billion above the ceiling. Since the new budgetary arrangement was clearly not effective, legislators decided in 1949 to move the deadline for budget resolution to May 1 (from

February 15). However, this date was past when most spending measures had already been enacted, so Congress did not even bother coming to a budget resolution for FY1950 (LeLoup 1980, 7). By 1950 the joint budget committee concept was abandoned completely.

The hasty death of this reform provision is attributed mainly to "resistance within Congress to ceilings on appropriations for favorite agencies and external spending pressures on the legislature" (Galloway 1953, 616–17). Representative Wright Patman (D-TX), described at the time as a leading opponent of the spending controls, argued that such limitations on appropriations would make it harder for Congress to direct special benefits to veterans, the aged, and other "deserving groups" ("Shaping New-Style Congress" 1946). Committee members, particularly Appropriations Committee members, resented the usurpation of their authority to set spending levels by simply "picking a figure out of the air." The concept proved unworkable because independent-minded committee chairs sought to avoid the constraints of a "well-meant but hopeless proposal" (Ippolito 1981, 47–48). Foremost among opponents of budgetary reforms were chairs of the money committees, largely supported by members wishing to avoid limits on their ability to provide benefits to their constituencies. Opposition to this form of fiscal control by members seeking to protect pet programs and unconstrained government spending would plague budgetary reforms for many decades.

The Rejection of Party Policy Committees

Moreover, reformers assumed that the most potent means of managing congressional decision making would be based on relatively dormant party structures. Although revolt against Speaker Joe Cannon was followed by a surge in party caucus authority to control chamber organization (committee assignments, House rules, patronage positions, etc.) and the policy agenda (through use of disciplinary measures, regulation of committee actions, and control of the Rules Committee as a de facto steering panel), the partisan tide shortly receded (Galloway and Wise 1976, 169–74). By the late 1930s, even a House Democratic Steering Committee intended to coordinate day-to-day legislative activities on many of the New Deal programs under consideration had withered, and much of the responsibility for policy leadership had shifted to the relatively autonomous committees (Galloway and Wise 1976, 178). The growing command of committee chairs over the policymaking process derived not only from the emasculated authority of party leaders to control the actions of their members, but also the expertise of these chairs after long years of service (most chairs of major committees had served between ten and thirteen congressional terms) and the entrenchment of the seniority system.

Committees were the locus of authority in the formulation and passage of legislation, and as such represented critical choke points for blocking legislative proposals. This became even more true as the conservative southern wing of the Democratic Party grew in the late 1930s and early 1940s, and their presence on prominent panels, particularly the Rules Committee, became a stumbling block for remaining portions of the New Deal agenda (Patterson 1967; Porter 1980). In 1936, southern Democrats represented only 29 percent of the majority party in the House, but by 1945 southerners constituted over 48 percent of chamber Democrats. The 75th through the 79th Congresses saw a Rules Committee dominated by a conservative coalition made up of southern Democrats—who equaled or outnumbered northern Democrats throughout this period—and conservative Republicans (numbering four or five). This alliance often used its committee domination and strategic position in the policymaking process to weaken or kill liberal proposals it opposed, like measures concerning fair labor practices and the minimum wage (e.g., see Robinson 1963; de Boinville 1982, 149–51).

Several reformers believed that by resurrecting the "moribund" party caucus organization (Galloway 1942) in defining the policy agenda of each chamber, Congress might more effectively confer with the president on important policy matters and regain the upper hand in directing federal policy. Authors of the NPA report felt that such party committees "would institutionalize within Congress a group with which the President or executive department heads could have regular communication without exposure to partisan politics" (Heller 1945, 14). Representative Estes Kefauver (D-TN) declared in his committee testimony that "particularly in times of great stress, there must be cooperation and constant liaison and understanding between the two branches of the Government" and saw party policy committees as the means to achieving this end. Since the La Follette-Monroney Committee fostered a perception of widespread support for this innovation among legislators and scholars alike, the panel included such provisions in its reform proposal to both chambers.

But there was no denying that party policy committees created to set chamber agendas and negotiate agreements with the president would, like the budget committees, develop and grow at the expense of individual committees and their policy autonomy. The proposal for the party agenda panels faced more opposition than the La Follette-Monroney Committee realized, and the concept never even made it to the House chamber. Part of the resistance to the Senate-approved bill, which delayed its consideration in the House for six weeks, was strong leadership opposition to these party policy committees because they would wrest chamber control from existing leaders and committee chairs (Byrd 1988; Rundquist 1985).

Roland Young, a congressional scholar and eventual member of the APSA congressional reform panel, several years earlier projected the mood of legislators toward this idea of partisan agenda committees:

> On the face of it, the reluctance of the party to commit its members to a program after full discussion and a two-thirds vote might seem like a victory for the freedom of the individual. In truth, however, it means that Congressmen prefer to be free to advocate local interests rather than be bound to vote for a broader national program. . . . From a national point of view, the ability of Congress to advocate local interests may not be wise, but it is practical from the viewpoint of the Congressman. No matter how much a Member of Congress may wish to vote nationally, he knows that to stay in power he must cater to his own constituency. (Young 1943, 95)

Eventually, Young's reading of the situation proved to be more accurate than that of the La Follette-Monroney Committee. As part of the price for admission to floor consideration in the House, Monroney and Dirksen were forced to abandon this provision of the original bill (Goodwin 1970, 21).[27]

The Rejection of "Docket Days"

Finally, a less severe means of limiting the ability of committees to control their agendas was the concept of "docket days" for committee hearings. The initiative would have forced committees to set aside regular periods during the month to hear testimony from sponsoring members for bills that panels had not previously acted upon. The intent of the reforms was to compel committees at least to consider additions to their legislative agenda that they had otherwise rejected. This measure was opposed by committee chairs and the Speaker, and, like the recommendation for party policy committees, it was forcibly deleted from the La Follette-Monroney Committee bill in order to secure House floor consideration.

However, the matter of "docket days" did not die there. Chris Herter (R-MA), reintroduced the idea on the House floor as an amendment to the newly trimmed reorganization plan. In its first consideration on the floor his measure for the inclusion of committee docket days passed on a voice vote. However, not to be overruled on a matter that he and committee chairs clearly saw as important, Speaker Sam Rayburn took the unusual step of speaking on the floor as a representative from Texas and made a short but impassioned plea to reject the Herter amendment. Specifically, Rayburn reminded members that such a provision would remove the ability of committees and their chairs to supervise their own policy direction, even if committee chairs, he admitted, can "be a little autocratic."[28] In its last action before the chamber rose to pass the revised La Follette-Monroney plan, the House voted to reject Herter's amendment.

Elimination of Private Claims: Updating Constituency Service

Finally, one of the more forgotten aspects of the LRA went further than any other provision to alter the way legislators served the needs of their constituents. The LRA shifted responsibility for resolving several different types of private claims on government from the legislative to the executive and judicial branches. The definition of what constitutes a private bill has shifted over time, but generally a private bill is one for the relief of private parties. This has constituted many different things, including immigration or nationality issues, claims against the federal government, correction of military records, or even commendations and special recognitions.[29] This alteration was not made because Congress wanted to avoid handling this form of constituency service. To the contrary, representatives frequently see opportunities to contend with private matters as "another golden chance to earn the gratitude of their constituents" (Berman 1964, 21). However, as the populations of congressional districts grew by more than 50 percent of what they had been at the turn of the century (from around 190,000 in 1900 to more than 300,000 constituents in the 1940s), members in the immediate postwar period made a strategic calculation that this time-consuming form of service to individual constituents had opportunity costs for their electoral prospects and that they would be better served by concentrating on other ways to provide for the needs of larger numbers of constituents.

American legislators had cultivated personal relationships with their constituents for electoral purposes long before even the emergence of careerist politicians in Congress. Swift (1987) identifies a considerable amount of constituency-oriented behavior in the early nineteenth century. As part of their "representative" role, members of Congress had taken on the responsibility of attending to the private matters of their constituents in dealings with government. Like their modern-day counterparts, members of Congress in the early nineteenth century often advertised and claimed credit for actions taken on behalf of needy constituents.

The LRA, however, was not the first congressional effort to curb the growing demands by constituents that legislators should handle private matters. In 1855, Congress established the Court of Claims and gave it authority to investigate contractual and other legal claims against the government and report them back to Congress. The court's powers were further expanded in 1883 and 1887 ("The Function of Private Bills" 1971).

However, these measures intended to improve the legislature's ability to deal with constituents' private matters did little to stop the flood of demands for personal attention. Brown claims that around the turn of the century there occurred "a significant increase in what might be called the purely personal duties of Congressmen, who became, indeed, almost the special agents in Washington of their constituents. They came to be called upon, more and more, to attend to innumerable matters unrelated to their legislative function, to obtain passports . . . report on claims against the government, to do the errands of influential persons in their congressional districts" (1922, 249–50; see also Dodd and Schott 1979, 63).

Private legislation leading up to the LRA showed a steady and undeniable increase in the proportion of legislation devoted to private matters. In the congressional terms immediately following World War I, private enactments only constituted about 20–30 percent of the bills enacted by Congress. But by the late 1930s, approximately 45 percent of enactments were private matters. Members of Congress expressed alarm at the increasing percentage of legislative work and resources devoted to the problems and concerns of individual constituents. Representative Robert Luce (R-MA) declared in 1932, "It is hard to see how any reasonable man with any sense of proportion can find ground for insisting that Congress continue to burden itself with the little bills [private legislation]" (1932, 819). By the mid-1940s, private claims represented more than 50 percent of the measures passed by Congress and almost one thousand enactments per term.

The concern that the rapid growth of this "petty business" could slow other legislative business to a halt was not unfounded. Although members had a long history of serving the individual needs of constituents, congressional districts were growing at an incredible rate. This unprecedented growth in constituent population was among the most distressing issues for reformers concerned about private bills. The APSA Committee on Congress specifically noted that the increasing size of constituencies was a primary reason why "the claims of constituents on the legislator's time have become incessant" (APSA 1945, 65).

By 1946, the fears that Luce had expressed more than a decade earlier about the all-consuming nature of private legislation were coming to a head. Galloway noted in a report after the 1946 reforms that "[f]rom the Seventy-sixth to the Seventy-ninth Congress [1941–1946] the proportion of private to total laws enacted rose from 39 percent to 55 percent."[30] When the La Follette-Monroney Committee finally heard testimony from legislators, one of the most common themes among House members was alarm over the growing demands from constituents concerning their private matters. The comments of Butler Hare (D-SC) were typical of members concerns over this form of constituent work: "I shall not attempt to show in any detail of the increased duties of Members of the Congress not directly related to their legislative responsibilities, but it is sufficient to say that for the past decade or longer there has been an increasing demand for service by constituents more nearly related to the administration of laws than in formulating and enacting bills into law." [31] Not surprisingly, Galloway demonstrated that House members bore the brunt of private demands by constituents—in the 80th Congress (1947–48), 85 percent of private bills introduced in Congress originated in the House. [32]

Elimination of several classes of private legislation was a change that by all indications (hearings testimony, floor debate, etc.) was favored with near unanimity. The LRA removed from congressional purview a large subset of private claims that concerned tort claims under $1,000 (Title IV); the construction, maintenance, and operation of bridges and approaches over navigable waters (Title V); and the correction of military and naval records (Title II, Section 207).

The purpose of these reforms was not to eliminate private claims handled by Congress, but to keep their number to a manageable level (Bennett 1967, 17). Immediately after the institution of the reforms in the 80th Congress, the number and percentage of private claims as a proportion of total laws sharply decreased. [33] As a result of the ban on these forms of private claims, the number of private bills introduced went from 3,772 in the 79th to 2,532 in the 80th Congress. Similarly, the ratio of private to total bills dropped from 32 to 21 percent. Carl Vinson (D-GA), the top-ranking Democrat on the House Armed Services Committee until 1965, estimated in July 1951 that the reform concerning the correction of military records alone had relieved Congress since 1946 of consideration of fifteen thousand such private bills ("The Function of Private Bills" 1971).

If private claims were so effective in serving the needs of constituents and assisting in an important aspect of Mayhew's electoral behavior—credit-claiming (1974a, 52–53)—why did members turn away from this legislative activity? Hill and Williams address this question in their study of the decline in private claims legislation from the Legislative Reorganization Act to the present. They find that it was not a decline in claims initiated by citizens or a dwindling need for credit-claiming by members that caused legislators to abandon this activity. Instead, they conclude from a series of interviews with staff members that legislators *simply no longer saw this kind of legislation as an advantageous electoral opportunity.* They found that, for many congressional offices, such legislation only affected a limited number of people, and with growing governmental responsibilities and stretched staffing resources, tremendous opportunity costs were incurred by devoting time to such narrow concerns (Hill and Williams 1993). Since district populations were growing rapidly, member and staff time could be better spent providing for the social and economic needs of a broader range of constituents through public enactments and pursuit of large-scale, government-funded projects.

Conclusion

The Legislative Reorganization Act afforded an opportunity for members of Congress to decide how they wanted to organize the legislative body. In the House, legislators were presented with the prospect of constructing more representative committees, imposing chamber-wide controls on spending, and introducing party machinery for defining legislative agendas. Ultimately, none of these changes took hold. Independent committees composed of members with shared and specialized interests retained their autonomy and utility as devices for reelection.

Despite the best intentions of congressional reform advocates after World War II to unify policy agenda-setting and strengthen the institution with respect to other branches of government, the enacted reform package did more to *weaken* central leadership and concentrate policymaking power in an even smaller number of dominant committees. At least prior to 1946, overlapping jurisdictions between committees meant that the onus for legislative coordination would, to a certain extent, be on the Speaker, who could determine which committee would have the right to consider a bill. The Legislative Reorganization Act, however, severely reduced this discretion by codifying many existing jurisdictions and merging several panels with overlapping boundaries, thus suspending the leadership's admittedly limited authority to determine the direction of legislation. The power of committees to exclusively control the direction of policy under their purview was further enhanced by other reforms, such as curtailing the use of special committees and significant increases in committee staffs (for more on this argument, see Huntington 1965, 20).

These alterations in the locus of policy authority were advantageous for a committee structure whose membership composition was barely touched by what seemed to be substantial reorganization of committee jurisdictions. In retrospect, changing electoral circumstances and increased careerism in the House around the turn of the century inspired the attractiveness of and dependence upon numerous committees to provide for the particularized needs of home districts. Securing federal funds for irrigation dams, post offices, or road construction projects was a means for a legislator "to prove himself successful in the eyes of the people back home" (Galloway 1946, 301). But instead of steering away from the petty details of constituent demands, as many had hoped Congress would do when it entertained reorganization, it altered the institution just enough so that it could serve constituent needs even more efficiently. One critic of the reforms argued that as a result of jurisdictional and staffing changes "it may be anticipated that the committees of Congress will be ready to dip into details [on legislation] to an extent never practiced before" (Harris 1946, 270). The perception was that instead of taking a more national focus in legislating, committees were delving even further into the specifics of policy for local interests.

Focusing on the details of constituent demands was, at least partially, what many members wanted their committees to do. The members of several committees had disproportionate district interests in the policy matters under their jurisdiction, so consideration of particularized needs was part of the strategy for helping their own reelection prospects. This membership pattern existed for many panels prior to the 1946 reforms, and remained even after several of the committees with specialized jurisdictions were merged together. Senator White's request to eliminate parochialism on committees was ignored entirely.

Of course, the rejection of reforms that would upset the existing institutional equilibrium went well beyond committee composition and would plague congressional reformers for decades. A frequent complaint at the time, even by Monroney, was that the reform package avoided what some considered the most profound structural problems facing Congress—the seniority system, the process of committee assignments, an obstructionist Rules Committee, and the Senate filibuster (Burns 1949; Monroney 1949). Ultimately, the reason reformers retreated from such controversial issues was that they were unlikely to succeed in altering such structures—particularly committee assignments and the seniority system in the House. Reformers, like Monroney and Dirksen, publicly claimed that the reason for not dealing with the issue of committee assignments and seniority was that they felt such internal party processes were outside the proscribed jurisdiction of their special committee.[34] Nevertheless, the Joint Committee had little problem providing for *party* policy panels in each chamber. However, it was later conceded that the La Follette-Monroney Committee wanted to go further on a number of points, panel seniority and assignments among them, but was "unable to get any substantial agreement on methods to improve the seniority system."[35]

Ultimately, defeats that the La Follette-Monroney proposal suffered before and during floor deliberation in the House (e.g., removal of party policy committees and "docket days"), as well as after passage of the LRA (e.g., the quick demise of budget reforms), were partially a result of reformers not accurately reading the mood of the House membership and, hence, misunderstanding the implications of institutional changes for the underlying motivations of members. Davidson claims that "it is questionable whether they [the La Follette-Monroney Committee] tapped a truly representative sample of lawmakers" when they held hearings on prospects for congressional reform. Members were so fixated on making changes to the legislature's structure and policymaking arrangements that they ignored implicit boundaries of their authority or the potential of the chamber to alter the reform package to perpetuate a committee system that already provided for their dominant electoral requirements. As Davidson (1990) notes, we will see the blinders of reform advocates contribute to the failure of efforts at structural change in the House in the years to come.

Chapter 6

Protecting Turf in a Reform Era: Distributive Politics and Congressional Committee Reform in the 93rd Congress

ONCE THE BASIC STRUCTURE OF THE HOUSE COMMITTEE SYSTEM was mapped out in the Legislative Reorganization Act of 1946, it remained largely unchanged through the end of the century. Chapter 5 discussed how the consistency in the configuration of committee jurisdictions quickly became one of the most reliable sources of electoral advantage for House members. As the salience of public policy issues shifted over time, legislators adapted the committee system to keep pace with the needs of their districts as well as their own reelection requirements. With rare exceptions, changes in the jurisdictional structure of House committees were incremental.

After 1946 there were only a small number of structural shifts in the House committee system (among the more notable was the creation of the Science and Astronautics Committee in 1958), but none were system-wide. Consideration of radical alterations was largely avoided until a sizable reform-oriented contingent was elected in the 1964 Lyndon Johnson landslide. Along with many incumbent liberals, the new, reform-oriented group of legislators encouraged several changes in congressional structure, ranging from calls for more equitable distributions of power within committees to exposing more aspects of congressional operations to public scrutiny. Many of the eventual changes in the early 1970s stemmed from the work of Senator Mike Monroney's and Representative Ray Madden's 1965 Joint Committee on the Organization of Congress. The Joint Committee considered and proposed several plans for restructuring House committee jurisdictions—division of the Education and Labor Committee, expansion of the Banking and Currency and Science and Astronautics jurisdictions, and so on. The failure of this panel to pass even minor reform proposals for a number of years is often attributed to widespread House opposition to jurisdictional alterations (Adler 1969, 196–98). Despite the failure of this effort to alter the House committee structure in any meaningful way, it laid the groundwork for a similar endeavor led by Representative Richard Bolling in the 93rd House (1973–74).

Perhaps never before or since have large-scale committee reforms been so extensively debated in the House as during deliberations over the Committee Reform Amendments of 1974. Over a two-year period, beginning in 1973, the effort to restructure the chamber's committee system included two months of hearings and statements by sixty-three members of Congress before the Select Committee on Committees, two weeks of hearings before the Rules Committee, and finally more than a week of extensive debate, including statements by twenty different members on the House floor. Throughout this period, relatively few statements appeared in the press regarding specific committee alterations, but behind the scenes there were flurries of internal congressional memoranda.

The extensive debate and wide range of potential jurisdictional changes provide an opportunity to learn more about individual members' preferences on reforms than at any other period of congressional history.[1] The two years of public deliberation and uncharacteristically well-kept records yield insight into the specific preferences of legislators on individual jurisdictional alterations.[2] Moreover, this information allows us to study the factors motivating members' reform preferences, in particular, the reasons why a majority of the chamber rejected the radical package of system-wide committee restructuring.

As with the reforms of the 1940s and similar efforts in the mid-1960s, proposals for restructuring the House committee system were largely predicated on notions of rationalizing an inefficient and outdated configuration of policy property rights. That is, the objective in altering the chamber's committee structure was, to many proponents, a means of eliminating unnecessary jurisdictional overlap and creating a "sensible" process of policy deliberation that considered more efficiently the opinions of opposing interests. However, this thoroughly single-minded ambition too frequently ignored the central incentive structure that is inherent in the legislature and had for decades been the defining factor in many questions of organizational structure—the seemingly instinctual political objective of reelection. This chapter recounts how efficiency arguments regarding the need for committee restructuring eventually gave way to members' core reelection motivations, resulting in a much weaker package of reforms than had initially been considered.

I begin with a brief history of the reform debate and subsequent battle over the restructuring package passed in the House during the 93rd Congress (1973–74). I then describe what I refer to as the "institutional theory" of committee reorganization, which is largely accepted as the conventional wisdom concerning the outcome of the reform proposals in 1974. In contrast, I assert that there is an alternative "reelection" explanation for why members preferred some alterations and rejected others. To test these two theories, I examine the deliberations concerning six specific jurisdictional changes in this period for evidence of legislators' motivations for supporting or opposing committee restructuring. Finally, I analyze the key roll-call vote for passage of the Hansen plan over the Bolling package of reforms.

The History of the Bolling-Hansen Committee Reforms

The history of the reform efforts in 1973 and 1974 are comprehensively recounted elsewhere (Davidson and Oleszek 1977; Sheppard 1985; Lowe 1976), so for now I provide only a brief outline.[3] Later I offer more detailed descriptions when discussing specific jurisdictional changes. The movement in favor of committee alterations that arose in the early part of the 93rd Congress (1973) did not occur spontaneously but had been in the making for many years and was an extension of reform efforts in the late 1960s and early 1970s. Just before the start of the 93rd Congress, members of the House seniority, Speaker Carl Albert (D-OK) and Minority Leader Gerald Ford (R-MI) among them, decided that it was time for the chamber to consider rationalizing what some saw as an antiquated, inefficient, and conflictual committee structure. A plan for the creation of a panel to do this was composed by Albert and senior Rules Committee Democrat and long-time reform advocate, Richard Bolling (D-MO), and was presented to the House at the beginning of the 93rd Congress. The plan triggered debate over whether an existing standing committee, like Rules or House Administration, might not be a better venue for consideration of committee reorganization than a new select committee. But ultimately the proposal was approved in the chamber in a 282–91 vote,[4] and the party leaders constituted this bipartisan committee with reform advocates and experienced parliamentarians.

The Select Committee on Committees (a.k.a. the Bolling Committee) went to great lengths to solicit the input of members and nonmembers (including political scientists, interest groups, trade and business associations, etc.) who wished to speak up on the issue of reforms. The committee heard testimony from more than sixty legislators. In addition to the hearings, the Bolling panel collected a large number of letters written by individual legislators, committee members conducted private interviews with their colleagues, and committee staff held similar interviews with the staffs of standing committees.

After months of careful consideration, the Bolling Committee released a 119-page report in early December 1973 that included a package of radical committee alterations, including the elimination of several standing committees and the restructuring of a number of other panel's jurisdictions. The proposal stimulated widespread and vigorous opposition from members and other interested parties over the next eleven months. In the wake of a flood of letters from affected legislators and groups, the Bolling Committee sent a revised report to the House in mid-March 1974.[5] The major changes from its earlier proposal included partial restoration of one previously eliminated committee and retreat from a few jurisdictional alterations, but profound structural change in the House committee system was still prevalent in the final plan.

Opposition to the revised Bolling proposal came from many quarters—individual legislators acting alone and as members of affected committees, interest groups, and committee and party organizations. To a certain extent, the fractured opposition solidified in a meeting of the Democratic Caucus at the start of May 1974. There, Phil Burton (D-CA) introduced a motion to refer H. Res. 988 to the party's Committee on Organization, Study, and Review (a.k.a. the Hansen Committee, after its chair Julia Butler Hansen of Washington) for review and recommendations to the Rules Committee Democrats. Opponents of the Bolling package saw the Hansen panel as the logical place to direct their efforts at killing the plan for widespread jurisdictional alterations. The Hansen Committee had been the party's instrument for considering and proposing changes in caucus rules in the prior few congressional terms, and, more important, it was composed of a majority of members who were publicly opposed to the Bolling plan.

The Hansen Committee solicited input from members of the Democratic Caucus and in closed-door deliberation devised an alternative proposal for committee restructuring, which they presented to the House in mid-July as H. Res. 1248. Among the major departures from the Bolling proposal were the retention of the Education and Labor and Post Office and Civil Service committees, expansion of Merchant Marine and Fisheries' jurisdiction, and fewer jurisdictional losses by Ways and Means. The Democratic Caucus then instructed its members on the Rules Committee to report both plans to the floor for debate. After a brief set of hearings and an attempt to kill the reform effort by a handful of Rules

Committee members, the two proposals were sent to the House.[6] This led to several days of debate on the House floor and a number of votes considering specific changes to the reform plans, after which the chamber accepted the Hansen substitute amendment by a vote of 203–165 on October 8, 1974.[7]

The Conventional Wisdom on the Failure of the Bolling Proposal

Historians of the Bolling-Hanson reforms usually claim that the demise of the more substantial Bolling committee restructuring package occurred at the hands of members who were seeking to protect the existing jurisdictions of their current committee assignments.[8] For example, Sheppard argues that efforts by liberal Democrats to reform traditional committee hierarchies in the late 1960s, which culminated in dispersion of authority to a broader group of legislators in the 1970 Legislative Reorganization Act, ultimately brought about the demise of the radical Bolling plan. Reforms instituted as part of the "Subcommittee Bill of Rights" limited the number of subcommittee chairs a member could hold, bolstered backbencher policy influence by mandating that every bill be granted a referral to a specific subcommittee, and strengthened subcommittee staff provisions. Sheppard contends that these changes vested a much larger number of junior legislators in the existing committee structure, and "[w]hen faced with an attempt to consolidate power—with unknown effects on personal careers—the new subcommittee chairmen allied with the old guard to defeat it" (1985, 187). Davidson and Oleszek make a similar assertion and also argue that adversely affected committee staff whose positions were threatened by Bolling changes mobilized outside support (executive agencies, clientele groups, etc.) to protect the existing policy monopolies (1977, 263).

The core concept in this perspective is that members who have invested numerous years in the current arrangement of committee jurisdictions will resist change simply because it upsets the power structure and their long-earned positions of policy authority. Apart from district interests in committee structure, legislators reject proposals for committee reorganization because of the disruptions to their positions of influence within the legislative body. The "institutional investment," of course, is more pronounced for those with a longer commitment to the established structure (senior legislators) and members of the ruling or majority party.

Scholars asserting this "institutional" explanation of the reform outcomes in the 93rd Congress do allude to the importance of opposition by outside interests (environmental groups, labor unions, etc.) in influencing members to spurn the Bolling plan. For instance, Davidson and Oleszek note that the Bolling proposal to eliminate the Merchant Marine and Fisheries Committee elicited a fierce defense from the relevant constituency groups. This, in turn, helped to generate a united resistance made up of committee members, representatives from port cities, and interest groups (1977, 158–59; more on this below). Most scholars, however, emphasize the institutional motivations for members' defense of existing committee jurisdictions more than the direct *constituency* connection to legislators' reform behavior. Explanations based on the institutional position of legislators do not usually point out that members, while protecting the turf of their committees, were also shielding their policy influence, established through a system of committee property rights, over federal programs that supplied funds to their constituencies.

The conclusion that the Bolling defeat represented the successful defense of committee turf is, in part, the result of how the panel framed the debate and public record. A thorough reading of the Bolling Committee record (hearings, markup, etc.) reveals that Bolling went to great effort to remove constituency or reelection considerations from decision making concerning committee reforms proposals. For instance, he specifically instructed committee staff to steer clear of political considerations when drawing up jurisdictional recommendations (Sheppard 1985, 124). However, Bolling also ordered his staff to analyze how different restructuring plans would affect each members' committee assignments. Conversely, William Cable, former Education and Labor staffer and one of only two informal Hansen Committee staff members, explicitly stated that the common thread in the jurisdictional alterations proposed by the Hansen panel was protection of both committee *and* constituency interests.[9]

The District Interests of Committee Members, 1973–74

Chapter 4 detailed the relationship between the jurisdictions of some House committees and their ability to direct specialized benefits to members' home districts for four congressional terms. Of course, such a distributive effect is probably not unique to that period; in fact, such relationships had existed a decade earlier. Evidence of a similar correlation would support the notion that legislators who were defending committee turf in 1973–74 were not only protecting their institutional power for its own sake, but may also have been safeguarding those funds that sustain local economies and subsequently help to maximize their electoral advantage.

Unfortunately, detailed data on the distribution of federal outlays to congressional districts similar to that compiled by Bickers and Stein are not available for this earlier period. However, *The Almanac of American*

Politics did for a short period (until 1974) calculate the level of federal funds from specific departments and agencies that were distributed to each congressional district from data on more than a thousand expenditure items broken down by counties and cities provided in the *Catalog of Federal Domestic Assistance* by the Office of Economic Opportunity.[10] These data are not as accurate or versatile as those used earlier. It is not, for example, possible to aggregate individual outlays to their specific committee jurisdictions. However, these data do provide us with a rough ability to judge whether there may be an additional fiscal incentive to protecting committee turf beyond the mere defense of institutional power. I purposely avoid any chicken-or-egg debate concerning whether increased funding from specific federal programs was a *result* of representation on a particular panel or was the *impetus* for a representative to seek membership on that panel. I simply assume that disproportionately high levels of district funding from federal programs under a committee's control—whether derived from inherent district demand or just panel membership—are a sufficient motive to protect existing committee jurisdictional boundaries.

To compare the government benefits of committee members versus those of the chamber, I conduct an analysis employing the same Monte Carlo simulation on difference-in-medians used in chapter 3. To determine the proper committees of jurisdiction for each federal department, I examined two things: for the statutory jurisdictions of each panel, I utilized policy boundaries stated in House Rule 10. For the more informal, "common law" jurisdictions (King 1997), I examine the frequency of mentions of each department name (or its major subagencies) in the subject category of the CIS Congressional Committee Hearings Index. The funds going to the congressional district from a particular department for the median committee member from 1972 are compared with the same amount for the median member of the chamber. The difference-in-medians test is used to analyze whether the committee median might be considered an outlier when compared to ten thousand randomly assigned panels of the same size. Again, these tests are less sensitive than means tests (*t*-test) to the influence of outlier observations, and, like the tests on district characteristics, they allow one to examine the proper two institutional bodies—the committee and the chamber.[11] The null hypothesis is that committee members receive federal benefits from departments under their jurisdiction at approximately the same level as the average member of the entire legislature.

The results of the median tests are provided in table 10. In every instance one finds that the median dollars directed to the districts of committee members from each federal department under their purview is

Table 10 Distribution of Federal Funds by House Committee and Executive
Department, 1972

Committee	Department or Agency	Committee Median ($millions)	Chamber Median ($millions)	*p*-Value
Agriculture	Agriculture	69.91	20.68	.00
Banking and Currency	Housing and Urban Development	9.62	6.62	.00
Armed Services	Defense	178.76	112.63	.00
Education and Labor	Health, Education, and Welfare	161.81	15.68	.38
Interstate and Foreign Commerce	Health, Education, and Welfare	152.73	15.68	.82
Ways and Means	Health, Education, and Welfare	162.36	15.68	.31
Interior and Insular Affairs	Interior	5.29	1.16	.00
Interstate and Foreign Commerce	Transportation	16.03	14.57	.14
Public Works	Transportation	16.98	14.57	.08
Joint Committee on Atomic Energy (House members only)	Atomic Energy Commission	1.35	0.17	.12
Science and Astronautics	National Aeronautics and Space Administration	2.21	0.70	.01

SOURCE: Data on congressional district outlays from Barone et al. 1974.

greater than the median for the floor, and for many of these panels the difference is quite substantial and statistically significant.[12] For example, the median level of funding from the Department of Agriculture (DoA) going to Agriculture Committee members is almost $70 million as compared to the floor median of about $21 million. As the significance tests show, its quite likely that committee members receive disproportionate DoA benefits. Similar findings obtain for the Department of Defense and Armed Services Committee; the Department of Housing and Urban Development (HUD) and the Banking and Currency Committee; the Department of Interior and the Interior and Insular Affairs Committee; and the National Aeronautics and Space Administration (NASA) and the Science and Astronautics Committee. One also finds similar disparities for the Atomic Energy Commission and the House members of the Joint Committee on Atomic Energy and the Department of Transportation and its two main principals—Interstate and Foreign Commerce and Public

Works—though with not quite as decisive significance values. While the committee medians for funding from the Department of Health, Education and Welfare—the agency with the most fragmented authority— were substantially higher than the chamber median, the wide variance in the level of district allocation from this federal department prevented these differences from producing dramatic significance values.

Although it cannot provide conclusive evidence of a direct relationship between committee turf and members' constituency interests, this analysis does suggest that there is a greater incentive than simple defense of institutional power for committee members to resist jurisdictional restructuring. As with previous analyses, there is a strong relationship between legislators' committee assignments and the funds directed to their districts from federal agencies and departments under the influences of those panels. It seems likely, therefore, that legislators avoid alterations in jurisdictional arrangements that might disturb these established relationships.

Constituency Advocates and Committee Reforms

To what extent, therefore, do institutional and electoral/distributive factors influence the decisions of legislators regarding committee reorganization? Previously, the problem in examining the issue of jurisdictional reforms in the House has been that it is often difficult to uncover the preferences of individual legislators on specific changes (for a recent effort at this, see Schickler, McGhee, and Sides 2001). Until the reform efforts of the mid-1990s, no systematic surveys had ever been conducted of members' preferences over specific changes to committee property rights. In lieu of such surveys, we rely on a combination of information on members' revealed reform priorities and roll-call votes on selected jurisdictional alterations.

Since the reform effort in this period unfolded over a relatively long period of time—almost two years—it is possible to discover who were the most zealous advocates and opponents of specific jurisdictional alterations by examining the public declarations and statements regarding individual reform proposals made in several different venues. To determine the widest range of reform positions for as many representatives as possible, I searched several sources for unambiguous statements by individual members for or against specific jurisdictional changes. The places where members were most likely to display their preferences over jurisdictional alterations were Bolling Committee testimony, "Dear Bolling Committee" and "Dear Colleague" letters,[13] Rules Committee testimony,

House floor debate, party caucus debate, statements inserted into the *Congressional Record,* private interviews conducted by Bolling Committee members, and comments reported in news outlets that closely cover congressional events.[14]

More than 350 statements concerning specific jurisdictional changes were made by 170 different members.[15] I examine six specific jurisdictional changes that were under consideration during the 93rd Congress: (1) abolition of the Merchant Marine and Fisheries Committee, (2) abolition of the Post Office and Civil Service Committee, (3) division of the Education and Labor Committee into two panels, (4) consolidation of all transportation jurisdictions into the Public Works Committee, (5) creation of an Aging Committee, and (6) abolition of the Internal Security Committee. These were among the most important jurisdictional alterations considered during this period and were the focus of the bulk of public statements concerning reform preferences. Moreover, except for the Aging Committee, these proposed jurisdictional alterations caused the most contentious disputes in the reform debate, where groups of adversarial legislators were most clearly defined and could be easily identified.[16] In some cases—transportation, aging and internal security— evidence concerning the preferences of legislators on jurisdictional changes is supplemented by a relevant roll-call vote. Finally, I examine how the factors thought to influence members' preferences about individual committee changes affect their positions on the overall reform packages through analysis of the final vote for passage of the Hansen plan. For each reform proposal, I provide a brief review of the history and issues surrounding the controversy, an assessment of the committee and constituency interests of the proponents and opponents of the restructuring, and a logit analysis of the relevant roll-call if one was taken.

Merchant Marine and Fisheries

Debate over the future of the Merchant Marine and Fisheries Committee (hereafter MMF) went from discussion of its outright elimination to strengthening and expansion of its existing jurisdiction. Rumors that the Bolling Committee was considering abolition of MMF prompted its chair, Leonor Sullivan (D-MO), to give an impassioned statement before the panel in defense of her committee's important work. As it turned out, the rumors were confirmed when the Bolling Committee's draft report released in late 1973 reallocated MMF's jurisdiction among a number of new and existing committees (Agriculture, Foreign Affairs, Public Works, and the new Energy and Environment Committee). After a furious campaign in defense of the committee, coordinated by both maritime and environmental groups as well as members of Congress (Lowe 1976, 47; Davidson and Oleszek 1977, 195; and "House Committee Reform Proposals" 1974), the Bolling Committee relented and restored a considerably weakened MMF panel.[17] MMF had an even more friendly audience in the Hansen Committee, which recommended no jurisdictional losses whatsoever and even one small gain. This proposal was eventually accepted in the final legislation.[18]

The relative success of maritime and environmental interests in not only forcing a partial retreat by the Bolling Committee but in ultimately restoring the entire authority of MMF is directly attributable to the influence of the maritime industry and unions and their ability to apply pressure on legislators through their geographic concentration and campaign contributions (Levine 1975; Davidson and Oleszek 1977, 160–61). Former Bolling Committee staff members Davidson and Oleszek argue that the maritime interests had been growing even more politically powerful in the early 1970s because of expanding ocean port facilities and the Merchant Marine Act of 1970, which helped revitalize the industry with tax benefits and shipbuilding and operating subsidies (Jantscher 1975, 40). The maritime industry regarded the current MMF as its chief advocate in Washington and feared that a "multi-interest" panel, such as Public Works, might be less concerned with maintaining the generous subsidies and protection the industry was currently enjoying (Sheppard 1985, 156; Davidson and Oleszek 1977, 158).

The influence of maritime interests and the importance of shipping-related subsidies to constituencies is obvious when examining the characteristics of members who supported and opposed the retention of this panel. Thirty-four members made statements in support of retaining MMF, as opposed to 7 against. The 34 supporters included a substantial portion of the committee itself (13 of the 39 MMF members), including Chair Sullivan, ranking Republican James Grover, and 3 of the 5 subcommittee chairs. But as was demonstrated earlier, committee membership was also strongly associated with district interests. Of the MMF members who voiced their support for the panel, several had major maritime interests in their home constituencies.[19] Sullivan's south St. Louis district sat along the western bank of the Mississippi River, and the city was the most active port on the river north of New Orleans. One of her district's largest employers was Pott Industries, which repaired ships and other rivercraft. Bob Eckhardt's working-class district in Houston included the entire length of the Houston Shipping Channel that made this largely inland city, with its neighbor, Galveston, the third busiest port in America. Two other supportive members of MMF were John Dingell from Detroit (one of the more active ports on the Great Lakes) and Mario Biaggi from New York City (the most active port in the country).

It should not be surprising that nonmembers of MMF from districts with intense maritime interests supported maintaining the panel. Several advocates represented active port cities. Lindy Boggs's New Orleans district contained the second largest port in the nation, and the district's two largest employers were the Avondale Shipyards and Lykes-Youngstown, a deep-sea transportation company. Bill Green from Philadelphia and John Hunt from Camden, NJ, were neighbors across the Delaware River and represented the bulk of the port activity in both cities. The maritime industry was not easily ignored in Hawaii, and consequently the International Longshoreman's and Warehousemen's Union (ILWU) was very influential politically in Spark Matsunaga's Honolulu district.[20] The largest single private employer in James Burke's south Boston district was General Dynamics' Quincy Shipbuilding Division (nine thousand employees). Similarly, William Whitehurst's Norfolk district not only depended upon its enormous naval installations, but also on jobs from one of its largest employers—Norfolk Shipbuilding and Dry-dock. Two members from Baltimore (the fifth most active American port) were defenders of the MMF Committee—Parren Mitchell and Marjorie Holt. Mitchell's newly created Seventh district included large portions of Edward Garmatz's old congressional district—and Garmatz was the previous chair of MMF. To draw an even closer connection to district interests, Mitchell and Whitehurst were quite explicit in their February letters to the Bolling Committee that their concern in maintaining this maritime panel was based on the port activity in their constituencies. Other advocates for MMF included a number of members from coastal congressional districts (without large ports): Alphonso Bell (representing the entire Los Angeles coastline), Chet Hollifield (Santa Barbara), and Bill Chappell (Daytona Beach).

Of the seven members who promoted the discontinuation of the MMF Committee, only two came from active port cities. Ed Koch's midtown and upper east side of Manhattan constituency did not include very many people employed in the maritime industry and was not likely to be affected noticeably by this jurisdictional alteration. Conversely, Thomas Ashley, a Democrat from Toledo, did have direct interests in maintaining a maritime panel—Toledo is one of the most active ports on the Great Lakes, and Ashley was a MMF member. Ashley, however, stated that he supported the transfer of his committee's jurisdiction to facilitate "coherent consideration of national policy with respect to environmental protection, transportation, . . . etc.," but most of the letter is a defense of his other committee assignment—Banking and Currency. The other four members were either from inland districts—James Stanton (Columbus,

OH) and Dale Milford (Dallas)—or members of the Bolling Committee from coastal districts with no sizable port activity—Meeds (northwest WA) and Steiger (central WI).

Post Office and Civil Service

The experience of the Post Office and Civil Service Committee (hereafter PO) is similar in many ways to that of Merchant Marine and Fisheries. Post Office Chair, Thaddeus Dulski, along with second-ranking Democrat David Henderson, testified before the Bolling Committee, after buzz that their committee was also being considered for the chopping-block. Like MMF, the rumors of PO's demise were confirmed when the draft Bolling proposal provided for the reassignment of its jurisdiction among the Government Operations and Standards of Official Conduct committees, and the newly proposed Labor Committee. A similar campaign to save the panel ensued, undertaken by postal and public employee unions and committee and noncommittee legislators. However, unlike MMF, the effort to compel the Bolling Committee to restore the jurisdiction of the PO panel was not successful, and the final Bolling proposal persisted in its abolition. Fortunately for advocates of the postal committee, the Hansen panel saw fit to not only spare the committee but to augment its jurisdiction with authority over the Hatch Act, population, and intergovernmental personnel issues.[21] In the end, the House elected to retain PO with a slightly expanded jurisdiction.

The similarity between the experiences of Post Office and Merchant Marine and Fisheries should not be surprising. Like MMF, PO had a well-defined constituency—postal and federal employees—where ties between the committee and the clientele group had been fortified by legislative changes years earlier. In 1970, Congress passed the Postal Reorganization Act which shifted authority over postal rates and salaries from the committee to the Board of Governors for the U.S. Postal Service and the Postal Rate Commission. However, the panel did retain general oversight over the Postal Service and the working conditions and salaries of all other federal employees (Fenno 1973, 283). This change removed one of the two traditional "strategic" policy objectives for the committee—opposing all postal rate increases for the benefit of postal users—but left in place the other strategic premise—maximum pay and benefit increases for federal employees (Fenno 1973, 64). The result of the reform was that any conflicting relationships that members had with respect to advocacy for postal users through influence over rates was eliminated, and the work of the panel focused almost entirely on its traditional clientele group, federal and postal employees. Federal employee organizations, such as the National Federation of Federal Employees and the American Federation of

Government Employees, feared that transfer of this committee's jurisdiction to other panels, even the potentially friendly Labor Committee, would seriously disrupt long-established and protective relations with the current committee and might eventually result in policy trade-offs on matters hitherto unassociated with federal employment issues (Davidson and Oleszek 1977, 166).

Scholars of congressional reforms have disagreed about the origin of opposition to eliminating the PO Committee. On the one hand, Bolling Committee staffers Davidson and Oleszek acknowledge the lobbying effort of interested unions in opposing this panel's demise but assert that defense of the committee came largely from a small number of its members who had made substantial investments in it—specifically in subcommittee chairs. On the other hand, Davidson and Oleszek argue that Bolling perceived that much of the opposition to eliminating PO was pro forma and originated with PO staff (Davidson and Oleszek 1977, 167). Bolling claimed during the markup of H. R. 988 that the opposition from legislators was prompted by constituency groups. He stated, "I am not mentioning names of members at this stage, but it is clear that the Civil Service government employee unions, the postal unions have suddenly become very active and very upset . . . [and] very vocal down there through their representatives." [22]

Evidence from PO supporters generally sustains the contention that its defense was based mostly on protection of committee membership and institutional power. Of the fifteen members who stated their support for retention of this committee, eleven were PO members. This included the panel chair, Dulski, and four of the five other subcommittee chairs. However, as Fenno demonstrated this panel was among the most attractive committees for members seeking protection of constituency/district interests. He argued that for "Post Office members, the distinctive, dominant personal goal is reelection through constituency service" (Fenno 1973, 9). Not surprisingly, Post Office members had a higher average percentage of constituents employed by the federal government (1.70 percent) than the chamber average (1.57 percent). Among the four noncommittee members supporting preservation of PO was Spark Matsunaga, whose Honolulu district had one of the highest levels of federal employment in the country (4.40 percent)—this district was in the top ten with respect to federal employment outside the Virginia and Maryland districts surrounding Washington, DC.

Education and Labor

Warranted or not, the Bolling proposal to split the Education and Labor Committee into separate panels was eventually seen as the most serious threat to the political influence of labor unions, and was fiercely fought by the trade groups and their legislative advocates. The initial Bolling proposal calling for division of this committee mobilized vigorous and vocal opposition once the unions (particularly the AFL-CIO) and congressional labor advocates realized that a panel exclusively devoted to labor issues might be not only marginalized with respect to House policy deliberation, but also weakened in its ability to logroll with education advocates for passage of favorable legislation (Democratic Study Group 1974, 16).[23] The Bolling Committee did make some minor adjustments to the jurisdictions of the two newly proposed panels, but in its final report did not back away from its initial plan. Not surprisingly, the Hansen panel, which included a number of senior Education and Labor members,[24] chose to retain the committee intact with some minor jurisdictional adjustments. The Hansen proposal was eventually accepted by the chamber.

As much as any reform proposal, division of Education and Labor agitated passionate defenders on both sides—sixteen members vigorously supported the status quo, while eleven members spoke in favor of the committee's partition. Eleven who favored retaining the committee were panel members, including several high-ranking Education and Labor Democrats—Perkins, Ford, O'Hara, and Thompson. However, as emphasized above, defense of committee turf was not in many cases completely detached from advocacy of district interests. As shown in chapter 3, this committee was heavily overrepresentative of blue-collar and union-oriented districts, and members often expressed a strong pro-labor bias in matters before the committee and chamber. For example, the committee's median COPE score in 1973 was far higher than that of the floor.[25]

Among the committee members who defended the current jurisdiction of Education and Labor were several whose districts had 40 percent or greater employment in blue-collar jobs (the floor mean was 34.5 percent)—these included O'Hara and W. Ford (auto industry in Detroit and surrounding areas); Hawkins (electronics and aerospace manufacturing in Los Angeles and San Fernando Valley); Perkins (coal mining in eastern Kentucky); Brademas (auto industry in northern Indiana); Daniels (textiles in Jersey City); and Dent (steel industry in the Pittsburgh area). In addition, some defenders were nonmembers from areas with high blue-collar employment and active labor movements: Leonor Sullivan and William Clay (auto and rail manufacturing, meat packing, maritime in St. Louis); John Dingell (auto industry in Detroit); Spark Matsunaga (maritime and textiles in Honolulu); and John Melcher (mining in eastern Montana).[26] The median labor support score (COPE) of the group of Education and Labor advocates was even higher than that of the committee itself, boosted by such strong labor advocates as Dingell, Sullivan, and Claude Pepper.

The group of opponents of the existing Education and Labor arrangement did not have nearly the same labor or blue-collar credentials as their adversaries. Advocates of the committee's division included some high-profile reform proponents, including the Minority Leader, Gerald Ford, and three Republican members of the Bolling Committee: David Martin, Albert Quie, and William Steiger. Quie and Steiger also happened to be members of Education and Labor. Few of this group of eleven hailed from districts known for strong union activity, and for the most part they represented districts comprising suburban and rural farming communities (Martin, western Nebraska; Quie, southeast Minnesota; Steiger, central Wisconsin; G. Ford, central Michigan; William Chappel, northeastern Florida; Bill Dickinson, southeastern Alabama; Delbert Latta, northwest Ohio; and Phil Landrum, northeastern Georgia). Landrum, a conservative southern Democrat, was fairly well known for his antilabor legislative battles. In his earlier years, when still a member of Education and Labor, Landrum cosponsored the Labor Management Reporting and Disclosure Act in 1959 (Landrum-Griffin), which for the first time imposed government regulations on the internal operations of labor unions (Lee 1990).[27] The eleven vocal opponents of the existing Education and Labor Committee had a very low median labor-support score (COPE) of 25.8.

Interestingly, two advocates of the Education and Labor split did have fairly strong labor credentials: Donald Fraser from Minneapolis and Jonathan Bingham from New York City. These two had been part of a small group of liberal, pro-reform Democrats who were staunch supporters of the Bolling Plan.[28]

Transportation

Perhaps the one major jurisdictional alteration where the Bolling Committee was most successful was in the area of transportation. In an effort to rationalize transportation jurisdictions that were fragmented among a number of panels, the Bolling Committee initially recommended that all transportation policy matters (rail, aviation, maritime, mass, etc.) fall under the purview of the Public Works Committee. After the battle over and eventual restoration of the Merchant Marine and Fisheries Committee, the final proposal of the Bolling Committee still consolidated all other transportation issues within the Public Works panel. The Hansen Committee further trimmed this proposal when it capitulated to Harley Staggers's (D-WV) pleas to restore railroad jurisdiction to the committee he chaired—Commerce. The controversy continued during the floor debate, when Republican Commerce Committee member Dan Kuykendall (TN), offered an amendment to scrap the proposals and restore the existing and fractured transportation jurisdictions. The amendment was rejected in a close 239–172 roll-call vote, and eventually the scaled-back jurisdictional merger within Public Works proposed in the Hansen plan was accepted.

The initial effort to consolidate disparate control over transportation issues, like other proposals for jurisdictional change, was based on the premise of policy coherence and efficiency. At the time, the Commerce; Banking and Currency; Merchant Marine and Fisheries; and Public Works committees all had jurisdiction over major transportation policy issues. There are two plausible explanations for the eventual success of this jurisdictional alteration: one based on the notion of protection of institutional power, and the other derived from the concept of distributive politics. Advocates of the notion that jurisdictional reforms were largely rejected during this time because affected committee members were battling to defend institutional turf might hypothesize that this jurisdictional triumph was a result of transportation's marginality with respect to the core issues of the potential "loser" committees. That is, panels likely to lose portions of their issue domain through transportation consolidation did not fiercely challenge this reform because these issues were not central to their members' needs. This is precisely the argument that King makes as to the reason Commerce Committee members were willing to relinquish their transportation issue policy rights (King 1997, 67).

Conversely, a distributive perspective on this jurisdictional change would hold that loser committees defend their turf because they have members with constituency interests in this policy arena. But ultimately the decision to move the policy matter into another committee's jurisdiction is made because an even greater number of members have likely constituency gains resulting from the change. That is, more legislators would benefit from a consolidated nucleus for transportation policymaking than would benefit from fragmentation of this policy matter among several panels.

It was clear from the start that fashioning a more coherent transportation policy apparatus was going to be a sensitive constituency issue for many members. John Culver (D-IA) asked during markup of the Bolling proposal, "How do we achieve a balanced transportation system in the absence of trying to harmonize this crazy pattern of irrational subsidization based upon constituent self-interest pressures without any real corresponding relationship to the overall national public interest?"[29] Examination of the advocates and opponents of transportation consolidation

Table 11   District Interests of Supporters and Opponents of Transportation
Consolidation

	Mean Percentage in District Employed in Transportation	Mean Percentage in District using Public Transport for Work Commute
Consolidation supporters (N = 9)	3.69	8.20**
Consolidation opponents (13)	4.37*	2.38
Entire house (435)	3.53	3.28

* Difference is statistically significant from chamber at $p \leq .05$.
** Significant at $p \leq .01$.

unequivocally shows that committee members were defensive of their committee turf. Of the thirteen members stating *opposition* to transportation consolidation, all but one—David Martin, vice chair of the Bolling Committee—were members of either the Commerce or Banking committees, and none were Public Works members. Similarly, of the nine members *supporting* consolidation, five were on Public Works, and only one was on either Commerce or Banking—Ed Koch (Banking).

At the same time, however, there were fairly unambiguous constituency reasons for these members' preferences on transportation consolidation. Similar to alterations in the maritime, federal employment, and general labor jurisdictions, transfer of transportation issues from established committee arrangements would upset long-standing relationships that such interests (transportation unions, surface transportation companies, airlines, etc.) had with relevant committees and their members and would introduce uncertainty into future policy considerations (Adler 2002). Representatives with significant district interests in maintaining these established relationships were also members of these key committees and were most likely to oppose the jurisdictional shifts. Table 11 shows that the thirteen legislators who vocally opposed the transportation consolidation represented districts with disproportionately high levels of employment in transportation as compared to either consolidation supporters or the floor. As an example, Bill Cable recounts that Commerce Committee Chair Staggers "complained mightily that we're [the Hansen Committee] going to ruin him politically" if their plan did not "put his trains back from West Virginia."[30] Staggers had recently ensured that one of AMTRAK's two new turbo trains on the Boston-to-Washington, DC, corridor was rerouted to run from Washington, DC, to Parkersburg, WV.

On the other hand, consolidation was likely to mean more coordinated federal policy on transportation issues and potentially significant improvements in the system of public transportation subsidies and regulation. This would be appealing to legislators representing districts dependent upon or seeking expansion of public transportation. During the Bolling markup, William Steiger (WI) argued in favor of a coherent transportation policy for urban areas.[31] As table 11 demonstrates, supporters of consolidation were much more likely to represent districts with significantly greater dependence upon public transportation; they were members from such large, public-transportation-oriented cities (at the time) as New York, Dallas, San Francisco, and Minneapolis.[32] Opponents of consolidation came from cities significantly less dependent upon public transportation—Detroit, Columbus, Seattle, St. Louis, and Houston.[33]

The same motivations that account for the positions of the most vociferous transportation consolidation supporters and opponents also seem to explain much of the chamber-wide vote on the Kuykendall Amendment to the Hansen proposal. Apart from the constituency and committee interests, I also test a number of member characteristics that are likely to influence reform preferences—seniority, party, and ideology. Higher institutional seniority and Democratic Party membership are likely to prejudice a legislator against institutional changes because of long- and short-term investments in an electorally beneficial status quo. Additionally, liberals had for years been battling with senior conservatives for control of major committees and the policy process (Rieselbach 1994), so they are expected to have supported more radical reform efforts that would shake up current committee structure.[34]

Table 12 offers a logistic regression analysis of this floor vote, where a vote in favor of the amendment would have restored the existing configuration of transportation jurisdictions and rejected the Hansen consolidation proposal. First, I note that Commerce Committee members were much more likely to support the amendment, while Public Works members were much more likely to oppose it. This offers further rejection of the institutional argument for the success of this jurisdictional reform. Members of the Commerce Committee, at least, were not passive in the face of jurisdictional losses and did oppose transfer of transportation issues. Moreover, even when I control for the protection of committee turf, I still find that district interests have a significant influence on the vote of members for or against the amendment. As expected, representatives from districts with high employment in transportation were more likely to reject transportation consolidation and vote for Kuykendall. Conversely, members from central cities were supporting consolidation

Table 12 Logistic Regression of Transportation Consolidation Vote (Kuykendall Amendment)

Variable	Transportation Vote	Wald
Constant	−0.97	2.03
	(0.68)	
Commerce Committee	4.40***	18.18
	(1.03)	
Banking Committee	−0.19	0.19
	(0.43)	
Public Works Committee	−2.62***	12.20
	(0.74)	
Percentage employed in transportation	0.20*	3.45
	(0.11)	
Central city (dummy)	−0.50*	2.95
	(0.29)	
Percentage commuting on public transportation	0.03	1.12
	(0.03)	
Republican	−0.52	2.33
	(0.34)	
Seniority	0.08***	7.43
	(0.03)	
Ideology	2.43***	20.98
	(0.53)	
−2 log likelihood	414.421	0.67
Model chi-square	137.64 ($p \le .000$)	

NOTE: $N = 411$ cases; standard errors are in parentheses.
   $*p \le .10$
  $**p \le .05$
 $***p \le .01$

and voting against Kuykendall. Interestingly, the percentage of constituents who commute using public transportation did not seem to play as important a role in the votes of the overall chamber membership as it had among vocal consolidation supporters. Partisanship did not have much influence on this vote, but more conservative and senior members were more likely to vote in favor of Kuykendall and reject this significant jurisdictional reform.

Aging

Although not a jurisdictional change seriously considered by either the Bolling or Hansen committees, the creation of a separate committee to handle issues of concern to elderly Americans was suggested during the early consideration of the committee reforms in 1973. The notion of at least a Select Committee on Aging was offered by a number of members in testimony before the Bolling Committee and proposed again in a "Dear Colleague" letter by Bill Young (R-FL) in September 1974. Finally Young offered an amendment for an Aging Committee to the Hansen proposal on the House floor on October 2, 1974. After brief debate, the amendment passed by a roll-call vote of 323–84, and the Select Committee on Aging came into being in the 94th Congress (1975–76).[35]

Supporters of the proposed committee faced no significant institutional losses from this jurisdictional shift and were well positioned to signal concern for the needs of certain constituents by championing the issues of aging Americans. Only one of the eight proponents for the Aging Committee had a seat on a panel that would lose any jurisdictional influence—Heinz, who was a member of Commerce. There were no Aging advocates on the Education and Labor Committee, which would have been the biggest jurisdictional loser. Moreover, many of these proponents represented districts with considerable percentages of older constituents. Young's St. Petersburg district was the heart of Florida's retirement community at the time and had the oldest median age of any district in the country—48.1 years old. Several other Aging supporters represented some of the top fifty oldest constituencies—Ed Koch (New York City), Dante Fascell (south Miami), and John Heinz (Pittsburgh). Of the three declared opponents of the Aging committee, two were members of Education and Labor—John Dent and John Brademas. All three—the third being Peter Frelinghuysen—were in lowest 40 percent of congressional districts with respect to median constituent age.

Similar committee and constituent motivations help to explain the positions of members' votes on the Young Amendment. In the analysis of this roll-call (table 13), we see that Education and Labor members were much less likely to support an Aging Committee, but loss of jurisdictional influence on other committees did not significantly influence this vote. As they did in the transportation vote, and as I expected, more senior members supported the status quo. But, more important, controlling for these other effects, I also find a statistically significant relationship between the median age of one's constituents and their vote on the creation of an Aging Committee. The older the constituency, the more likely a representative was to support a new Aging Committee.

House Internal Security Committee

The jurisdictional change most likely to divide the House along ideological lines was the proposal to abolish the long-controversial House

Table 13   Logistic Regression of Aging Committee Vote (Young Amendment)

Variable	Aging Vote	Wald
Constant	−1.58 (1.34)	1.40
Commerce Committee	−0.09 (0.46)	0.04
Education and Labor Committee	−1.28*** (0.40)	10.15
Ways and Means Committee	0.08 (0.54)	0.02
Median age of district	0.11** (0.04)	5.62
Republican	0.58 (0.39)	2.24
Seniority	−0.12*** (0.03)	14.37
Ideology	0.27 (0.49)	0.30
−2 log likelihood	370.70	
Model chi-square	40.93 ($p \leq .000$)	

NOTE: $N = 407$ cases; standard errors are in parentheses.
  *$p \leq .10$
 **$p \leq .05$
***$p \leq .01$

Internal Security Committee (HISC; formerly known as the House Un-American Activities Committee). With the exception of the potential to gratify political organizations back home, this panel had little in the way of constituency benefits. Its primary and limited jurisdiction was to investigate "subversive" groups and to report any appropriate legislation. After listening to HISC Chair Richard Ichord (MO) passionately defend his panel, the Bolling Committee decided that it was time to rid the House of what many considered a congressional embarrassment. Furthermore, they reassigned HISC's jurisdiction to the liberal-dominated Judiciary Committee. This was the worst of all possible recommendations for conservative legislators, who feared that Judiciary would simply ignore the traditional mission of this panel. HISC supporters therefore campaigned either to restore the committee or to have its jurisdiction transferred to what some considered a more conservative committee, Government Operations. The Hansen Committee yielded to the latter suggestion in its reform package, but a dissatisfied Ichord eventually appealed to the entire chamber on October 2, 1974, in an amendment to the Hansen proposal to restore HISC altogether. The Ichord Amendment passed after spirited debate, 246–164, but the committee was abruptly expunged by the Democratic Caucus at the start of the 94th Congress (1975–76).

Beyond the committee investment of members—which was significant for only a small number of legislators—there was a more significant ideological nature to the question of HISC's existence. In many ways the endurance of this panel after numerous efforts to eliminate it reflected legislators' views on the role of government in a democracy.[36] It should not be surprising, therefore, to discover that members' preferences on this question are almost purely driven by their ideological beliefs. Seventeen members spoke for retaining the Internal Security panel, including eight of the nine members of the committee itself. Among the other HISC defenders were several members who had conservative credentials and/or came from very conservative districts—William Bray, a Republican from Indianapolis (described by Barone, Ujifusa, and Matthews [1974] as one of the most conservative major cities in the nation); Jack Edwards, a Republican from Mobile, AL; John Hunt, a Republican from New Jersey and an ardent defender of Nixon during the ongoing Watergate investigation; and Thad Cochran, a Republican from Jackson, MS.

One HISC member was among the twenty legislators calling for this committee's end—the liberal catholic priest, Robert Drinan. Drinan had vowed to abolish the committee since he had been assigned to it as a freshman in 1971 (Davidson and Oleszek 1977, 187). Not many Government Operations members called for HISC's abolition,[37] but eight Judiciary members supported its elimination. Among them were some of the chamber's most left-wing members, who hailed from many of the most liberal parts of the country—John Conyers from Detroit, Don Edwards from northern California, and Elizabeth Holtzman and Charles Rangel from New York City. A number of the non-Judiciary members who spoke for HISC's abolition also were well-known House liberals from similarly leaning districts—Henry Reuss from Milwaukee, Donald Fraser from Minneapolis, Michael Harrington from north Boston, and Ed Koch and Bella Abzug from New York City.

The ideological nature of the question of HISC's existence was also quite apparent when the entire chamber voted on Ichord's amendment to the Hansen plan. In a statistical analysis of the roll-call vote (see table 14) I find that, with the exception of a member's party affiliation, ideology is the only other variable that explains this vote. Conservatives, obviously, were strong supports of retention of HISC, while liberals voted against it. Interestingly, once I control for ideology, Republicans were *less* likely to vote in favor of retaining HISC. Even when measures of the constituency characteristics are added to the model—a measure of ideology (percent

Table 14 Logistic Regression of House Internal Security Committee Retention Vote (Ichord Amendment)

Variable	HISC Vote	Wald	HISC Vote	Wald
Constant	4.30*** (0.92)	22.03	−4.47** (1.96)	5.21
Internal Security Committee	1.61 (1.31)	1.53	1.55 (1.31)	1.40
Judiciary Committee	0.06 (0.63)	0.01	0.07 (0.63)	0.01
Govt. Operations Committee	−0.26 (0.49)	0.27	−0.27 (0.49)	0.31
Nixon vote percent 1972	—		−0.01 (0.02)	0.01
NeedLabor[a]	—		−0.05 (0.13)	0.14
Republican	−3.08*** (0.58)	28.52	−3.08*** (0.59)	26.96
Seniority	0.06 (0.05)	1.80	0.06 (0.04)	1.83
Ideology	11.92*** (1.31)	83.30	11.94*** (1.48)	64.70
−2 log likelihood	237.276		237.117	
Model chi-square	305.19 ($p \leq .000$)		305.35 ($p \leq .000$)	

NOTE: $N = 410$ cases; standard errors are in parentheses.
[a] NeedLabor measures the degree to which a district ranks high on both union membership and blue-collar employment.
  *$p \leq .10$
 **$p \leq .05$
***$p \leq .01$

of Nixon vote in 1972) and a measure of district labor orientation (Need-Labor is the same as the measure used in chapter 3, combining state union membership and district blue-collar employment)—there is no change in effect of party or ideology.[38]

Final Vote on the Hansen Proposal

Decision as to the restructuring plan that the House would accept (if any at all) finally came to a vote late in the evening of October 8, 1974. The chamber had resolved the details of the Hansen and Martin amendments, and the House was faced with the choice of either accepting one of these alternatives or taking a vote on the Bolling proposal. The special rule for consideration of the legislation on the floor as prepared by the Rules Committee arranged that if either the Hansen or Martin substitution amendments were passed, the issue of committee reforms would be settled, and no vote would be taken on the Bolling plan. Members of Congress are of course strategic actors, and this voting arrangement was a prime opportunity for opponents of major committee restructuring to act as such. Votes in favor of the Hansen proposal were likely to come from one of two types of members:

Group A   Legislators who wished to protect against what they perceived to be enormous *committee* and *constituency* losses contained in the Bolling plan. Many Bolling opponents knew that a sizable minority of Democrats might support this radical reform plan along with the majority of Republicans, who would be attracted by a number of "sweeteners," such as provisions for minority committee staff. Therefore, the expected utility calculations of some of these representatives dictated that passage of their second-ranking preference (Hansen) was better than risking a vote on and possible passage of their least preferred outcome (Bolling).

Group B   Legislators who had significant *committee* and *constituency* gains to be made by passage of either the Bolling or Hansen alternatives, so would vote for both to avoid their least preferred outcome—no reform package passing at all. This latter group was made up of members such as those who supported the creation of a standing Small Business Committee.[39]

Given this configuration of preferences and the voting agenda as defined by the Rules Committee, the Hansen proposal would win as long as the combination of Group A and B legislators was larger than the group that considered only the Bolling proposal acceptable (Group C).

With this in mind, I analyze the 203–165 vote for passage of the Hansen proposal with respect to the institutional and constituency interests of members. As with the previous analyses of votes on individual jurisdictional reforms, institutional and distributive theories make separate predictions about the effects of different variables on members' vote choice. The institutional approach contends that members will vote according to their committee interests. That is, members of committees who were facing massive jurisdictional losses under the Bolling plan but significantly fewer losses under the Hansen plan (Group A) would be likely to vote in favor of the Hansen plan. This group included members of the Commerce, Education and Labor, Internal Security, Merchant Marine and

Fisheries, Post Office and Civil Service, Ways and Means, and Joint Atomic Energy committees.[40] Similarly, members of panels that were going to see large jurisdictional gains under both Hansen and Bolling (Group B), would vote in favor of either plan. This set includes members of the Public Works and Small Business committees. Members with long-term and majority party investments in the current committee system would be much more likely to vote in favor of the plan that made minimal changes in the institution than one that undertook radical reconstruction. Conversely, members who would experience *desired* jurisdictional gains only under the Bolling plan[41]—Foreign Affairs, Interior, and Science—were more likely to vote against the Hansen plan.[42]

The distributive model, on the other hand, predicts that beyond protection of institutional powers accrued through longevity or membership to particular committees, members would also vote along with their district interests in favor of either retaining panels that were important to their constituents or creating new panels that would benefit their districts in the future. For example, members representing districts with significant maritime interests were more likely to support the Hansen plan, which would make only minimal jurisdictional adjustments to the Merchant Marine Committee, than the Bolling plan, which would entail considerable jurisdictional losses. The same logic would hold for members from districts with tremendous federal employment, extreme transportation interests, and strong labor interests.[43]

Analysis of the Hansen vote (table 15) reveals evidence that *both* institutional and constituency interests played a part in members' decisions on system-wide jurisdictional restructuring, similar to the previous votes on individual committee reforms. Membership on only two committees—Post Office and Ways and Means—that were identified among those that would take major losses with the Bolling but not the Hansen plan (Group A) are significant in influencing legislators to vote in favor of the latter. Controlling for other factors, membership on other Group A panels plays little part in legislators' vote calculus. Similarly, membership on a panel that would gain large jurisdictional responsibilities under either plan influenced members of Small Business to support Hansen in significantly large numbers, but did not do the same for members of Public Works. Conversely, belonging to a committee that would make gains only under the Bolling Plan was effective in inducing members of Foreign Affairs and Science to oppose Hansen, but not members of the Interior and Insular Affairs Committee.

Looking at the constituency interests of members, I find that legislators representing districts with the greatest interest in the jurisdictions of panels that would take the largest hits under the Bolling plan were signifi-

Table 15   Logistic Regression of Hansen Committee Reform Proposal Vote

Variable	Hansen Vote	Standard Error	Wald
Constant	2.31	(1.47)	2.48
Committees to lose under Bolling Plan (Group A)			
Education and Labor Committee	0.35	(0.46)	0.56
Internal Security Committee	−0.21	(0.87)	0.06
Interstate and Foreign Commerce	0.53	(0.84)	1.48
Merchant Marine Committee	0.65	(0.52)	1.55
Post Office Committee	1.25**	(0.58)	4.68
Ways and Means Committee	2.31***	(0.81)	7.93
Joint Atomic Energy	0.75	(1.08)	0.48
Committees to gain under either plan (Group B)			
Public Works Committee	−0.26	(0.44)	0.35
Small Business Committee	1.13*	(0.64)	3.12
Committees to gain under only Bolling Plan (Group C)			
Foreign Affairs Committee	−0.78*	(0.48)	2.61
Interior Committee	0.38	(0.43)	0.77
Science Committee	−0.88*	(0.48)	3.32
Constituency Characteristics			
Major port (dummy)	1.13**	(0.49)	5.32
Percent employed by federal govt.	0.31***	(0.12)	6.86
Percent employed in transportation	−0.02	(0.11)	0.05
Percent commuting on public trans.	0.03	(0.04)	0.77
Central city (dummy)	−0.04	(0.34)	0.02
NeedLabor[a]	0.11	(0.11)	1.00
Republican	−3.17***	(0.45)	50.46
Seniority	0.06	(0.04)	2.63
Ideology	3.41***	(0.63)	29.39
−2 log likelihood	364.07		
Model chi-square	134.18 ($p \leq .000$)		

NOTE: $N = 368$ cases.
[a]NeedLabor measures the degree to which a district ranks high on both union membership and blue-collar employment.
  *$p \leq .10$
 **$p \leq .05$
***$p \leq .01$

cantly supportive of the Hansen proposal. Even controlling for the effects of committee membership, representatives from port districts or those with significant federal government employment were much more likely to vote for passage of the Hansen plan. However, I do not find any significant effect of transportation or labor characteristics on members' votes on committee reforms. As expected, majority party investment in the committee status quo swayed Democrats to favor Hansen and Republicans to oppose it, but seniority had no statistically significant effect. On the other hand, ideology was very important in this vote, with liberals opposing Hansen's less radical alterations and conservatives supporting them. Additionally, a sensitivity analysis on the logit coefficients reveals that having a port or very high federal employment in one's district changes the probability of voting in favor of the Hansen plan at the same level as being a member of the Small Business, Ways and Means, or any other committee found to have a statistically significant effect on the reform votes.[44]

Conclusion

The prevailing wisdom on House committee reform efforts in the mid-1970s has been that the failure to pass the radical Bolling plan for jurisdictional restructuring was a result of legislators protecting their positions of institutional power. Members with different levels of career investment in a long-established system of committee property rights manipulated chamber and party rules to whittle away support from a proposal that some believed would "rationalize" a fractured and incoherent committee system. However, others simply thought the Bolling plan would severely disrupt the spheres of jurisdictional power that members had worked for years to protect. The institutional approach contends that the eventual passage of a significantly weaker reform package was based on members' willingness to, as Davidson and Oleszek put it, "accept half a loaf" in order to prevent possible passage of a bill that might truly upset the established order.

While this explanation seems adequate on its face, it ignores much of what political scientists have long contended about the committee system and how legislators view its structure. Legislators do not simply accrue seniority, and hence a greater investment in the existing institution, for its own sake. They have a number of goals—making good public policy, political influence, higher office (Fenno 1973; Deering and Smith 1997)—but none can be achieved unless they first secure their own survival. The legislative process can be lengthy and frustrating, and achieving institutional influence or a higher elected position can take years. Through experience, legislators know that the best way to ensure their longevity is through careful attention to the needs of those who elect them. As we learned, this is what has driven the consistency of the modern committee system since its establishment in the 1940s, and this is what also helped to sustain its structure as it came under fire in the 1970s.

Evidence from a number of proposals for restructuring committee jurisdictions in the 1970s reveals that considerably more than simple defense of established committee seniority motivated the opposition. The most vocal proponents and opponents of jurisdictional alterations were not only committee members defending jurisdictional turf, but also vocal legislators with strong constituency interests in specific jurisdictional configurations. Almost as frequently as "high-need" representatives protected the jurisdictions of their own panels, there were "high-need" representatives defending the policy property rights of panels on which they had no assignment. This trend occurs not only for the most zealous jurisdictional adversaries but also, as roll-call analyses revealed, for the less vocal rank-and-file when faced with chamber-wide decisions on specific jurisdictional alterations.

Of course other factors, such as party affiliation, ideology, and seniority played important parts in shaping the reform preferences of members. However, the effects of these variables were not always consistent across roll-call votes on specific changes. For instance, the single variable that perhaps best comprises the conventional wisdom on opposition to the Bolling plan—member seniority—seems to show no influence on how legislators finally voted on the Hansen plan after accounting for other factors. Nevertheless, the evidence presented here strongly suggests that, besides the institutional interests of members, concerns for district needs that affected legislators' choices on committee structural changes were also important.

Chapter 7

Committee Reforms under Partisan Politics

BY THE MID-1990S, POLITICAL CONDITIONS WITHIN CONGRESS
had changed considerably from what they had been two decades
earlier. The influences of more cohesive partisan policy programs
and a widening gulf between the ideological centers of the parties
came to characterize much of normal congressional operations. Efforts at structural change within Congress were not immune to the
influences of party-oriented strategies and agendas. The strengthened partisanship that consumed much of the way the House operated by the middle of the decade also shaped the way the chamber
considered, rejected, and eventually resurrected committee reforms
from the start of the 103rd Congress (1993–94) to the transition to
Republican control in the 104th Congress (1995–96).

This chapter examines how the familiar electoral considerations
of individual legislators intertwined with increasingly influential
partisan factors to alter how committee reorganization was treated
by the House in 1993 and 1994. I begin by reviewing evidence concerning the rise of conditional party government and expectations
about the way this should affect how legislators approach the issue
of committee restructuring. In the following section I study the circumstances surrounding the Joint Committee on the Organization
of Congress in 1993–94 and the factors contributing to the ultimate
failure of the committee reform proposals in the 103rd Congress.
Next I describe the transition to Republican rule in the House after
the 1994 elections and the dilemma the GOP faced regarding elimination of standing committees. I propose three potential criteria for

selecting panels to be abolished, based on notions of institutional efficiency, partisan policy objectives, and partisan electoral needs. Ultimately
I show that the confluence of intensified conditional party government
and the district investments of individual members in the existing configuration of committees produced a slight variation on what had previously
been seen as congressional reform fettered by electoral considerations.
Here, electoral requirements do stifle reform efforts, but the leverage
takes on a much more partisan character as caucus leaders are constrained to attend to the electoral needs of their membership as a whole
rather than on an individual level.

The Rise of "Conditional Party Government"

The decade of the 1980s saw considerable changes in the elements of congressional structure that make up what Aldrich and Rohde (1995) call
"conditional party government." Unlike the periods leading up to and
during the congressional reform movements of the 1940s and 1970s, internal party structures, or "party in government" (Aldrich 1995), had by
the mid-1980s firmly entrenched itself as a determining factor in House
operations.[1] To explain how strong caucus structures established the direction of reorganization efforts in the mid-1990s, I return to the subject
of partisanship and its role in legislative organization and policy agendas.

   As hypothesized earlier, efforts at congressional reform and committee
reorganization should take on a much more partisan direction if two
main conditions are met: (1) policy preferences within the party delegation are relatively homogeneous, and (2) deep and substantial divisions
exist in policy agendas between the parties. Evidence of the growth in
these conditions leading into the 1990s has been offered elsewhere, but
let me recount some of the highlights. With respect to party homogen-
eity, Rohde notes the increasing convergence of preferences among Democrats on various types of roll-call votes (procedural, appropriations,
non-appropriations, etc.) starting in the mid-1980s (1991, 52). Cox and
McCubbins's slightly different tack on party unity taps caucus support for
the policy agenda set by party leadership (1993). They similarly find a
dramatic increase in support for Democratic Party leaders beginning in
the late 1970s, with an especially profound redirection of the policy preferences among southern Democrats. Several authors have gauged the
gradual drift of southern Democrats back into the mainstream of the party
since the mid-1970s—Rohde does so through use of party unity scores
(1991, 55–58), and Poole and Rosenthal do this through their NOMINATE
ideology scores (1997). Poole and Rosenthal subsequently demonstrate

that the moderating shift in southern Democratic ideology is a likely result of large-scale retirements by conservative Democrats that led either to occupation of their seats by Republican legislators or by considerably more liberal Democrats (Poole and Rosenthal 1997, 79). Many authors account for the latter change through the "re-enfranchisement" of blacks in the south as a result of the Voting Rights Act of 1965 (Carmines and Stimson 1989). Similarly, Cox and McCubbins also find a shift toward support of the Republican leadership among GOP rank-and-file at about the same time, though this trend is not quite as dramatic as that in the Democratic Party (1993, chapter 6).

With regard to interparty division, Cooper and Young study partisanship using a measure that summarizes the frequency and strength of party unity votes in each congressional term. They determine that House partisanship in the mid-1990s hit a postwar high (1997, 256–57).[2] Likewise, Groseclose, Levitt, and Snyder use "inflation-adjusted" Americans for Democratic Action (ADA) scores to describe a growing polarization of policy preferences in the mid-1990s between House Democrats and Republicans—a division that they note had been widening since the early 1980s (1999, 41–42).[3]

Finally, in the most comprehensive study of conditional party government to date, Aldrich and Rohde (1998) use two different scales of legislator ideology (Poole and Rosenthal and Heckman-Snyder) and several summary measures of the distribution of ideal points for House members to illustrate the strengthening conditions for CPG. Again, they find that the breach between Democratic and Republican ideal points began to widen in the mid-1970s (identified by examining the difference in the party median positions and the declining overlap of party ideal points), and simultaneously intraparty preferences converged (identified through analysis of the deviation of members' ideal points from the party median).[4]

Since the elements of CPG are stronger in the 1990s than in any other postwar period, I expect to see a different approach to congressional reorganization. Along the lines of previous work on CPG, I hypothesized in chapter 2 that, once these conditions are met, party members will allocate increased power and resources to the caucus leadership to undertake actions that are potentially beneficial to them and to their future electoral prospects. These actions may entail not only a unified and coherent legislative agenda, but possibly even a reordering of legislative structures to facilitate the advancement of that agenda. Thus, "congressional reform" is likely to take on a much more partisan flavor. Rules are changed or perhaps committee jurisdictions are rearranged, but such actions are purposive. Legislators engage in reorganization under these conditions because it will help to advance a partisan policy program or help fellow party affiliates to win elections. The question is, How do the process and outcome of committee reforms differ under conditions of escalating party polarization? The next section examines how the concerted efforts of the Democratic Party to protect the policy interests of its electoral coalition restricted and ultimately doomed the efforts of reformers and the Joint Committee on the Organization of Congress to institute changes in the committee system during the 103rd Congress. I begin by describing the reform mood leading up to the creation of the Joint Committee and some of the work of that panel. I then analyze how and why the Democratic leadership inhibited those efforts.

A Joint Committee . . . Again

Following the reform efforts of the 93rd Congress and reinvigorated by the election of seventy-five mostly liberal Democratic freshman in the post-Watergate election of 1974, reformers further advanced their cause by instituting several changes during the next congressional term. Alterations included modifications in caucus rules, including caps on the number of committee and subcommittee leadership posts legislators were permitted to hold, as well as partisan-oriented changes, like caucus selection of Appropriations subcommittee chairs and redistribution of committee staff to help advance the majority agenda. The most significant jurisdictional alteration in this period was the elimination of the House Internal Security Committee at the start of the 94th Congress (1975–76).

Eventually, reform advocates reopened the difficult issue of energy jurisdictions in 1980, forcing the creation of another Select Committee on Committees headed by Representative Jerry Patterson (D-CA). As with transportation jurisdictions in the 93rd Congress, the Patterson Committee recommended consolidation of energy policy matters within the domain of a proposed Energy Committee. But in a fashion reminiscent of the jurisdictional battles just a few years earlier, committee and constituency advocates fiercely opposed this change, and ultimately the recommendation died. Ironically, one of the fears opponents of the Patterson proposal had was that, as Phillip Burton (D-CA) articulated it, "[O]ver the long term, members of the producing states are likely to get on the energy committee, as members of agriculture districts get on the agriculture committees," and the Energy Committee would soon become another constituency-dominated panel (Rosenbaum 1981, 73).

The reform mood in the House withered after the failure of the Patterson proposals, but slowly reemerged following a number of public scandals and forced early retirements from the House in the late 1980s. First came the resignation of Speaker Jim Wright (D-TX) resulting from allegations of ethical improprieties concerning a book contract and his abuse of office, followed soon after by Majority Whip Tony Coelho's (D-CA) resignation, also resulting from allegations of ethical misconduct. Not long after, in late 1991, more disgrace was brought on the House with the disclosure of widespread check-kiting by legislators at the House bank. About the same time, revelations of irregularities and mismanagement in the House post office led to accusations of drug peddling and embezzlement by legislators. Dan Rostenkowski (D-IL), the high-profile and influential chair of the Ways and Means Committee, was eventually implicated in the scandal that led to his conviction and removal from office.

As the 1992 election approached, public pressure was mounting for Congress to take action and "clean house." The Democrats and Speaker Tom Foley (D-WA) were especially pressured to initiate efforts at congressional reform out of a fear that the combination of sixty-five mostly Democratic retirements (the highest retirement rate in the entire postwar period) and an increasingly aggressive Republican electoral organization would capitalize on the legislature's negative publicity to take a significant number of seats away from Democrats. Foley needed to rebuff the perception that Democrats, with nearly forty years of continuous control of the House, had become complacent in the face of a growing public perception of corruption and abuse of legislative power. In March of 1992, Foley declared his support for a proposal by Lee Hamilton (D-IN) and Bill Gradison (R-OH) to create a bipartisan joint committee to study possible reforms in the structure and leadership of both chambers. The measure passed both houses later in the summer of 1992. The new Joint Committee on the Organization of Congress (JCOC) would convene after the swearing-in of the 103rd Congress in January 1993.

Support for Jurisdictional Restructuring

The statutory limit of a one year life-span meant that the work of the JCOC had to get underway immediately. The panel held thirty-six hearings between January and July 1993, taking testimony from 243 witnesses, 133 of whom were members of the House of Representatives.[5] From the start there were indications of broad support for significant alterations to the committee system. Like its namesake almost fifty years earlier, the Joint Committee believed that a large share of its mission was to make the committee system more "efficient and responsive" and to equalize "a very uneven distribution of power and workload among chamber committees." To Co-chair Hamilton, rearranging committee policy authority and jurisdictions was a "key part of reform."[6]

At least thirty-seven legislators recommended some amount of substantial change in the configuration of House committee jurisdictions: either a "rationalization" of the committee system or creation of parallel committee jurisdictions in the two chambers.[7] However, in most cases member statements were relatively vague as to what *specific* jurisdictional changes were needed. The comments of David Price (D-NC) were typical of those by many legislators: "I believe [we] need to revisit what proved to be the most difficult and least successful reform effort of the 1970s, namely the simplification and rationalization of committee jurisdictions."[8] Price went on to describe how a system of corresponding committee jurisdictions in the House and Senate has proven to be beneficial on Appropriations matters and would have aided in the passage of legislation such as banking reform in the late 1980s and early 1990s.

Additional support for profound reorganization of the House committee system came from other quarters, including separate groups of freshman Democrats and Republicans, as well as the liberal Democratic Study Group.[9] But, like the proposals of individual legislators, their recommendations were ambiguous about the details regarding which committees needed restructuring. Similarly, a JCOC survey of House members found that more than half (54 percent) supported a "comprehensive realignment of the committee system," 29 percent favored a "more modest consolidation of selective committees," and 12 percent favored "just a few jurisdictional changes" (Evans and Oleszek 1997, 94). Again, there were no details about specific committees or jurisdictions to be altered.

On the other hand, members generally defended the status quo in comments before the Joint Committee concerning the particular jurisdictions of several committees. Of more than fifty such statements, a sizable proportion were either by chairs or the ranking minority members, who defended their panel's turf or sought expansion of the committee's current issue boundaries, including remarks by Representatives de la Garza (Agriculture), Dellums (Armed Services), Gonzalez and Leach (Banking, Finance, and Urban Affairs), Dingell and Moorhead (Energy and Commerce), McDermott (Ethics), Clinger (Government Operations), Rose (House Administration), Fields and Studds (Merchant Marine and Fisheries), Clay and Myers (Post Office and Civil Service), Mineta and Shuster (Public Works and Transportation), Combest (Intelligence), LaFalce and Meyers (Small Business), and Montgomery (Veterans' Affairs). It was not uncommon for the defense of jurisdictional boundaries by committee leaders to have been (in part, at least) motivated by district interests.

Hamilton recalls that this was the case for Studds's defense of his Merchant Marine and Fisheries Committee. He stated that "Gerry [Studds] was a liberal, progressive member . . . you could hardly recommend a reform he wasn't for. But he fought this proposal [for elimination of the maritime committee] tooth and nail [because] Merchant Marine and Fisheries was a powerful committee for his constituency." [10]

Once the JCOC wrapped up its information gathering, it moved on to formulate the reform package to be presented to both chambers. In August 1993 the four leaders of the committee met in private to draw up a draft bill, or "chairman's mark," from which the entire panel would work during the markup later in the year. Several months later, in November, the House and Senate panel members held separate markups to debate their own version of the bill for chamber consideration. That finished, the JCOC leadership introduced the plans to their respective chambers at the start of the second session in 1994,[11] with the House version sitting in the Rules Committee for several months. Not until the threat of a discharge petition did the Democratic leadership break off a less controversial portion of the bill for separate floor consideration.[12] The bulk of the reform package came before the Rules Committee for consideration initially in August and then again in September 1994. As Rules Democrats began to debate amendments, such as a ban on proxy voting and eventually an alternative committee restructuring plan, Foley called committee Democrats away from the markup for consultation. Later that day Chairman Moakley adjourned the Rules Committee, and it never considered the JCOC's proposal again (Evans and Oleszek 1997, 73–75). This figured to be the end of any consideration of congressional reform during the 103rd Congress.

The Failure of Committee Restructuring in the 103rd Congress

How do we understand the failure of committee restructuring during the 103rd Congress in light of broader electoral and partisan considerations? The answer offers the first signs of how the standard reelection motivation of legislators interacts with the partisan inclinations of the majority caucus as a whole to limit the boundaries of structural reform. Several authors offer explanations as to why the House demurred from even simply considering committee reorganization. They range from a lack of leadership, majority party enthusiasm, or compelling public pressure for system-wide reforms, to opposition by committee chiefs or fractured party preferences both on the Joint Committee and in the chamber as a whole regarding specific jurisdictional changes (Evans and Oleszek 1997; Davidson 1995b, 1999). None of these explanations is incorrect, but behind them may lie an elementary electoral motivation not too different from what was seen in previous generations, but with a more profound partisan stake.

Despite the overwhelming sentiment among House members that something needed to be done to restructure the committee system, reorganization of jurisdictions never seemed to be a viable issue in the reform effort. To understand the failure of the chamber to take on the matter of jurisdictional realignment, I concentrate on three critical junctures where the House, or more appropriately the JCOC and party leadership acting on behalf of the House, had an opportunity to consider and advance committee restructuring but chose not to. These three instances are (1) the deliberation over the chairman's mark, (2) the markup of the House version of the JCOC proposal, and (3) the consideration of the reform bill in the Rules Committee. I analyze the actions and motives of those who halted the progression of the reform proposals and study how they comport with the electoral and partisan propositions on committee restructuring.

The Chairman's Mark

When the four leaders of the JCOC sat down to draw up its first version of the reform bill, they were confronted with a tremendous amount of information concerning committee reorganization. The panel collected volumes of testimony, and its staff had extensively surveyed the mood of the members of Congress toward the reform effort. Even if most of the data gave little detail as to members' specific preferences for jurisdictional reshuffling beyond a vocal preference for the status quo, the JCOC had numerous recommendations in a commissioned study by the Congressional Research Service as well as a detailed report from a group of prominent political scientists under what was called the Renewing Congress Project.[13] Yet in spite of this information and their seemingly genuine commitment to congressional reform, deep divisions erupted between the Democratic (Boren and Hamilton) and Republican committee leaders (Domenici and Dreier), specifically over the issue of jurisdictional reorganization. Boren and Hamilton opposed the inclusion of any substantial restructuring of committee issue jurisdictions, and ultimately the chairman's mark included a minimal plan for considering the abolition of committees that would kick in only after elections. This market-driven, or what was called an "incentive-based," approach triggered a review of a committee's status if during the assignment process at the beginning of the congressional term it attracted less than half of its total membership from the previous term. Under proposed reforms, the matter of membership size was likely to be a more serious issue than in the past, since the Joint Committee also recommended stricter limitations on the number of committee assignments members could hold. Other issues involving the reshuffling of committee jurisdictions, like moving specific policy issues from one jurisdiction to another or criteria for adding new panels to the committee system, were excluded from further consideration.

Hamilton stated that the Democratic co-chairs feared that consideration of jurisdictional restructuring would cause so much conflict among legislators (as it had in the mid-1970s) that it would be impossible for *any* rules changes to move forward and would doom the entire process.[14] Clearly this was a reasonable prophecy and likely an accurate one; as the outcome of the markup of the House reform bill reveals, there was more motivating Democratic Party opposition to a debate over jurisdictional changes.

House Markup

Jurisdictional restructuring was broached again during the markup of the JCOC proposal by its House members. Vice Chair Dreier introduced an amendment to the existing reform plan that included a radical set of jurisdictional rearrangements, including the abolition of the District of Columbia, House Administration, Merchant Marine and Fisheries, Post Office and Civil Service, and Small Business committees, whose policy jurisdictions would be placed under the purview of other existing panels. Deliberation on this amendment became one of the more contentious moments during the House markup. Hamilton and David Obey (D-WI) were especially offended that they had barely seen Dreier's proposal, let alone discussed it prior to the markup session. Hamilton opposed the plan in a subcommittee roll-call, and it was eventually defeated on a partisan 6–6 vote. He claimed that the proposal was not a serious effort at reform and stated that because of its "complexity" and "political sensitivity" he again feared that such a plan would condemn the entire reform effort on the floor.[15]

However, it was not simply a fear of compromising support on the floor that motivated Democratic opposition. Notes from a series of meetings that Hamilton held with the caucus leadership prior to the markup reveal that the JCOC co-chair was under orders from the party leadership not to allow any plan for jurisdictional reorganization to move forward. Speaker Foley's instructions were that Hamilton should find a way to defer any serious consideration of jurisdictional restructuring during the JCOC markup. Foley suggested that it was acceptable to discuss the matter, but that ultimately Hamilton should recommend that the topic deserved further study. Perhaps, Foley suggested, Hamilton should recommend that a new committee be created to look into the topic of jurisdictional change.[16]

Deliberation in the Rules Committee

Finally, the demise of the reform package and any chance for consideration of jurisdictional restructuring occurred in the House Rules Committee during late summer of 1994. By this point, Foley's obstruction of consideration of jurisdictional changes was beginning to crumble even within the Democratic Party. Rules Committee Democrat Anthony Bielenson (CA) had prepared two packages of jurisdictional changes that closely resembled the plans Dreier wanted to introduce to the committee (Evans and Oleszek 1995, 11).[17] When it became apparent that a small number of Democratic votes along with the support of Republicans might result in passage of some of the new reform amendments, Foley called the Democrats away from the committee for a private caucus. After this meeting Chair Joe Moakley (D-MA) adjourned the markup.

The Democratic leaders' opposition to allowing consideration of jurisdictional reforms stemmed from several related factors. To begin with, Foley, a veteran of the conflicts during the Bolling-Hansen era, sought to avoid the bitter battles that had characterized the reform effort in the 1970s (Evans and Oleszek 1997, 59). As speaker, Foley had relatively little ability to manage his committee chairs, and such a battle would have paralyzed the party's ability to advance Clinton's policy agenda, specifically his health care plan.[18] The 103rd Congress was the first unified Democratic government since the Carter administration, and they had hoped to seize the opportunity to alter federal policy in a number of important issue areas. Foley was so fearful of the potential fallout of a jurisdictional debate that he even attempted to prevent jurisdictional changes from being part of the authorizing mandate for the JCOC, but the bill's sponsors, Hamilton and Gradison, refused to support the plan altogether if this was done. Foley subsequently backed away from this proposal.[19]

On a broader scale, however, the Democratic leadership recognized that there were significant constituency ramifications to any consideration of committee restructuring. For instance, one panel that had long been a target for elimination was the District of Columbia Committee. The delegate for the District, Eleanor Holmes Norton, stated her grave fear for the perpetuation of this panel once the chairman's mark with the "incentives-based" proposal was reported.[20] Norton's concern was that placing a premium on the number of committee assignments would leave this panel with far fewer, if any, members, and make it immediately vulnerable to the possibility of elimination. Foley specifically recognized that abolition of this committee would have profound negative consequences for the party among District residents: "A howl will go up if [the] District of Columbia [Committee] is absorbed elsewhere . . . D.C. residents will argue that they can't get statehood, Delegate votes are challenged on revotes, Congress intrudes too much in D.C. affairs, and now you take away the only committee that stands up for the District."[21] The district has traditionally voted very heavily for Democratic candidates (see below).

Further statements made during the leadership meetings in October 1993 reveal that the Democrats' evasive strategy on the matter of jurisdictional alteration was to some extent driven by electoral considerations. For instance, the Democratic chiefs were fully aware that if they appeared obstructionist on the matter of reforms, this could come back to haunt them in the elections the following year. During one meeting of party leaders—Speaker Foley, Majority Leader Dick Gephardt (MO), Democratic Caucus Vice Chair Vic Fazio (CA) and Hamilton—the Speaker stated his concern that failure to demonstrate willingness to move forward on reforms in the wake of the numerous scandals and faltering public confidence in the institution would likely be used by Republicans and Reform party leader H. Ross Perot to attack incumbent Democrats in the 1994 elections. They were particularly concerned that such attacks would be directed at their large and vulnerable freshman class.[22] The Democratic leadership would, alternatively, pursue other types of political reform, specifically campaign finance reform, in order to demonstrate their willingness to alter "business as usual" in Congress.[23]

Democratic constituency concerns even played a significant part in the decision to adjourn the Rules markup. Waler Oleszek (Staff Policy Director of the JCOC) recalled that among Bielenson's reform plans was a proposal to eliminate the Veterans' Affairs Committee. Oleszek stated that a number of representatives from the Veterans of Foreign Wars and the American Legion were standing at the back of the Rules hearing room in an obvious attempt to demonstrate their great displeasure with this proposal. The Democrats were not looking to pick a fight with veterans' groups—an important and politically active demographic group with whom the party had been losing electoral support (see more on this point below)—and this contributed to Foley's motivation to abruptly end the hearing.[24] Oleszek stated that a similar demonstration of clientele group "concern" for the future of their patron committee occurred during the Joint Committee hearings on the Merchant Marine and Fisheries panel, when representatives of the maritime unions appeared in the hearing room while Chairman Gerry Studds testified.

Facing public pressure to "clean up" Congress, the Democrats proceeded to consider reorganization proposals with little serious consideration of jurisdictional realignment. Democratic leadership ultimately killed the entire process when it became apparent that a combination of

Republicans and reform-minded Democrats might prove to be a large enough coalition to pass some kind of reform package. In many respects it was fear of severe electoral fallout that provoked leaders to oppose changes in the committee system. The next section demonstrates even more profoundly how defense of the policy interests of important electoral groups affected the reform choices of Republicans in late 1994.

The Transition to Republican Control

Efforts at committee restructuring in 1994 did not end with the adjournment of the Rules Committee in September. Attempts to reorganize the House committee system simply changed venues with the elections. Here I examine the decisions of the Republican leadership after they won a House majority in the November elections and were faced with their own decree to eliminate one-third of the committees in the legislature. I describe what led up to this proposal and study the capacity of three different hypotheses to explain the reasons why just a few panels were cut off, while others that had been on the chopping block were spared.

Developing the Contract with America

In order to distinguish themselves from the long-ruling Democratic Party and to distance the GOP from any complicity in the numerous scandals that had plagued Congress over the previous five years, a number of Republican leaders devised the *Contract with America.* The *Contract,* with its ten catchy policy goals, was intended to signal to voters in the coming 1994 elections that the Republican Party had a coherent and coordinated vision for governing.[25]

The *Contract*'s provisions for congressional reorganization included a vague proclamation that the system of legislative committees in the House would be reduced by one-third (Gillespie and Schellhas 1994, 8). The plan gave no further detail on how this would be done nor which committees would be eliminated. However, to a certain extent, details on how the Republicans would handle reorganization had already been in the works. Minority Leader Bob Michael (R-IL) had named a twenty-six-member Leader's Task Force on Congressional Reform in March 1993.[26] Once it was clear that the JCOC would be unable to pass any meaningful committee restructuring, the Republicans called upon Dreier, Jennifer Dunn (WA), and Gerald Solomon (NY) to come up with a GOP reform plan that included provisions for reshuffling committee jurisdictions. Their proposals were eventually included in more general terms in the *Contract with America* (Davidson 1999, 74; Evans and Oleszek 1997, 84).

On the day after the election in 1994, Speaker-in-Waiting Gingrich called Dreier to request that he devise several specific committee reorganization options for consideration by the Republican Transition Team. Even before the November elections, a number of House committees had been cited by Republicans as being on the endangered list (Burger 1994b). A week after the elections, Dreier presented four prospective committee restructuring plans to the Republican leadership and the larger transition group. Dreier's plans ranged from relatively mild adjustments (Option 1) to revolutionary restructuring in committee organization (Option 4). The four plans are shown in table 16. His most conservative proposal eliminated only three panels, redistributed their jurisdictions among a number of existing committees, and merged two other panels. Dreier's most radical plan called for the elimination of one additional committee and, what was more important, the reorganization of the jurisdictions of almost every major panel.

Once these options became public knowledge,[27] they aroused a considerable amount of opposition among a number of high-ranking Republicans as well as interested parties outside of Congress (Hosansky 1994). Perhaps the most critical miscalculation made by Gingrich and the GOP leadership in its attempt to cut the number of committees was effectively announcing panel chairs while simultaneously deciding which of Dreier's options to implement (Burger 1994a; Clymer 1994). As Robert Walker (a close friend of Gingrich and a leader of the GOP transition) stated, once individuals were pegged for these committee leadership spots, they became "jealous guardians" of their jurisdictions.[28] Like previous efforts at jurisdictional restructuring, the visceral opposition of Republican legislators compelled the transition team to hear from prospective committee chairs complaining about adjustments to their future assignments.[29]

Sensing that prolonged debate over major jurisdictional restructuring could ignite a civil war among Republicans, Gingrich and a small group of senior Republican leaders chose to go with a minimal reorganization of committees that basically consisted of Dreier's first option. The reform plan included the elimination of the District of Columbia and Post Office and Civil Service committees and the transfer of their jurisdictions to the newly renamed Government Reform and Oversight Committee (formerly Government Operations); the abolition of the Merchant Marine and Fisheries Committee and redistribution of its policy property rights to the National Security (formerly Armed Services), Transportation and Infrastructure (formerly Public Works and Transportation), and Resources (formerly Interior and Insular Affairs) committees; and the slicing up of a few policy issues under the jurisdiction of the Energy and Commerce

Table 16 Rep. David Dreier's Proposals for Committee Restructuring During the Republican Transition, 1994

Committee	Option 1	Option 2	Option 3	Option 4
Agriculture		*Consolidate hunger issues*	Becomes Ag. Nat. Resources, and Envir. *Nutrition to Empowerment*	Becomes Agric. Resources *Nutrition to Empowerment*
Appropriations				
Armed Services			Becomes National Defense	Becomes National Defense
Banking			*Housing to Empowerment*	Becomes Banking, Finan. Services, and Small Business *Housing to Empowerment*
Budget				Becomes Budget and Econ. Forecasting
District of Columbia	Merge into Govt. Ops.	Merge into Govt. Ops.	Merge into Govt. Ops.	Merge into Reform and Govt. Oversight
Education and Labor		*School lunches to Agric.*	Becomes Empowerment	Becomes Empowerment
Energy and Commerce	*Railroads to Public Works*	*Railroads to Public Works* *Securities to Banking*	Becomes Commerce and Health *Railroads to Trans. and Infrastructure* *Envir. to Ag. Nat. Resources and Envir.* *Securities to Banking* *Energy to Science and Energy*	Becomes Commerce and Health *Railroads to Trans. and Infrastructure* *Envir. to Envir. and Nat. Resources* *Securities to Banking* *Energy to Science and Energy*
Ethics	Combine w/ House Admin.	Combine w/ House Admin.	Combine w/ House Admin.	Combine w/ House Admin.
Foreign Affairs				Becomes Intl. Relations
Govt. Operations				Becomes Reform and Govt. Oversight

Committee					
House Admin.	Combine w/ Ethics	Combine w/ Ethics	Combine w/ Ethics	Combine w/ Ethics	Combine w/ Ethics
Judiciary					
Merchant Marine	Abolish; divide juris.	Abolish; divide juris.	Abolish; divide juris.	Abolish *Envir. to Ag. Nat. Resources and Envir. Merchant Marine to National Defense Coast Guard to Trans. and Infrastructure*	Abolish *Envir. and fishing to Envir. and Nat. Resources Merchant Marine to National Defense Coast Guard to Trans. and Infrastructure*
Natural Resources				*Make into Ag. Nat. Resources and Envir. Energy to Science and Energy*	Becomes Envir. and Nat. Resources
Post Office	Merge into Govt. Ops.	Merge into Govt. Ops.		Merge into Govt. Ops.	Merge into Reform and Govt. Oversight
Public Works				Becomes Trans. and Infrastructure *Envir. to Ag. Nat. Resources and Envir.*	Becomes Trans. and Infrastructure *Envir. to Envir. and Nat. Resources*
Rules					
Science				Becomes Science and Energy	Becomes Science and Energy
Small Business				Abolish; juris. to Banking	Abolish; juris. to Banking
Ways and Means			*Welfare, child support, adoption assistance and foster care to Educ. and Labor*	*Welfare to Empowerment Medicare to Commerce and Health*	Becomes Revenue *Welfare to Empowerment Medicare to Commerce and Health*
Veterans' Affairs				Merge into National Defense	

NOTE: Data for table taken from Evans and Oleszek 1995. Entries in italics are proposals for partial jurisdictional changes.

committee among five different panels. According to Walker, the decision as to which committees would be eliminated, who acquired their jurisdictions, and the extent of other jurisdictional reshuffling was not made by the conference membership or even the more elite transition team, but by a considerably smaller group of senior GOP advisors—essentially an assembly of about half-a-dozen Republicans who devised the *Contract*.[30]

Facing the Dilemma

Deciding which committee to eliminate was clearly not easy, and Gingrich would have preferred not to make the decision if he could have avoided it.[31] Nevertheless, the choice about abolishing panels can be very instructive in how partisan and electoral considerations played an influential role in decisions concerning chamber structure. In this section I explore the ability of three distinct hypotheses to explain why certain committees were pegged for extinction while others were not.

As tempers flared both among Republican legislators and outside constituency groups concerning the potential restructuring of the House committee system, the Republican leadership was faced with a dilemma. In order to distinguish their agenda, Republicans had promised in the *Contract* that several congressional reforms would be passed immediately on opening day of the 104th Congress—including a severe reduction in the number of House committees. However, even the suggestion of this kind of reform had the potential to rip apart the caucus before it had taken office and impede the timely consideration and passage of the more salient policy objectives in the party platform. GOP leadership could therefore either scrap a major provision of a key promise in the *Contract*—a rather distasteful and embarrassing prospect—or find a minimally acceptable reform option that would at least nominally fulfill the promise of the *Contract* to cut the number of committees. Oppenheimer (1997) refers to this problem as the "reformers' pitfall"—in order to garner media and public attention and support, out-party reformers propose more extensive institutional changes than are politically feasible once they gain control of the legislative body.

As mentioned above, several panels were potentially on the chopping block following the election, either as part of the Dreier plan for jurisdictional restructuring or cited as such by a prominent party leader or aide. Many committees faced potential jurisdictional changes, mergers, or elimination—even some of the chamber's most influential panels. The threatened committees included Agriculture, Armed Services, District of Columbia, Education and Labor, Energy and Commerce, Government Operations, House Administration, Merchant Marine and Fisheries, Natural Resources, Post Office and Civil Service, Public Works and Transportation, Science, Small Business, Standards of Official Conduct (Ethics), Veterans' Affairs, and Ways and Means. Dreier pushed for the most extreme of his four options, adhering to a philosophy on committee reforms that he articulated during his work on the JCOC. Dreier believed that the best approach to jurisdictional reforms was wholesale change: "[I]f you start from scratch and propose a comprehensive [jurisdictional] realignment then members of those committees will support that approach. But not if those panels are the only ones targeted." [32]

To avoid embarrassing claims that their *Contract* was disingenuous or, worse yet, a campaign ploy, and also to forestall a potentially contentious and crippling intraparty battle over jurisdictional turf, the GOP leadership decided to implement the most painless feasible reforms with respect to elimination of committees (Sinclair 1999, 24; Davidson 1999, 77). This would fulfill at least in deed some of the reform provisions in the *Contract,* but ultimately Republicans did not eliminate the one-third that was called for in the *Contract.* That would have required the removal of no less than four more committees.

With their backs to the wall, Republican leaders had to select a minimal number of committees for elimination. The question with regard to the larger debate over committee restructuring is, Under what decision rule did the GOP leadership choose to eliminate the District of Columbia, Merchant Marine and Fisheries, and Post Office and Civil Service committees, but not others, like Small Business or Veterans' Affairs? I propose three plausible criteria for selecting committees to be eliminated. The first is based on institutional efficiency, the second on partisan policy utility, and the third on partisan electoral considerations. I explore each in turn, along with empirical evidence as to their ability to explain the choices made by Republican leaders.

Utilitarian Approach

Perhaps the simplest and least partisan criteria for trimming what was increasingly considered a bloated and inefficient committee structure was merely to eliminate panels that were most expendable on efficiency grounds. As with the reforms in the mid-1940s, the most painless means of consolidating committees would be to target those panels that were least active, whose work was not central to the functions performed by the legislature, or whose duties could most easily be subsumed by some other entity within the chamber. Members were significantly less likely to be affected by alterations that eliminated inactive or peripheral committees, which were unlikely to be crucial either to many members' personal political agendas or to the general policy program of the party.

To identify the chamber's most expendable panels, we begin with a

Table 17 Committee Activity as Measured by Days of Committee Hearings, Standing Committees (1989–1993)

	Committee	1989	1990	1991	1992	1993	Yearly Average
1	Appropriations	295[a]	306	289	295	292	295
2	Energy and Commerce	158	121	297	86	150	162
3	Foreign Affairs	187	157	171	117	150	156
4	Banking	111	142	107	94	111	113
5	Armed Services	130	114	116	114	67	108
6	Science	132	81	118	104	120	107
7	Ways and Means	98	77	120	73	114	96
8	Education and Labor	100	88	132	57	100	95
9	Government Operations	117	104	101	75	62	92
10	Judiciary	131	103	79	75	43	86
11	Agriculture	110	57	88	57	85	79
12	Merchant Marine	78	59	69	51	87	69
13	Public Works	59	84	79	55	64	68
14	Interior/Natural Resources	58	80	74	60	32	61
15	Small Business	50	46	67	41	66	54
16	Post Office	57	56	48	43	32	47
17	Veterans' Affairs	37	26	28	30	33	31
18	District of Columbia	19	7	15	8	6	11
19	House Administration	9	8	11	9	6	9
20	Standards (Ethics)	0	0	0	0	0	0

[a]Hearing days taken from Baumgartner and Jones's accounting of the CIS Index of Congressional Committee Hearings. The figure for each committee includes hearings held by subcommittees.

simple examination of "activity" as measured by the number of hearing days per year. These are listed in table 17 for every major standing committee (except Rules) in the five-year period (1989–1993) prior to the election of the GOP majority in 1994. Several panels are clearly very active; Appropriations leads the way with an average of almost 80 percent more days of hearings per year than the next closest panel, Energy and Commerce. Several other committees were extremely active by this measure (averaging more than a hundred hearing days per year). With the exception of Commerce, none of these panels was seriously considered for radical reforms or jurisdictional restructuring.

Of the panels mentioned for elimination, interestingly, several appear to have been fairly active—Merchant Marine and Fisheries (an average of 69 hearing days per year), Natural Resources (61), Small Business (54), and Post Office and Civil Service (47). Conversely, several panels stand out by this measure as ripe for removal, with few, if any, hearing days per year—Ethics (0), House Administration (9), District of Columbia (11), and, arguably, Veterans' Affairs (31).

This measure, however, is not an entirely unbiased gauge of committee activity or importance to the chamber or party's agenda, since, in part, an active hearings schedule is controlled by the committee itself. Thus a committee can affect the perception of its own importance by simply holding more hearings than are necessary for the legislation they produce. Therefore, to further capture the significance of a committee's workload to the duties and legislative responsibilities of its principal body, I focus on two alternative scales of activity—the number of public laws that were previously referred to each panel when they were originally offered as bills, and the number "major" public laws originally referred to the committee. The criteria for "major" or significant public laws are similar to those employed, for example, by Mayhew (1991) or Howell et al. (2000). For a measure of legislative importance, I rely on the "retrospective" significance that congressional reporters give to each particular enactment in the year-end summaries of congressional activity. Major enactments are simply those to which the *Congressional Quarterly Almanac* devoted at least fifty column inches of text in describing their content and passage.[33] The rankings are a rough gauge of the extent to which the chamber would consider the work of a particular committee critical to the institution's overall output at the time. Table 18 lists these two measures in the three pre-reform congressional terms for the ten committees considered to be most endangered.

Examining participation in the production of public laws, six committees stand out as particularly fruitful among this group. As with the measure of hearing days, the most active panels in this group as gauged by output of enactments include Natural Resources, Merchant Marine and Fisheries, Post Office and Civil Service, and Public Works and Transportation. However, they also include two committees not noted for tremendous hearings activity—House Administration and Veterans' Affairs. The Natural Resources Committee leads the way in the production of legislation by a long way with its duties in supervising the government's public land holdings.[34] After these more active panels, however, there is a drop in legislative productivity for such committees as District of Columbia and Government Operations, and very little evidence of legislative activity by the Small Business and Ethics committees.[35]

Turning to major legislation, once again I find Public Works and Transportation, Merchant Marine and Fisheries, Natural Resources, and possibly Veterans' Affairs among the most prolific panels, all averaging more than four major enactments per congressional term. Following close behind is the Post Office and Civil Service Committee, averaging three major enactments per term. Finally, several panels rank toward the bottom,

Table 18   Committee Production of Public Laws and Major Public Laws,
Endangered Committees (101st–103rd Congresses)

Committee	Public Laws			Major Public Laws		
	101st[a]	102nd	103rd	101st[b]	102nd	103rd
District of Columbia	8	6	6	0	1	0
Government Operations	7	5	8	1	0	3
House Administration	21	12	13	0	1	1
Merchant Marine	22	22	15	6	4	3
Interior/Natural Resources	95	80	69	4	6	3
Post Office	223	165	109	2	1	6
	(7)[c]	(20)	(14)			
Public Works	33	24	41	8	6	6
Small Business	3	2	2	1	2	2
Standards (Ethics)	1	0	0	0	0	0
Veterans' Affairs	6	19	13	1	9	5

[a] Number of public laws recorded as having been previously referred to this committee as noted in the House of Representatives' THOMAS database http://thomas.loc.gov.

[b] Number of "major" public laws recorded as having been previously referred to this committee as noted in *Congressional Quarterly Almanac*. Major enactments are those that received at least 50 column lines of text in the *Almanac*.

[c] Figure in parentheses is the number of "noncommemorative" enactments.

producing two or fewer major pieces of legislation each term—District of Columbia, Government Operations, House Administration, Small Business, and Ethics.

One final consideration for elimination of marginal committees is how easily each committee's legislative responsibilities could be assumed by other panels. That is, to what extent does a committee's jurisdiction overlap with that of other committees that could just as easily handle consideration of its policy issues. As a crude measure of jurisdictional overlap I examine the percentage of bills referred to each committee that were also referred to one or more other committees (often called "multiple referrals") in the 103rd Congress.[36] These data, provided in table 19, reveal that most of the committees facing potential elimination had a fairly well-defined field of issues that they solely controlled—approximately two-thirds of their legislative work was conducted without consultation or input from any other panel. However, two committees stand out as having shared a substantial part of their legislative duties—Government Operations (75 percent of bills were multiply referred) and House Administration (66 percent).

Table 19 Jurisdictional Overlap of Endangered Committees, 103rd Congress

Committee[a]	Percentage of Multiple Referrals, Public Bills (N)
District of Columbia	38 (39)
Government Operations	75 (277)
House Administration	66 (324)
Merchant Marine	36 (253)
Natural Resources	19 (498)
Post Office	37 (638)
Small Business	32 (57)
Veterans' Affairs	26 (177)

[a]Standards of Official Conduct (Ethics) is not included since it usually considers little or no legislation.

It is not surprising that Government Operations would rank highly on jurisdictional overlap, since much of its work is simply oversight of federal agencies. Nevertheless, this begs the question of why, under a need to pare down committees, oversight responsibilities for government agencies like the Department of Justice or Department of Transportation could not be shifted to the committees with authorizing jurisdiction over them—Judiciary or Public Works and Transportation, respectively.

From the examination of hearing days, production of public laws, and jurisdictional distinctiveness, I find little evidence that Republicans chose committees for elimination on efficiency grounds. Two panels ranked low on all three criteria, District of Columbia and Ethics, but only the former was selected for abolition. Though Ethics does not operate as do most standing House committees and therefore would rate poorly on many of these conventional measures, it also has a very limited role within the institution and could easily have been merged into the responsibilities of a different panel or chamber structure without upsetting any particular constituency group. This might have been an obvious choice for the Republican leadership under pressure to fulfill their reform pledge. In fact, early in the transition period, this was an argument touted by GOP leaders for the possible elimination of this panel (more on this below; see Burger 1994a). Other panels also rated poorly on two of the three criteria—Government Operations, House Administration, and Small Business—but none were selected for elimination. Conversely, of the two committees beside the District of Columbia panel that were selected for elimination, Merchant Marine and Fisheries, and Post Office and Civil Service, neither was significantly inactive or redundant as compared to several other, less important committees.

Given the measures employed here, I find little support for the utilitarian hypothesis of committee abolition during the Republican transition. Active and seemingly useful committees for the purpose of policy making were selected for abolition, while inactive and peripheral panels were spared.

Congruence with Partisan Policy Preferences

The discussion in chapter 2 of the partisan principles of legislative organization suggests the first of two potential party criteria for selecting committees to eliminate. As stated previously, the Cox and McCubbins cartel approach advises that party contingents on committees are seen primarily as agents of their parent caucus. They serve the needs of the party by acting as its specialized experts, pursuing caucus goals within their policy boundaries. Given this responsibility, parties have an incentive to ensure that the aggregate preferences of its members on specific panels comport with the central tendency of the caucus preferences. A party contingent on a committee with divergent policy goals can pursue policy objectives that may be contrary, possibly even harmful, to their fellow partisans' electoral prospects. Cox and McCubbins argue that parties will regulate those panel contingents whose aggregate preferences become unbalanced with those of the caucus (Cox and McCubbins 1993, 224–28).

Concern for the composition and activities of party subunits on committees is likely to be most acute in situations where the jurisdictions of those panels are likely to affect the reelection prospects of many, if not all, party members. These are committees that Cox and McCubbins identified as having *uniform* or *mixed* externalities; they include Appropriations; Armed Services; Banking; Energy and Commerce; Education and Labor; Foreign Affairs; Government Operations; House Administration; Judiciary; Post Office and Civil Service; Public Works and Transportation; Rules; Veterans' Affairs; and Ways and Means. While the panels of broad importance are likely to face the stiffest scrutiny under reform conditions because of their prominence, they are liable to face membership adjustments rather than elimination if the preferences of the party contingents are found to be incongruent with that of the overall party caucus. On the other hand, committees with *targeted* externalities—Agriculture; District of Columbia; Interior and Insular Affairs; and Merchant Marine and Fisheries—whose party contingents are found to be preference outliers, are more likely to meet a very different fate. While their policy responsibilities affect a considerably smaller number of members, therefore limiting the effects of contrasting preferences, elimination of such panels due to outlier contingents would also have a relatively minor influence on the party agenda.[37]

Therefore, faced with the unpleasant but unavoidable duty of eliminating at least some legislative panels, the GOP might have found it easiest and most efficient from a policy perspective to abolish those with previous outlier Republican contingents and those whose jurisdiction touched relatively few congressional districts. Additionally, since the caucus was becoming even more conservative after the election of seventy-three freshman in 1994 (Rae 1998), the party leadership would have found it even easier, if not necessary, to target for restructuring those committees that had been composed of outlier *liberal* Republican contingents. To examine this hypothesis, I first explore the ideological composition of the returning Republican members on each committee from the 103rd Congress. To capture ideology, I use Poole and Rosenthal's w-NOMINATE scores.

The ideology tests conducted are identical to the previous Monte Carlo simulations performed on the constituency-demand scores. Here the comparison bodies are *returning* Republican committee contingents and the entire *returning* GOP caucus.[38] The null hypothesis is that the median of Republican committee contingents is no different ideologically than the caucus median. The tests for all standing committees in the 103rd Congress are reported in table 20. The table provides the number of returning Republicans previously assigned to the panel, the median for that group, its numerical difference from the caucus median (the GOP caucus median is .40 on the NOMINATE scale), and the *p*-value for the difference-in-medians Monte Carlo test. A positive difference indicates a more conservative Republican committee contingent than the entire GOP membership, and a negative difference indicates a liberal contingent.

Several returning Republican committee contingents appear to be liberal outliers with respect to the caucus median. These include two panels with uniform externalities (Appropriations, and Post Office and Civil Service), one with mixed externalities (Foreign Affairs), and one with targeted externalities (Merchant Marine and Fisheries). Conforming to expectations about structural reforms driven by party policy motives, two of these four panels were eliminated (Post Office and Civil Service and Merchant Marine and Fisheries) and a third (Appropriations) experienced relatively strict management of its composition and activities by Republican leaders. Oversight of the Appropriations Committee included hand-picking the full committee chairman from four positions down the seniority ladder, radical alteration in the composition of the GOP contingent on Appropriations with the addition of eleven new members, and a requirement that all GOP members on the committee sign a "letter of fidelity" that bound them to follow the leadership's program of budget-cutting (Evans and Oleszek 1997, 120).

Two other panels need further mention. First, one committee seems to

Table 20 Tests of Ideological Outliers for Returning Republican Contingents on House Committees, 103rd–104th Congresses

Committee	Returning Republicans	W-NOMINATE Median	Difference from GOP Median	Significance Level
Uniform externalities				
Appropriations	21	.32	−.08[b]	.05
Budget[a]	15	.34	−.06	.21
Energy and Commerce	16	.42	+.02	.44
Government Operations	13	.40	.00	.51
House Administration	7	.43	+.03	.32
Post Office	8	.23	−.17	.01
Public Works	23	.41	+.01	.42
Rules	4	.53	+.13	.08
Science	20	.44	+.04	.14
Small Business[a]	17	.43	+.03	.23
Standards (Ethics)[a]	5	.29	−.11	.12
Veterans' Affairs	13	.42	+.02	.40
Ways and Means	11	.39	−.01	.44
Mixed externalities				
Armed Services	18	.41	+.01	.37
Banking	15	.41	+.01	.47
Education and Labor	15	.42	+.02	.31
Foreign Affairs	16	.33	−.07	.09
Judiciary	13	.44	+.04	.21
Targeted externalities				
Agriculture	18	.43	+.03	.21
District of Columbia	4	.51	+.11	.13
Merchant Marine	16	.30	−.10	.03
Natural Resources	13	.42	+.02	.37
Republican Conference	155	.40		

[a] Several committees tested here were not categorized by Cox and McCubbins (1993). These panels were classified by the author according to criteria outlined in Cox and McCubbins.

[b] A positive difference indicates a more conservative GOP committee contingent than the entire Republican membership, and a negative difference indicates a liberal contingent.

have had a Republican contingent that was a conservative outlier—Rules. It is understandable that the ideological disposition of this panel was not going to trigger substantial caucus action since: (1) given the ideological direction the party membership had taken as a result of the election, the caucus would not necessarily oppose a conservative contingent, and (2) in gaining majority control of the chamber, the GOP acquired some extra seats on the committee that it could use to alter the committee's ideological composition if it felt the need to do so (in this case, five seats, or more than one-third of the panel). In the other direction, the Republican Ethics contingent emerges as fairly liberal, though not to the same level of statistical significance as the others. This is partially due to the small number of returning members. (Preservation of this panel is discussed in more detail below.)

A further examination of the aggregate support for the party's agenda by Republican members on these committees simply confirms the findings of the tests conducted on ideology scores.[39] The partisan theory leads one to expect that the central tendency of GOP contingents should be at least as supportive of the party agenda as the median member of the caucus. Those committee contingents who are significantly less supportive of the party program are most likely to face reforms and possibly elimination. Simply comparing party unity medians for each Republican committee contingent with the caucus median demonstrates that the Appropriations, Post Office and Civil Service, Ethics, and Merchant Marine and Fisheries' contingents are the most incompatible with the Republican membership. Interestingly, Post Office and Civil Service, and Merchant Marine and Fisheries—two of the three eliminated panels—had the lowest party unity medians of all other Republican committee contingents.

The partisan policy hypotheses concerning committee reorganization fits relatively well with the Republican decision to eliminate specific committees, but still has a few holes. On the one hand, two of the three committees eliminated (Post Office and Civil Service, and Merchant Marine and Fisheries) were among the handful whose previous GOP contingents were on the far liberal end of the caucus's ideological spectrum and were weak supporters of the party agenda. Along the same lines, another liberal outlier (Appropriations) had strict checks imposed upon it but was not eliminated because of its significance in the policymaking process. On the other hand, two other panels previously composed of more liberal Republicans faced relatively few reforms (Foreign Affairs and Ethics). Additionally, the third committee abolished (District of Columbia) was a panel whose party contingent had been among the more conservative in the House and had been one of the strongest adherents to the party agenda.

One further note was that the Post Office and Civil Service Committee was eliminated even though it was considered, at least by Cox and McCubbins, as a panel with uniform externalities. Though technically the committee does fit the criteria for uniform effects, in that every congressional district has postal workers, their numbers are quite small per district, and clearly a few districts have more federal employees than others (particularly those near the District of Columbia or containing large federal facilities, like the National Institutes of Health, the National Institute of Standards and Technology, etc.). Moreover, this panel is more clientele-oriented than most of the others in this group, and could reasonably fit into the *targeted* externalities group.

Partisan Electoral Considerations

The final perspective on the decision to eliminate committees from the House system is based upon the electoral needs of Republican candidates and the party generally. Unlike the previous hypotheses, where decisions about institutional organization are made in accordance with the policy program of the party, this perspective takes a more direct approach to the link between legislative structure and partisan electoral prospects. Rather than assume that decisions as to configuring committee jurisdictions are driven by policy priorities and conformity to the caucus's ideological center, I propose that such decisions are based in this period on the party's desire to bolster its electoral coalition. That is, choices as to which committees to maintain or abolish are driven by consideration of those groups who vote for and financially support (or oppose) the party.

Why should one expect a shift toward congressional reforms that are based upon partisan electoral consideration in this period? As has already been established, the 1990s saw more intense "conditions" for party government (intraparty policy unification and interparty ideological division) than had been experienced in six decades or more. This intense partisanship also included more centralized party planning and coordination of House campaign messages and financing (Pitney and Connelly 1996; Sinclair 1998). A number of researchers have noted the increased effort of GOP "Hill" committees (the National Republican Congressional Committee and the National Republican Senatorial Committee) in conducting polls, producing campaign ads, buying media time, and training candidates during the early 1990s (Herrnson 1998; Jacobson 1997; Balz and Brownstein 1996; Aldrich and Rohde 2001). Moreover, Republican leaders such as Gingrich, who headed the conservative political action committee, GOPAC, and Bill Paxon (R-NY), chair of the NRCC, took a much more active role in fostering and recruiting better qualified GOP candidates for House races and in coordinating fund-raising among Republican incumbents (Jacobson 1997; Gimpel 1996). Damore and Hansford (1999) find that Republican campaign committees acted in a strategic manner when providing election resources in the early and mid-1990s, "target[ing] those candidates with the best probabilities of winning instead of allocating party resources in a somewhat more equitable manner as appears to be the case with the Democrats" (383). These were adaptations from earlier periods when campaigns had little coordination with central party leadership, and in some cases candidates would even try to distance themselves from the activities of their fellow partisans (Herrnson 1998; Jacobson 1997).

Centralization of party electoral machinery increased dependence of the rank-and-file upon the caucus for electoral assistance and consequently inflated the leadership's responsibility to care for members' re-election prospects in a wide variety of situations. Therefore, when House Republicans backed themselves into a position that forced them to reorganize jurisdictions and even cut committees, partisan electoral needs would necessarily have to be taken into account. The new GOP leadership would balk at eliminating committees that served the demands of groups supportive, both electorally and financially, of its candidates' campaigns. Alternatively, it would be relatively eager to abolish panels whose work served groups supportive of its opponents.

To examine this proposition, I explore the circumstances surrounding the decision to retain or eliminate five standing House committees: the District of Columbia, Merchant Marine and Fisheries, Post Office and Civil Service, Small Business, and Veterans' Affairs committees. These five committees, by most accounts, were in the greatest danger of elimination.[40] In the end only three of these panels were abolished. To understand the partisan electoral ramifications of each panel's jurisdiction, I analyze the financial contributions of pertinent political action committees (PACs), the party affiliation or voting patterns of relevant clientele groups, and their important political or electoral activities with respect to the two parties and their House members or candidates for office.

DISTRICT OF COLUMBIA COMMITTEE If elimination of committees was based upon partisan electoral considerations, selection of the District of Columbia Committee was a relatively straightforward decision for House Republicans. Relations between District of Columbia residents and members of this committee had been historically antagonistic. For years, going back even to the 1940s, the committee was dominated by southern Democrats, led by staunch conservative and segregationist, John McMillan (SC). During McMillan's chairmanship, the committee opposed most bills that would have the result of benefiting the capital's population largely on racial grounds. This intransigence included steadfast hostility to legislation concerning home rule for the District of Columbia. With McMillan's defeat for his House seat in the 1972 elections, the panel's leadership was turned over to an African-American, Charles Diggs (D-MI), and the composition of the committee's Democratic contingent quickly changed to one much more sympathetic to the plight of the District's majority black constituency. However, not long after enactment and implementation of the District Home Rule Charter in 1975 (which

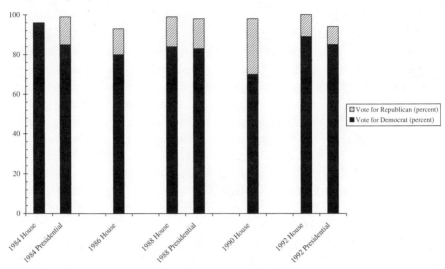

Figure 8   Presidential and House votes in the District of Columbia, 1984–1992
SOURCE: Official election results from the Clerk of the House of Representatives
http://clerkweb.house.gov/elections/election.htm.

turned over a good portion of the territory governance to its district council and mayor), talk among DC politicians and the committee turned to
the issue of statehood (Harris 1995).

The concept of the state of "New Columbia" has always been particularly unappealing to Republicans, since its realization would mean two
additional senators and one representative who would almost assuredly
be Democrats. Figure 8 shows the voting patterns of the District of Columbia in the three presidential and five congressional elections prior to
1994. Voters in DC are clearly partial to the Democratic Party by a wide
margin. In fact, since DC residents were granted the right to vote in presidential elections in 1961 (the Twenty-third Amendment), they have never
given more than 28 percent of their votes to a Republican candidate, and
anything over 15 percent is quite rare.

GOP antagonism toward the District is readily apparent in the composition of Republican contingents on the DC Committee. Since the death
of ranking minority member Stewart McKinney (R-CT) in 1987, the Republicans had not assigned a pro-District legislator to the panel. Republicans clearly expressed their disassociation from voters in the District
when the issue of DC statehood came up for a vote in 1993. Every Republican on the panel voted against the measure in committee, and the

same was true for 172 of the 173 Republicans who voted on the legislation on the House floor.[41]

Republicans were clearly not beholden to, nor did they seek electoral support from, the majority of voters in the District of Columbia. While Speaker Foley confirmed during consideration of the Joint Committee proposals in the 103rd Congress that the Democrats had considerably more to lose if they alienated this tremendously supportive constituency by eliminating the DC Committee, the Republicans knew that they had almost nothing to gain by its perpetuation. The GOP had little reason to give district advocates a venue with potential Democratic Party supporters for their statehood bid. If forced to cut panels, the GOP could abolish this committee with few electoral concerns.

MERCHANT MARINE AND FISHERIES COMMITTEE Unlike the District of Columbia panel, Merchant Marine and Fisheries had constituency ties with the two major political parties that were in some ways more ambiguous. On the surface, the Democratic Party had strong ties with large portions of this committee's clientele—particularly maritime unions and conservation groups.[42] Examining the geography of congressional districts, we find almost 20 percent of Democratic-controlled districts in the 103rd Congress were in locations that included all or part of the twenty-five most active American ports. By comparison, only 8 percent of Republican districts included such centers of maritime commerce.

On the matter of electoral support in the form of campaign contributions, House Democrats were the beneficiaries of three-quarters of the nearly $2 million in campaign contributions from maritime labor groups during the 1994 election cycle.[43] Among the major contributors were the Marine Engineers Union and Seafarers International Union, both among the top fifty most generous PACs of any kind in 1994, and both contributed more than 90 percent of their money to Democrats. Additionally, Democrats were by far the greatest beneficiaries of money from environmental groups. The League of Conservation Voters and the Sierra Club, the two largest campaign contributors among conservation PACs in the 1994 election cycle, gave more than 95 percent of their collective $1.3 million to Democratic candidates. Since not all giving by conservation groups is intended for issues under the purview of the maritime panel, I examine contributions just to Merchant Marine and Fisheries members. Not surprisingly, all of the more than $50,000 in contributions to committee members from these two environmental groups went to Democrats.

The other major clients of this panel, maritime-related corporations and trade associations, were also substantial campaign contributors, giving House candidates almost $1.3 million for the same election cycle. However, these PACs did not show the same partisan orientation as the maritime labor groups. While the marine industry did give slightly more money to Democratic candidates than Republican candidates (55 to 45 percent), this division of contributions more accurately reflects a pattern of giving in accordance with the parties' proportional control of the legislature. Makinson and Goldstein reveal that the overall pattern of business PAC campaign giving during the 1994 elections is very similar and equally politically pragmatic—about 52 percent of contributions went to Democrats (1996, 24).

Regardless of the overall pattern of electoral and political support that generally leaned in the direction of the Democratic Party, this committee had always had an important constituency-oriented jurisdiction for a small cadre of members of both parties. In many ways this fits the standard of a classic constituency committee whose jurisdictional benefits cross partisan lines. As Democratic members on the panel have overrepresented maritime interests (ports, coastal areas, etc.), so have Republicans. Table 21 reports many of the different district interests of returning committee Republicans with respect to the jurisdiction of the Merchant Marine and Fisheries panel. Most of these GOP members had been strong supporters of the committee's survival in the past. For instance, in his 1993 JCOC testimony, Representative Don Young of Alaska advocated eliminating the Natural Resources Committee—a committee he was due to chair if the Republicans took control of the House—over abolishing the maritime panel, where he was slightly further down the seniority ladder.[44]

Once reports surfaced among caucus members and in the press of the possible termination of the Merchant Marine and Fisheries Committee under the new GOP leadership, maritime groups and interested legislators mobilized a spirited letter-writing and lobbying campaign to save the panel, similar to the movement formed during the 93rd Congress.[45] On November 15, 1994, eight senior Republican members on the committee appealed to Gingrich and his leadership group to save the panel on the grounds of its importance to their respective districts (Evans and Oleszek 1995, 16). In one of the most important signals of the changing nature of committee reform in this partisan era, the GOP leaders ignored the petition of this small group of Republicans with constituency concerns in Merchant Marine and Fisheries and killed the panel.

On the whole, the Republican Party and most of its members had relatively little to gain from a committee whose major clientele groups overwhelmingly supported the Democrats. Only one relevant constituency—maritime corporations—used a political strategy of supporting

Table 21 Constituency Interests and Related Committee Assignments of Returning Republican Members of the Merchant Marine and Fisheries Committee

Member	District Interest in Committee	Related Committee/Subcommittee Assignment in 104th Congress
Jack Fields (TX)	District formerly included the Houston Ship Channel	Resources Committee (Chair)
Don Young (AK)	Oil exploration and shipping, wildlife matters	Fisheries, Wildlife, and Oceans Subcommittee
		Coast Guard and Maritime Trans. Subcommittee
		Water Resources and Environment Subcommittee
Herbert Bateman (VA)	Shipbuilding (military and civilian)	Military Readiness Subcommittee (Chair)
		Water Resources and Environment Subcommittee
H. James Saxton (NJ)	Shoreline safety and ocean dumping	Fisheries, Wildlife, and Oceans Subcommittee (Chair)
Howard Coble (NC)	(Coast Guard veteran)	Coast Guard and Maritime Trans. Subcommittee
Curt Weldon (PA)		
Wayne Gilchrest (MD)	Shoreline safety and ocean dumping, marine manufacturing	Fisheries, Wildlife, and Oceans Subcommittee
		Water Resources and Environment Subcommittee
Randy Cunningham (CA)	Shoreline safety	
Jack Kingston (GA)	Shoreline safety	
Tillie Fowler (FL)	Shoreline safety, marine transportation	Coast Guard and Maritime Transportation Subcommittee (Vice Chair)
Michael Castle (DE)		
Peter King (NY)		
Lincoln Diaz-Balart (FL)	Shoreline safety and ocean dumping, marine manufacturing	
Richard Pombo (CA)	Marine transportation	
Charles Taylor (NC)		
Peter Torkildsen (MA)	Fishing industry	Fisheries, Wildlife, and Oceans Subcommittee

both parties, and this behavior seemed to exist no matter who controlled Congress *or* what institutional venue was given to its issues. In a concession to individual Republicans with genuine district concerns in policy matters formerly under the purview of the maritime committee, many of them were assigned to high-ranking posts on subcommittees that acquired those policy jurisdictions (see table 21).

POST OFFICE AND CIVIL SERVICE COMMITTEE The similarities in the Republican decision to eliminate both the Post Office and Civil Service and Merchant Marine and Fisheries committees resonate with the parallel fates shared by these two endangered panels twenty years earlier. To begin with, the political ties of Post Office and Civil Service's major clientele group were similarly with the Democratic not the Republican Party. However, the political bonds of postal groups were even more unequivocal than the maritime interests. This partisan imbalance reflects itself most vividly in the party affiliation of government employees, as shown in table 22. Government employees generally leaned quite heavily toward the Democratic Party in the decade prior to the 1994 elections—two-thirds identified themselves as affiliated in some way with the Democrats.[46] Focusing specifically on federal postal workers, I find that although they are more evenly divided between the two major parties, their inclination is still toward the Democratic Party, as is the general population in this period.[47]

Like the partisan orientation of government employees, the campaign contributions of federal employee PACs were also undeniably directed at the Democrats. Nine out of ten dollars from such major donors in the 1994 election as the National Association of Letter Carriers, the National Association of Retired Federal Employees, and the American Postal Workers Union (all among the top fifty most generous PACs that election cycle), were directed to Democratic candidates. In all, the postal and federal employee groups dispensed over $3.3 million in the 1994 election cycle alone. Almost the same lopsided pattern of giving by federal and postal employee PACs holds for the $8.4 million such groups contributed to congressional candidates in the 1990 and 1992 elections.

The political connection between this committee's constituency and the two major parties is perhaps most clearly seen in the battle over revisions to the Hatch Act. Enacted in 1939, the law prohibited federal employees from actively participating in partisan elections in almost any manner, even when off-duty (except for individual campaign contributions). Contemporary efforts by Democratic congresses to revise the Hatch Act and allow federal employees to participate in partisan elections or even hold party posts were continually scuttled by Republican presi-

Table 22   Partisan Affiliation of Selected Economic and Social Groups

Group/Years of Surveys	Identify as Democrats (%)	Identify as Republicans (%)	Number of Respondents	Chi-square Significance
Government workers[a]				
1984–1994	61.1	30.5	457	.00
Postal workers[b]				
1984–1994	47.6	41.8	186	.51
Self-employed				
1984–1994	39.9	46.2	1,631	.00
1990–1994	38.4	47.4	708	.00
Veterans[c]				
1984–1989	49.6	39.2	768	.50
1990–1994	42.1	46.8	494	.01
General population				
1984–1994	48.8	38.3	16,702	
1984–1989	50.7	36.9	9,283	
1990–1994	46.3	40.1	7,419	

NOTES: Data gathered from 1972–1996 General Social Survey Cumulative File. Political party affiliation taken from "partyid" variable, where the three categories of partisan identifiers (strong, not strong, and near) are aggregated. Pearson Chi-square significance as to independence from the general population asked the same question.

[a]Respondents who identified their industry of employment as general government (code 901). By default this group includes state and local government employees.

[b]Respondents who identified their occupation as either post masters (code 017) or in postal jobs (codes 354–357).

[c]Respondents who identified themselves as having been on active military duty for at least two consecutive months.

dents (Ford in 1976, Reagan in 1988, and Bush in 1990). Even from the start of the 103rd Congress, Republicans viewed the Hatch Act revisions, along with two other legislative proposals at the top of the Democratic policy agenda, as purely partisan. GOP critics worried "that a politicized federal work force will become a bulwark of the Democratic Party." On the other hand, Democrats saw relaxed restrictions on the political work of federal employees as a likely boon for the party. Representative Albert Wynn (D-MD) declared that "the federal workforce is a major potential source of manpower in campaigns . . . no question that it's likely to be an asset to the Democratic Party" (Alston 1993). Following Clinton's inauguration, the first act taken by the Democratically controlled Post Office and Civil Service Committee was to pass its proposal for Hatch Act revisions, which allowed limited political involvement by federal workers. The measure was reported to the floor even before the panel's membership had been finalized in January 1993. The Hatch Act revisions bill had 260 cosponsors, of whom 231 were Democrats. An attempt to advance the measure on the floor of the House under suspension of the rules failed when the previously supportive Republican coalitions vanished—only 28 of 168 voting Republicans supported the legislation.[48] The bill eventually did pass both chambers after some partisan skirmishes in the Senate and was signed by the president in October 1993.[49]

This relatively large constituency group of the Post Office and Civil Service Committee—federal employees in 1994 made up approximately 4 million potential voters—could not even marginally be considered part of the GOP's electoral coalition. Federal employees most often voted for Democrats, and their unions and trade associations overwhelmingly supported Democrats with large campaign contributions. As Republican reform advocate Dreier saw it, "[Federal employees] weren't the traditional constituency of the Republican Party. [The] Post Office [Committee] was important to the unions. With the kind of sway that the unions had with Democrats and not Republicans it was a natural for them to defend it." [50] Conversely, the GOP membership of the House often demonstrated that it would resist relaxation of restrictions on the political activity of federal employees. Clearly, House Republicans would not be concerned to provide for the policy needs of government workers, and their leaders would hardly worry about electoral fallout from elimination of the Post Office and Civil Service Committee.

SMALL BUSINESS COMMITTEE Whereas the relationship of federal employees with the GOP was anything but amicable, the opposite was true for the small business community. The community of small businesses and the Republican Party often shared the same policy goals. The battle over the Clinton administration's health care initiative during the 103rd Congress (1993–94) brought small business interests and the GOP closer together. Both the Republican Party and major small business associations, like the National Federation of Independent Business (NFIB) and the Chamber of Commerce, strongly opposed the Clinton Health Care Plan. The NFIB, with its politically active membership of six hundred thousand small business owners, was a leader in mobilizing to defeat what potentially could have been a costly public policy change for independent businesses (Shaiko and Wallace 1999).

The long-standing relationship between the GOP and small business was further solidified prior to the 1994 elections when Republican leaders began formulating the *Contract with America*. Several Republican officials, including Gingrich aide Christie Carson and pollster Ed Goeas, stated that the NFIB and Chamber of Commerce were among the five most important outside groups consulted during formulation of the *Contract*, and the NFIB served as the leader among outside groups (West and

Loomis 1999, 115–16). Consequently, the *Contract* promoted this sector of the economy by including proposals for a number of "small business appreciation" tax cuts. Perhaps a further reason for the close relationship with the GOP was that NFIB President and CEO S. Jackson Faris formerly served as the head of the Republican National Finance Committee. Many of the staff that he brought on board when taking his position at the NFIB had been aides or consultants to the Republican Party (Shaiko and Wallace 1999, 25).

Direct electoral ties between the small business community and the GOP are undeniable. At the core of that relationship is the party identification of individuals who own small businesses. The self-employed are strongly biased in the Republican direction when compared to the general electorate. Table 22 shows that over 46 percent of those who identify themselves as self-employed had for the decade prior to the 1994 elections also identified themselves as Republicans, compared to just under 40 percent identifying with the Democrats.[51] Over the same period, only about 38 percent of the general population identified with the GOP. The partisan identification of the self-employed was even slightly higher for the period between 1990 and 1994—a trend that also existed in the electorate as a whole, but was more profound among the self-employed.

Republican dependence on the support and resources of the small business community in the 1994 elections went well beyond the ballot box. The small business community was a critical entity in the provision of resources to Republican candidates in the 1994 election. Examining only political action committees that specifically identify themselves as representing small businesses (i.e., not including trade associations for industries in which small businesses make up a large percentage of the members, like the National Restaurant Association, etc.), I find that they gave 80 percent of their nearly $600,000 in campaign contributions in the election cycle to Republican candidates. These contributions were well coordinated with the Republican leadership's strategy of winning control of Congress—more than 60 percent of NFIB's contributions went to GOP challengers or open-seat candidates. Additionally, one claim was that the NFIB gave "money and manpower to eight of every ten Republican winners in closely contested races, including the large, breakthrough class of freshmen" (Weisskopf 1996, 26; Sinclair 1998, 87–88). Consequently, as election returns rolled in on the night of November 8, 1994, showing surprising GOP gains, Haley Barbour, chairman of the Republican National Committee declared, "The Republican Party is the party of small business, not big business; the party of Main Street, not Wall Street" (quoted in Shaiko and Wallace 1999, 18).

In addition to their dependence on the votes and contributions of the small business community, Republicans were also hopeful that their involvement in passage of provisions of the *Contract* would continue well into the new congressional session. Dreier recalled that GOP leaders were counting on the abilities of the small business community to mobilize at the local level to "gin up support . . . for votes on Contract issues. They [the NFIB] were going to send out letters in swing Democratic districts to get members to vote for items in the *Contract*."[52]

In the weeks that followed the election, the Republican leadership, confronted with the necessity of cutting committees, were presented with the option of eliminating the Small Business panel. According to leadership insider Robert Walker (R-PA), many Republicans were keen on cutting the committee, since it was felt that a subcommittee could adequately handle its issues and, furthermore, many of the policy matters of concern to small businesses were already under the purview of the Commerce and Government Operations committees.[53] Despite this view, Republican leadership chose to retain the Small Business Committee. Several accounts at the time stated that a heavy lobbying campaign by small business groups convinced GOP leaders that abolishing the panel would "send the wrong signal to entrepreneurs" (Cooper 1994b) and that this group was one of the "party's primary constituencies" (Roman 1994b; Pincus 1994; Hook and Cloud 1994). In interviews well after the decision, one senior Republican staff member claimed that this was "not a constituency that the party wanted to mess with. . . . They [small business groups] were not going to be appeased by placing this jurisdiction within the bailiwick of another panel and giving them a subcommittee. This would be seen as a devaluing of their issues."[54] Walker similarly recounted that such an action was thought to be "a slap in the face of small business."[55]

One frequently repeated justification for retaining the panel was that Jan Meyers (R-KA) stood in waiting to become chair of the Small Business Committee, and the GOP did not want to be seen as eliminating the "only committee to be chaired by a woman" (Roman 1994b). This seems a curious argument considering the following: (1) Nancy Johnson (R-CT) was also in line to become the chair of the Ethics Committee, after ranking minority member Fred Grandy (R-IA) abandoned his House seat for an unsuccessful bid for the Iowa governorship. Johnson was the most frequently mentioned member for this leadership post (Kahn 1994; Tin 1994) and was ultimately given the chairmanship. (2) The Republican leadership did not hesitate to skip over the chain of seniority to grant chairmanships to three members who were not the most senior Republicans on their panels. Had appointing a woman to a chair's post been a specific priority for the GOP leadership, they could have done this on any of a number of panels and still eliminated the Small Business Committee. In particular, Jennifer Dunn (R-WA) was mentioned as a potential chair of the House Administration Committee (Jacoby and Kahn 1994) and Marge Roukema (R-NJ) was well positioned for a leadership position as the third-ranking member on both the Banking, Finance, and Urban Affairs and Education and Labor committees.

Unlike the District of Columbia, Merchant Marine and Fisheries, and Post Office and Civil Service Committees, the Small Business Committee had a group of strong supporters who would have offered serious resistance had the GOP chosen to eliminate it. The party had for years cultivated a close working relationship with this sector of the economy and its major trade associations. When the small business community realized that this panel was potentially on the chopping block, it mobilized to remind the Republican leadership that this committee would not go down without severe ramifications. By all indications from the GOP leadership, this message was clearly received.

VETERANS' AFFAIRS COMMITTEE Plans to abolish the Veterans' Affairs (VA) panel appeared as early as the summer of 1993, when the Renewing Congress Project advocated folding jurisdiction over veterans' matters into the purview of another committee with broader responsibilities (Mann and Ornstein 1993, 23–24). The VA committee was noted as being endangered several times during the transition period (Burger 1994a; Pincus 1994; Cooper 1994b), and although eliminating this panel was not part of any of the four plans Dreier presented to the transition team or Republican leadership, he did state later that it was part of his design for committee restructuring.[56]

If any committee epitomized "bipartisanship," it was Veterans' Affairs. Neither party had any interest in upsetting this enormous block of voters. In the mid-1990s there were twenty-six million veterans in the United States, and they have always been fairly evenly distributed across all congressional districts. With the exception of a small number of urban congressional districts, just about every location in the country consists of between 8 and 13 percent veterans—a relatively sizable voting bloc no matter the party affiliation or ideology of the member of Congress. The bipartisanship on veterans' issues manifested itself continually on matters before Congress and the committees that deal with the Department of Veterans' Affairs (formerly the Veterans Administration). Rarely has the House Veterans' Affairs Committee ever had trouble crafting legislation that attracted a majority of both Democratic and Republican support either before it was reported out of committee or once it reached the floor. Occasionally skirmishes between the parties ensue on veterans' legislation, but they have generally been over peripheral policy issues like health coverage of abortions for female veterans as part of a bigger veterans' health care package.[57]

Regardless of the incentives for both parties to care for the interests of veterans, the Republicans had one significant advantage over the Democrats with respect to this population—the GOP had gained the edge in political support from military veterans. During most of the 1980s voters identifying themselves as veterans affiliated with the Democratic and Republican parties at about the same levels as the general electorate (see table 22).[58] However, around 1990 the partisanship of veterans began to move significantly in a Republican direction. Perhaps not so coincidentally, this shift in veteran party identification toward the GOP came very soon after President Ronald Reagan broke his pledge to eliminate at least two Cabinet-level departments and endorsed legislation to elevate the Veterans Administration to a Cabinet-level department in 1989. This act by the Republican president was done in the face of protests by several lawmakers and supporters of veterans' groups that the elevation was not needed. Regardless of the motivation for the elevation of the Veterans Administration, in the four years prior to the 1994 elections, the plurality (nearly 47 percent) of veterans claimed to identify with the Republican Party—a significant difference from the general population.

As one close observer of the post-election reforms stated, "[T]he Republicans did not want to pick a fight with veterans groups."[59] This was a big constituency that carried a large number of votes across all congressional districts and had recently begun to shift in a Republican direction. As with support for the small business community, the party leadership did not want to signal to veterans that their issues were not important to them by eliminating the Veterans' Affairs Committee.

OTHER COMMITTEES These five committees were not the only ones facing a potentially ominous future under the new Republican regime. Among the remaining committees, two panels—Ethics, and Energy and Commerce—were most frequently mentioned as being considered for drastic jurisdictional changes. The Ethics panel was being positioned to become a subcommittee of the House Administration Committee (Roman 1994a; Burger 1994a). However, the besieged Democrats shamed the Republicans into sustaining the panel over an impending ethics investigation of Gingrich's own book deal and links between his political action committee (GOPAC) and a college course he had been teaching. Senior

Democrats, particularly Minority Whip David Bonior (D-MI), took every opportunity to highlight the irony of Gingrich contemplating the elimination of a committee that was preparing to undertake an inquiry into allegations against him. In order to extinguish the matter and quell the political embarrassment, Republican leadership quickly retreated from the proposal to eliminate the Ethics panel (Evans and Oleszek 1997, 98; Cooper 1994a).

The Energy and Commerce Committee, with its enormous and wide-ranging policy boundaries, was also under threat that its jurisdictions might be raided by aggressive members of other panels. This possibility was not taken lightly by incumbent committee Republicans who had long waited, and some would say "suffered," under the chairmanship of John Dingell (D-MI) for their turn at the helm of this powerful committee (Cooper 1994b). Wishing to avoid engaging the Republican Party in a protracted battle over the jurisdiction of this panel, the party leadership lopped off a small portion of its policy boundaries and distributed them to a number of other committees (Evans and Oleszek 1997, 97). The GOP leadership declared, and the press frequently echoed, that the Commerce Committee lost 20 percent of its jurisdiction (Victor 1995). However, Groseclose and King (1998) claim that 20 percent is an exaggeration. Their examination of Commerce hearings activity as a gauge of jurisdictional breadth reveals that the issues removed from the purview of the Commerce panel amounted to less than 5 percent of the committee's work. Additionally, Groseclose and King note that among the jurisdictional reallocations imposed during the Republican transition, two important changes "can be attributed to the distributive-politics instincts of other committees" (148). Food inspection issues were acquired by the Agriculture Committee, whose members' districts had much to gain from relaxed regulations. Similarly, Resources took authority over the Trans-Alaska Pipeline at the same time Don Young, the only House member from Alaska, became chair of that panel (see also Gugliotta 1994).

Conclusion

In this chapter I contend that, although there have been sharp increases in House party polarization and caucus authority over the legislative process, party politics has not completely subsumed the progression of structural reform in the system of committee jurisdictions. Parties certainly played a larger role in congressional organization and operations in the 1990s than in any other major reform periods examined. Partisan structures had greater influence in how legislators campaigned for office and financed their reelection bids, how the legislature defined its political agenda, and how it made decisions about rules and procedures. Specifically, the party leadership became the center of decision making when the chamber faced choices about committee restructuring. Under the Democrats in the 103rd Congress, caucus chiefs commanded the actions of the JCOC, set the agenda for the reform debate, and were ultimately responsible for terminating reform proposals once it was evident that they could no longer ensure the outcome would benefit the party as a whole. For Republicans, the party leadership was responsible for every aspect of decision making concerning jurisdictional changes during the transition to the 104th Congress.

Additionally, some evidence connects the reform choices of the Republican leadership to the party's policy preferences (Aldrich and Rohde 1997a, 1997b). In accordance with the characterization of partisan theory, Republican contingents on at least two of the three committees chosen for elimination were among those most discordant (in the "wrong" or liberal direction) with respect to the aggregate preferences of the entire caucus membership. Additionally, one important committee that also had an extremely liberal contingent, Appropriations, sustained a number of substantial checks by the party leadership. In many ways, these discoveries point to a radically different approach to congressional committee reforms than that of earlier periods.

However, the growing intensity of conditional party government does not tell the entire story of committee reorganization in the 1990s. Though party institutions and partisanship were increasingly influential in congressional operations and decisions concerning legislative structure, they could not completely trump the innate reelection incentives that traditionally shape and constrain efforts at committee reorganization. Evans and Oleszek show that, as in earlier periods, "[d]uring the 1990s, the main impact of clientele incentives was the blocking of a comprehensive overhaul of committee jurisdictions" (1997, 168). In the 103rd Congress, the House Democratic leadership resisted attempts at meaningful jurisdictional reform partly because of its fear of upsetting clientele groups that remained important to its electoral coalition. Even stronger indication of electoral motivations can be seen in the GOP decisions to eliminate House committees as it rearranged structures for the 104th Congress. Republican leaders had no problems in choosing to abolish committees that served traditionally Democratic constituencies like federal employees, maritime and environmental interests, and DC residents, but they were much more reluctant to eliminate panels oriented around policy matters important to Republican patrons, like the small business community or increasingly supportive military veterans (Davidson 1995b).

Most important, however, this chapter demonstrated how reelection considerations that had long shaped decisions about the reorganization of legislative committees changed under conditional party government. As party organization and its leadership became more integral to all aspects of legislative operations, including the electoral campaigns of individual members, decisions concerning the operational structure of the legislative body could not avoid considering party members' electoral prospects. If members are going to relinquish decision making about committee reorganization to caucus chiefs, as they do with many other aspects of congressional operations under conditional party government, leaders must not act in ways that will hinder their partisan colleagues' prospects at the polls. Electoral considerations still constrain the ability of the legislature to reshape its committee system, but under a stronger partisan regime this inhibition increasingly comes in the form of collective electoral considerations of the entire party membership, rather than an amalgam of individual electoral needs.

Additionally, the nature of the linkage between the reelection imperative of legislators and the choices about structure appears to have changed in the contemporary Congress. That is, reelection motivations affecting the organization of the legislative institution no longer simply derive from a need to serve the economic and social demands of constituents through committee work, but have evolved into an additional quest to maintain or increase campaign assistance such as contributions and campaign workers. Though still assuming a partisan element to the strategy, members increasingly protect existing jurisdictional turf not only to distribute government benefits to their home districts, but also to protect their "donor base," or "fund-raising." [60] As members of Congress become more partisan, so do the battles over congressional organization that have campaign finance implications. Despite what we traditionally believe about congressional campaigns, Hamilton declared, "You win elections by contributions not by votes." [61]

Furthermore, by linking individual distributive/electoral needs of legislators with heightened conditions of partisanship, we gain further insight into the interplay between the partisan policy preferences and partisan electoral rationales for committee reorganization during a transition in party control of the chamber. For example, while serving as a minority party, the Republicans are likely to care little about the composition or policymaking role of committees that do not address the needs of client groups in the core Republican electoral coalition. Moreover, these marginalized committee contingents may even become "congressional Siberia" for minority party members whose policy preferences conflict with the caucus center. However, if the caucus gains a majority status and is compelled to eliminate committees, as the Republican caucus did in late 1994, selecting committees to eliminate is easy. The party can abolish panels that it has traditionally treated as peripheral. In an era of strong parties, electoral concerns still shape how the chamber treats the issue of committee reorganization—it simply takes a more macro-partisan perspective.

Chapter 8

Conclusion:
Beyond "Institutional Navel Gazing"

BATTLES OVER COMMITTEE JURISDICTIONS ARE SOME OF THE fiercest confrontations among members of Congress. Walter Oleszek, a life-long Hill staffer and veteran of several reform committees, described the fights over panel property rights during the early 1970s as probably the most bitter and mean-spirited that occurred in the House, far more contentious than the skirmishes over the Vietnam War that were occurring at about the same time. He stated that members threatened revenge if jurisdictions were rearranged, no matter how long it took.[1] Similarly, David Dreier claims, half-jokingly, that he still eats alone in the Member's Dining Hall on Capitol Hill for his part in the modest jurisdictional changes at the start of the 104th Congress. In describing how legislators react to proposals for jurisdictional changes, Dreier said, "You would have thought I was threatening their wives . . . people would prefer to give me their first born rather than give up a portion of their committee jurisdiction."[2] Hence, it is no wonder that the system of legislative committees has been markedly resilient over time. Except for a few minor adjustments—Military Affairs and Naval Affairs now make up the Armed Services Committee, and the Merchant Marine and Fisheries Committee no longer exists—the powers and specifically the jurisdictions of committees doing the bulk of the work in the House in the mid-1940s have changed remarkably little over the last half-century (Galloway 1946).

Despite the constancy in the chamber's busiest and most important panels, many still claim that the overall institution of legislative committees is not what it used to be—committee chairs have less power, there is greater reliance on staff for decision making, parties set the over-all chamber agenda, and more legislating is done through "unorthodox" methods than ever before (such as task forces, leadership decreed legisla-tion, etc.; see Sinclair 1997). While some scholars focus on shifts in com-mittee powers imposed as part of the Republican takeover of the House after the 1994 elections (Smith and Lawrence 1997), others trace the de-mise of the committee system back much further. One recent observer of Congress remarks that seeds for the destruction of committee power were planted in the 1960s, when President Johnson's landslide election "al-lowed him to define the terms of debate" in subsequent political matters and to skirt the authority of old-style Democratic committee barons (Co-hen 1999).

The perception of the demise of committees, however, is not universal among congressional scholars. For instance, while Groseclose and King acknowledge that the period immediately following the start of 104th Congress (the first hundred days) was in many ways distinct from the nor-mal functioning in the House legislative process, thereafter "committees operated much as they have for one hundred years" (1998, 136). Specifi-cally, they argue that the chamber's reliance upon nontraditional law-making practices like ad hoc task forces was short-lived and that legis-lators still funneled their energies into committees that retained much of their independence and agenda-setting capacity (see also Hall and McKis-sick 1997).

By any of several measures, one would have trouble making the case that two or even four years after the "Republican revolution" committees are simply marginal players in the policy process, even though the cham-ber operates under what is still seen as a relatively controlling party or-ganization. For instance, an examination of legislative accomplishments during the 105th Congress (1997–98) considered to be most important by the political reporters in the *Washington Post* (Dewar 1998) and the *New York Times* (Seelye 1998)[3] shows that House leadership rarely, if ever, skirted the authority and jurisdiction of its standing committees. For ex-ample, the Ways and Means Committee was an integral player in the re-form of the Internal Revenue Service; the Education and the Workforce Committee was critical in reauthorizing higher education programs and expanding Head Start; the Judiciary Committee restructured immigration programs to provide more visas for highly skilled immigrants; the Judici-ary and Commerce committees together strengthened pressure on foreign countries that engage in religious persecution and restricted taxation on Internet commerce; and, of course, the Transportation and Infrastructure Committee was one of the two most important actors (the other being its

Senate counterpart, the Environment and Public Works Committee) in producing the enormous transportation act. And committees are still the vital actors in day-to-day legislation on relatively routine issues like funding for agriculture research, extensions of federal vocational education programs, and reauthorizations of the Superfund program.

The Electoral Foundation of Committee Stability

The remarkable durability in the legislative committee system is hardly an accident and has occurred in spite of concerted and well-organized efforts at reform and increasing party involvement in chamber rules and procedure. I have not only argued here that there is considerable stability in the House system of legislative committees but have uncovered some of the reasons for that stability. Owing to distinguishing features of the American political and electoral system—particularly single-member legislative districts and plurality elections—legislators are not only responsible for representing their own constituents but are rewarded for doing so over the interests of the nation as a whole (Stewart 1989). Thus, a legislator who is a successful advocate for the needs of her home district is almost invariably seen as helping to ensure her own individual reelection. As a result, members of Congress have fostered a structure in the legislative process that can both effectively govern and afford the flexibility needed to bolster relations with constituents for legislators who desire reelection.

The argument presented here concerning the stickiness in authority and jurisdiction of legislative committees is based on two primary factors. First, though committees can perform different functions at different times for various political actors (individual legislators, the party caucus, the chamber, etc.; see Fenno 1973; Maltzman 1997), one of the fundamental duties of representatives as committee members is to serve the particularized needs of their constituents. This involves securing assignment to a committee with the capability of controlling federal programs and agencies important to the economic and social needs of the district, protecting the current flow of benefits directed to the district, and seeking new ways to promote the well-being of constituents. Gaining special consideration and benefits for one's district is done within the representative capacity of a legislator's duties, but undeniably such activity serves a reelection function.

The implications from the research presented here do not exclude other explanations of legislative structure and the role of committees. To the contrary, proponents of a reelection theory of congressional organization have never contended that this theory correctly characterizes all forms of policymaking in the U.S. Congress or its system of committees.

Most probably, different theories work in concert to improve our understanding of congressional operations. For example, the partisan approach to congressional organization contends that the majority contingent on a committee is responsible for serving the electoral needs of its parent caucus as a whole (Aldrich and Rohde 1997a; Cox and McCubbins 1993). But facilitating the caucus effort to retain its majority status may not necessarily mean following a strict caucus policy agenda. On numerous policy matters the majority party may quite possibly have no single electorally maximizing policy program. Additionally, as some studies of conditional party government have previously asserted, the most beneficial approach for the electoral prospects of the party as a whole may be *to allow* members of particular committees to provide for the district needs of legislators with highly interested constituencies (Hurwitz, Moiles, and Rohde 2001). Of course, what may be foremost in this partisan responsibility is for committee members to ensure their own reelection.

Second, because legislators are so profoundly conscious of the electoral effects of institutional arrangements when chamber rules and procedures are developed or evolve, we can expect them to be equally conscious of the potential reelection fallout of significant and sudden changes to those arrangements. If members of Congress partially depend upon congressional organization to maximize their likelihood of reelection, then preferences during reform periods should be influenced by this same reelection motive. Evidence presented here demonstrates that even the seemingly united and focused policy agenda of a strong party structure, which may implicitly include a prescription for rearrangement of policy-making institutions (such as the Republican *Contract with America*), will itself fall prey to the more basic individual reelection and constituency needs of legislators.

Constituents and the Details of Committee Jurisdictions

Since this study asserts that a reelection element operates in legislative opposition to structural changes in the House, the findings come close to suggesting that the arrangement of congressional committee jurisdictions and powers is relevant to constituents; that is, voters would notice if the existing structure of policy property rights were changed. On its face such a proposition seems somewhat far-fetched. Representative David Obey (D-WI) made this very claim in the 1993 House markup of the Joint Committee reform bill. He declared, "If we were going to reform the committee structure, what I think we would do is attack the people's agenda rather than engage in institutional navel gazing. I don't think that the public much cares whether surface transportation, for example, is in the

Commerce Committee or in Public Works. I don't think they care whether that Merchant Marine Committee exists or not. I don't. I don't pay any attention to that committee." [4]

But the suggestion that constituents know or care about the jurisdiction or powers of congressional committees is not unreasonable. The legitimacy of this claim derives from two perspectives. First and most directly, it may be legitimate to expect that at least *some* specialized segments of a constituency are keenly aware of the configuration of committee jurisdictions, the composition of those committees, and their policymaking powers. Although few individuals in Obey's rural northwestern Wisconsin district may have known or cared much in 1993 about the existence of the Merchant Marine and Fisheries Committee, one can argue that sizable numbers of voters in Helen Bentley's Baltimore district, Jack Fields's Houston district and Lynn Schenk's San Diego district had an acute interest in the powers and policy purview of this panel. In the same vein, it is easy to believe, for example, that substantial constituency groups in Pat Roberts's expansive western Kansas district understood much about the inner workings of the Agriculture Committee, that numerous voters in Owen Pickett's Norfolk, Virginia, district cared about the business and composition of the Armed Services Committee, or that many constituents in James Hansen's rural western Utah district had concern for the powers of the Interior and Insular Affairs Committee. This is why such groups often lobby on their representative's behalf to secure assignment to these valuable committee slots and are so vocal when a panel is threatened by jurisdictional rearrangements. While awareness of the inner structure of congressional policymaking is not likely to be universal across legislators' constituents, it may encompass a large enough portion of the district population to cause a real problem for reelection if the legislator neglects such voters' concerns.

Second, and more indirectly, constituent interest in the details of jurisdictional organization may exist in a latent form such as that identified in Arnold's (1990) study of the electoral calculations in legislative decision making. While on some levels Obey is correct that a fair number of constituents care little if surface transportation matters are controlled by Public Works or Commerce, they may nevertheless notice if a jurisdictional shift means that their representative can no longer secure much-needed federal funds and programs. As described in this study, members of committees with jurisdiction over federal programs and agencies important to their particular districts go to great lengths to build policy and procedural expertise that will position them to consistently provide benefits and special consideration for their constituents. Similarly, representatives not assigned to such a committee will work just as hard to establish relations with members of the relevant panels for the same reason—to provide for district needs. Even though constituents may not directly care that a policy issue is being reassigned to a new panel, neither of the above-mentioned groups of legislators is likely to embrace structural changes that would disrupt established lines of communication and policy authority that play an integral role in securing reelection.

Other Theories, Other Reforms

Implicitly, any argument in favor of a reelection base to the organization and output of congressional committees at least partially rejects alternative explanations of legislative organization. In fact, in many places this study unequivocally rejects core arguments of theories of congressional structure based on informational and partisan principles. For instance, the informational contention that committees are populated so as to avoid the advocacy of district interests over the needs of the legislature as a whole is repeatedly rejected for many committees over a long period of time through examination of the constituency characteristics of committee members.

But more important, I contend that at several moments in modern congressional development, legislators who had to choose how they would organize committees as critical policymaking structures almost always preserved existing arrangements. Often the choices were explicitly between retaining structures that afforded opportunities for legislators to provide for the acute economic or demographic demands in their districts or rearranging decision-making structures along grounds that altered communication between the committee and its parent body or increased partisan influence on committee activities. For example, in the mid-1940s representatives could have consolidated legislative panels and imposed severe fiscal limitations that were to encourage policy expertise in committees and grant greater chamber control over budgetary decisions, at the cost of decreasing the distributive underpinning of many panels. In essence, neither of the two proposed changes occurred—many committees remained overrepresentative of high-demand constituencies, and after a few years the House gutted the provisions of the budgetary reforms. What I contend in this study is that not only was the status quo largely sustained in all of these critical institutional junctures, but the impetus for legislators' inclination toward the existing structure was based largely on their reelection imperative. Even as parties have become a much stronger influence in institutional organization and policy direction, reelection needs are still central in considering committee jurisdictional arrangements.

More recently, the issue of rearrangement of committee policy property rights resurfaced at the start of the 107th Congress. The jurisdictions of three House committees were being considered for modification— again a call for the splitting of the Education and the Workforce Committee, and a request to shift portions of the Commerce Committee's jurisdiction to the Banking Committee (Pershing 2000). In the end, the Republican majority dropped the thorny issue of splitting the Education and the Workforce panel and shifted a relatively small portion of the Commerce panel's jurisdiction to a renamed Financial Services Committee (formerly the Banking Committee), mainly to solve a dispute over chair succession on the Commerce Committee.[5] An examination of committee hearing days over the prior two congressional terms (the 105th and 106th Congresses) reveals that transfer of this fraction of Commerce's jurisdiction represented a loss of less than 6 percent of the panel's issue agenda. Nevertheless, the move worried some Commerce members with ties to the securities industry, so they were expected to request and receive waivers that would enable them to serve on both panels (Barnett 2001).

As noted in chapter 1, the outcomes of the reform cases examined here are heavily skewed toward instances where the movement for institutional change failed. There are important reasons for this bias in the reform outcomes I explore. Foremost, because I examine only formal efforts at committee jurisdictional reorganization, by definition I look only at unsuccessful reform bids—this is the only outcome that occurred with regard to these kinds of system-wide legislative rearrangements.

This is not to say that more informal or common-law shifts in policy property rights did not occur, as King describes with the Commerce Committee (King 1997). For that matter, I do not deny that even a few formal jurisdictional changes occured in each of the periods I examine. However, I do contend that most of the alterations were no more than marginal with respect to the macro-configuration of policy property rights in the House. We are only now starting to learn how to measure changes in the policy control of committees over time. While the research of Baumgartner, Jones, and colleagues has shown that the work of congressional committees (measured through the subject matter of hearings activity) has diversified over time (Baumgartner, Jones, and Rosenstiehl 1997), I contend that much of the common-law expansion of committee jurisdictions has come with the introduction of new issues into the legislative agenda of Congress and less as a result of the actual transfer of responsibility for policy arenas between committees.

But beyond the consideration of jurisdictional changes, there is the obvious question of how my approach informs our understanding of outcomes in other reform circumstances. Certainly some reform efforts have been successful at altering institutional arrangements in Congress; perhaps the best examples are the non-jurisdictional changes in the 1970s. It is not clear whether reelection/constituency motivations influenced members' preferences on changes such as the process of selection of committee chairs, the "Subcommittee Bill of Rights," or enhanced Speaker powers. Scholars like Dave Rohde (1991), and Eric Schickler (2001) and co-authors (2000) have explored the *policy* motivations of legislators in promoting and consenting to these institutional alterations. To my knowledge, no one has contrasted these explanations of members' reform preferences with ones based on the reelection imperative, but this does not necessarily mean that a distributive approach will add significantly to our existing understanding of these legislative changes. Clearly, there are limitations to the kinds of reforms that the reelection perspective will be able to explain.

What is most interesting about these successful reforms is that a significant number of them were promoted and developed by party-based organizations, particularly the liberal Democratic Study Group, rather than formal, chamber-wide committees. Additionally, in several instances the actual structural changes were instituted at the level of the party caucus rather than the chamber. This raises an important question: What is it about party-based reform proposals that made them more successful in this period? Could the demise of structural changes regarding committee jurisdictions be rooted in the decision to use formal, bipartisan, chamber-wide (or even cross-chamber) reform committees? A quick glance at what occurred at the start of the 104th Congress indicates that this is probably not the entire answer. GOP reform advocates were in the strongest position of any group of caucus-based institutional entrepreneurs in modern congressional history. Structural changes (*specifically* ones regarding jurisdictional changes) had been part of the party platform endorsed by nearly all members of the new caucus; the highest ranks of leadership had endorsed reforms; and if the process of selecting committee chairs was any indication, it appeared as though the new Republican leadership would be able to institute whatever structural rearrangements it wished. Yet, despite all of that, GOP reformers could only muster the elimination of three committees with very heavy Democratic constituencies—a far cry from the proclamation party reform advocates had inserted into the *Contract.*

Conversely, the utility of the reelection perspective in explaining outcomes with regard to legislative reforms is not limited to debates over committee jurisdictions. Other realms of congressional structure exist (not explored here) for which the same reelection approach would quite effectively explain the persistent lack of success in altering rules or institutions. For instance, one does not have to read too much between the lines to appreciate that continual resistance to meaningful alterations in the laws governing how congressional campaigns are financed is largely driven by legislators' fears as to how changes will affect their reelection prospects or the electoral fortunes of their party as a whole—a point alluded to in the previous chapter. As the pursuit of campaign contributions has taken an increasingly prominent place in the management of congressional elections, this aspect of the electoral connection has bled into considerations of institutional arrangements.

Similarly, the persistent opposition and undermining of measures meant to control the growth of federal expenditures (such as provision in the LRA in 1946, the Gramm-Rudman-Hollings Act, and amendments in the late 1980s, etc.) can often be attributed to the desire to protect district interests and federal dollars directed to members' districts. As noted in the analysis of reforms in the 1940s, legislators strongly resisted the imposition of a supervisory budget committee because it impinged on the autonomy of legislative committees to determine spending for programs under their authority. These two areas of potential institutional change warrant further examination with an eye to the insights offered by existing theories of legislative organization. The strength of the reelection instinct in members of Congress makes it likely that this motive lies behind the failure of structural reforms in other realms of congressional politics.

Lessons Learned for Committee Restructuring and Beyond

Of the many lessons to draw from this analysis, one of the more important may not be completely surprising to congressional scholars—that efforts at congressional reorganization do not occur in a vacuum.[6] What may be best for the institution as a whole on any number of grounds, "efficiency" being the most common objective of reformers, is frequently not what the chamber adopts in the end. Pessimism about Congress's ability to alter its established practices and structures has a long history and has often been based on a belief that members will defend entrenched constituency-oriented interests (Burns 1949). Legislators are rational and astute political actors who surely understand the ramifications of proposed changes for their own electoral survival and political careers. Reform proponents who ignore the reelection motivation when proposing alterations to the structure of the policy process are bound to meet with considerable resistance.

The implications drawn from these experiences have an "aggregate" lesson for advocates of structural change in committee jurisdictions—the more committee jurisdictions a reform plan alters, the more political toes are stepped on, and the greater the likelihood of active resistance. Omnibus reorganization proposals simply serve to solidify the assembly of a winning coalition *in opposition* to profound structural changes. This is not to say that reform efforts directed at a small number of committees have a greater likelihood of success—witness the failure of the Patterson Committee to create an Energy panel in 1980. To the contrary, the message is simply that wholesale efforts at committee reorganization, no matter how well-intentioned, will result in broadening the potential pool of opponents.

Therefore, advocates of radical reform in congressional organization should heed one of two words of caution. First, unless absolutely necessary, proposals for structural changes in congressional procedure should strenuously avoid a direct assault on the matters of committee power and the jurisdictions of specific panels. As we have learned, legislators invest heavily in their assigned committees and the benefits they can draw from them, and they are likely to aggressively resist perceived or real attacks on those power bases. Such reform efforts are seen not only as adding uncertainty to decision-making outcomes, but also as direct attacks on members' established strategies for reelection. The institution's efficiency can more easily be increased by less threatening alterations directed at such things as the role and size of staff and the distribution of powers among committee and subcommittees. Ultimately, of course, definitions of "efficiency" are in the eye of the beholder.

If the first situation is unavoidable, and alterations to committee authority and policy property rights must be undertaken, then reform advocates who seek support would be most successful if they could make a persuasive case that rearrangement of the policy issues that committees control will somehow "improve" either the process by which legislation is considered or the outcome of federal policy itself. That is, reformers must be able convince their colleagues that changes will either enhance their abilities at representation or will come with some kind of concessions or offsets that can provide assistance in their reelection strategy. Thus far, however, procedural entrepreneurs have never successfully made such arguments. While this approach concedes an explicit link between representation and reelection, the reality of our form of congressional structure and system of elections cannot be denied.

Notes

Chapter 1

1. Joint Committee on the Organization of Congress, "Bipartisan Leadership Session," October 28, 1993 (staff summary of meeting).

2. King's analysis categorized the subject matter of all committee hearings by issue areas. His study reveals that in the four years prior to the committee reforms, the issue areas that were transferred to other panels generally made up 5 percent or less of the committee's annual activity.

3. This theme goes as far back as McConachie (1898) but is now a staple of the congressional politics literature. Among the more prominent recent examples are Cox and McCubbins 1993; Krehbiel 1991; King 1997; and Maltzman 1997.

4. Occasionally a member may ask for suspension of the rules to pass a bill without committee consideration, but this is uncommon.

5. Sinclair reports that the percentage of "major measures" bypassing committees is slightly higher than 5–10 percent, but again, this varies with the circumstances of the congressional term and is still extraordinary (1997, 14–15).

6. The agenda-setting power of committees is often considered conventional wisdom in congressional literature. Yet, beyond a few theoretical and case studies (e.g., Denzau and Mackay 1983; Epstein 1997; Evans 1995; Krehbiel 1985), we know little about its extent or scope over time or across issue areas.

7. In addition to the bicameral reorganization efforts, Senate attempts at structural reform also included two Temporary Select Committees to Study the Senate Committee System (the Stevenson Committee in 1976–77 and the Quayle Committee in 1984).

8. Drawn from Baumgartner and Jones's coding of Congressional Information Service (CIS) Congressional Hearings Index CD-ROM (1998), as well as data collected by the author. Note that since the study spans more than fifty years of congressional history, it necessarily includes numerous committee name changes. In most cases I use the name for each committee that is appropriate for the period under discussion.

9. Tullock (1981) specifically examined stability in policy equilibria, but the stability question has begun to creep into work on congressional structures (Ainsworth and Sened n.d.). Tullock's work inspired a number of responses like those by McCubbins and Schwartz (1985) and Ostrom (1986).

10. One interesting side note is that frequently the most comprehensive and insightful examinations of committee reform efforts in Congress come from political scientists with firsthand knowledge of the process as participant-observers: these include works by individuals like George Galloway (1946), Roger Davidson and Walter Oleszek (1977), Burton Sheppard (1985), and Larry Evans and Walter Oleszek (1997).

11. Details about rational-choice work on legislative structure are addressed in chapter 2.

12. See Rieselbach (1978, 1994) and Welch and Peters (1977) for studies of the various aspects of congressional reform.

13. See similar comments by George Goodwin (1970, 19).

14. While these statements referred to packages of institutional changes that went beyond mere alterations in the committee system, jurisdictional changes were a major part—often considered the keystone—of the reform efforts.

15. King 1997 also identifies these three reform instances as the most important with respect to potential for statutory jurisdictional change, *along with one other*—the 1980 House Select Committee on Committees, formed to consider alterations in energy jurisdiction. While I give passing treatment to this other reform movement (chapter 6), its scope is limited compared to that of the three more substantial reform junctures. (Also, much of King's study focuses on the jurisdiction of the House Energy and Commerce Committee, which worked extensively on energy policy.) Nevertheless, the outcome of the 1980 energy reorganization effort was still the same—the committee's reform proposals were largely rejected in favor of the status quo.

Chapter 2

1. Public Law 31, 106th Cong., 1st sess. (May 21, 1999).

2. Public Law 33, 105th Cong., 1st sess. (August 5, 1997).

3. For the sake of parsimony, I set aside for now the notion of a zero-sum competition for limited governmental budgets. This is a debatable point, particularly during periods in which Congress has faced few or no meaningful statutory boundaries on its overall spending. The above example of the emergency supplemental appropriations is an excellent illustration of how members of Congress have evaded legislated budget limits.

4. Shepsle (1986) also treats other equilibrium institutions, like procedures for vetoes, consideration of revenue-raising legislation, and the role of the vice president in Senate proceedings, that are stipulated in the Constitution and so face even higher hurdles for alteration.

5. To simplify things, I combine two separate but closely related hypotheses concerning committee recruitment and composition, since the implications are the same for committee composition.

6. Below I address caucus control of committee assignments and explain why parties may be served by assigning legislators to committees according to district needs.

7. It is precisely the legislative exchange offered in the agriculture example that distributive theory best explains—particularistic policy decisions concerning benefits accruing mainly to members of the same committee. Committees composed of members with different policy objectives would find it easiest to enforce agreements for support of benefits to each other's districts because such proposals can simply be packaged into one bill.

8. "Divided government" refers to the circumstance where the presidency is controlled by one party and one or both chambers of Congress are controlled by the other party.

9. Scholars have also explored another possible motivation for the genesis of some kinds of congressional reforms—the policy objectives of certain groups of legislators

might be hindered by existing deliberative structures and rules. This has been shown to be a plausible explanation for members' preferences concerning alterations in committee hierarchy and democratized procedures during the 1970s (see Rohde 1991; Schickler, McGhee, and Sides 2001).

10. See Zelizer (forthcoming) for an in-depth discussion of the individuals who have shaped the rules and structure of Congress over the last half-century.

Chapter 3

1. An active interim period was precisely the case for members of the 105th Congress, who were left to consider President Bill Clinton's impeachment between the November 1998 elections and the start of the 106th Congress in January 1999.

2. Formally, the last step is that each caucus-approved slate of committee assignments is presented to the chamber for a floor vote.

3. Assignment-request memos and letters were gathered from House Speaker Carl Albert's collection of materials for organizing the 94th Congress (1975–76). Elections for this congressional term resulted in one of the highest turnover rates in the House for the postwar period—13.3 percent—and were likely to reveal one of the more active periods of reshuffling of both incumbent and freshman committee assignments.

4. Lawrence, Maltzman, and Wahlbeck (1999) also note the influence of "external endorsements" in gaining desired committee assignments, though they concentrate on a much earlier historical period.

5. The Appropriations; Rules; Ways and Means; Commerce; Public Works; Science; Post Office; House Administration; Government Operations; and Veterans' Affairs committees.

6. The Agriculture; District of Columbia; Interior and Insular Affairs; and Merchant Marine and Fisheries committees.

7. The Judiciary; Foreign Affairs; Education and Labor; Banking; and Armed Services committees.

8. It should be noted that interest-group ratings, like ADA scores, and NOMINATE scores are usually highly correlated (the .9 level or better: Krehbiel 1991; Poole and Rosenthal 1985, 1997). The initial advantage of some NOMINATE scores was that they are comparable across congressional terms; however, Groseclose, Levitt, and Snyder (1999) have produced an algorithm to make the same intertemporal adjustment for ADA scores.

9. For a notable exception, see Londregan and Snyder 1994.

10. Pickett, a member of the Armed Services Committee, chose not to run for reelection in 2000. Not surprisingly, his successor in the Second Congressional District, Edward Schrock, also gained assignment to Armed Services in his freshman term.

11. These tests (described in Hogg and Craig 1995, 508–13) compare the median of a distribution (here, the committee members) with that of a fixed number (the actual chamber median). One calculates the difference of each score in the distribution with that of the floor median and ranks the absolute value of the differences. The ranks are given positive or negative signs depending on whether the member's ideology score was greater or less than the floor median and then summed. If this value is greater than a critical value determined by the size of the sample, then we can reject the null hypothesis that the medians are equal.

12. In experiments comparing tests using both means and medians, I discovered, as one might expect, that findings of difference-in-means tests were occasionally sensitive to extreme outliers. That is, a member whose level of constituency need was extreme and in the opposite direction from the majority of the panel would pull the committee

mean away from its "central tendency." This resulted both in Type I errors (finding outlying committees when there were none) and in Type II errors (not finding outlying committees when they were actually extreme).

13. Evidence from Speaker Albert's files for committee assignments in the 94th Congress.

14. Deering and Smith list District of Columbia, House Administration, and Standards of Official Conduct as "unrequested" committees—assignments that are generally undesirable and not sought after by most members. They also list Post Office in this category, but Fenno's interviews and research compelled him to consider it a constituency panel.

15. Browne (1995) uses a concept similar to my notion of district profiles in examining legislator interest in agriculture policy.

16. The phrase refers to the committee chair and ranking minority member who served during this pre–budgetary reform era and were seen to have instituted this practice of "non-advocacy" in subcommittee assignments.

17. Even Fenno, who is frequently cited as the primary advocate of the older "guardian" model of Appropriations behavior, gives a certain amount of credence to the belief that subcommittee assignments *prior to the budgetary reforms* in some ways conformed to members' distributive needs (1966, 140). Fenno eventually reconciles these seemingly opposing goals a few years later when he states that the objective of reelection for Appropriations members is usually subordinated to the aim of institutional power procured through service to the needs of the chamber (1973, 4).

18. This criterion disqualified the Budget; Internal Security; Standards of Official Conduct; Science, Space, and Technology; and Small Business committees. It also allows me to include panels eliminated by the Republican changes at the start of the 104th Congress.

19. This criterion excluded the House Administration; District of Columbia; and Rules committees.

20. Conducting a study of each committee's hearings to determine "common law" jurisdictions for this entire time period, as was done for individual committees in King 1997 and Baumgartner et al. 1994, is beyond the scope of this study.

21. Seven states in the 89th Congress, twenty-five states in the 90th Congress, nine states in the 99th Congress, and six states (affecting nine districts) in the 104th Congress. Even though a large share of these off-year redistrictings are accounted for here, there were others for which no new Census data could be located.

22. Aggregation was completed through a combination of maps and descriptions of congressional district boundaries published in *Congressional Directories* and in Martis 1982 for "whole-county" districts. For counties that were divided into several districts (primarily those including large cities, like Los Angeles or Cook counties), or partitioned into districts that contained part of more than one county, I employed a coding system that utilized the *Congressional District Atlas* for 1960 (which contained the boundaries of districts for the pre-1962 apportionments; United States Bureau of the Census 1960) and Michael Dubin's detailed maps of congressional districts. I am grateful for Mr. Dubin's generosity in granting access to his previously unpublished maps. Urban counties that contained multiple congressional districts were divided geographically and demographically according to their respective number of districts. For example, the proportion unemployed in Los Angeles County in the 1950s was utilized as the proportion unemployed in the 15th–26th districts of California, which encompassed the county in that decade. In several instances counties were divided among two congressional districts, but these county portions made up only *part* of an entire district. In those instances, the sum of the populations of all the other counties in the

district was subtracted from the population of the entire district (as provided in the *Congressional Directory*) to estimate the population contained in the divided county, and thus the proportion of the county within that district.

23. In a few cases "lowest" values on the measure were considered to be the "highest" demanders: for example, median district income for Education and Labor or population per square mile for the Interior and Insular Affairs Committee. In these instances the standardized scores were multiplied by -1 to reverse their effect on the additive scales.

24. This technique makes the important assumption that the component measures have "equal" effects on a legislator's sense of interest in the benefits provided by a specific subcommittee. For example, this would mean that the percentage in a district employed in farming is *equally as important* in measuring need for benefits provided by the Agriculture Committee as the percentage living in rural farming areas. While this is not always the case with all component measures employed here, there is no obvious means of determining proper weights.

25. I conducted standard, two-sample, difference-in-means tests (*t*-tests) on all of the individual component measures. For the most part, the *t*-test results confirm those of the more robust Monte Carlo method.

26. The first year of analysis varies from one committee to the next due to the availability of constituency data and the consistency of the committee and its jurisdiction before and after the Legislative Reorganization Act of 1946.

27. The strongest and most consistent of the individual components of this committee's demand scale, according to the means tests of components, was the measure for the foreign-born proportion of the population.

28. Occasionally, we see large fluctuations in the *p*-value for a committee from one term to the next—such as that for the Banking Committee in the 85th Congress. Because members can be distributed broadly across the measure of district demand and the tests rely on panel *medians,* the departure or arrival of just a small number of members could result in large swings in *p*-values. This phenomenon is even more pronounced in the smaller Appropriations subcommittees.

29. The Postal Service, however, does have a history of being used to provide government benefits to legislators' districts for electoral gain. See Kernell and McDonald (1999) for an early history of this phenomenon.

30. See Cox and McCubbins (1993, 193) for elaboration of the "duty" nature of the Veterans' Affairs Committee.

31. Republicans have traditionally considered Commerce among its "exclusive" committees because of its broad jurisdictional powers.

32. Due to the limited availability of subcommittee rosters and the use of slightly different constituency information, tests do not include all Appropriations subcommittees going back the mid-1940s.

33. Large scale swings in the *p*-value of certain subcommittees at different periods (e.g., Energy and Water in the 96th–98th Congresses) are due to the relatively small size of these panels. During the early period examined, Appropriations subcommittees averaged about eight members, but have more recently tended toward twelve members. Therefore, replacement of just a few members can drastically change the subcommittee's median score.

34. Officially, Taber had retired at the end of the 87th Congress, and Ben Jensen (R-IA) became ranking minority member for the 88th Congress.

35. This statement was made in reference to Krehbiel's (1991) analysis using general ideology scores (ADA scores), but he later supports this assertion with an examination of jurisdiction-specific voting scores.

Chapter 4

1. Public Law 178, 105th Cong., 2nd sess. (June 9, 1998).

2. Public Law 240, 102nd Cong., 1st sess. (December 18, 1991).

3. Large portions of the federal bureaucracy were shut down in 1995 and 1996 because President Clinton and the Republican majority in Congress could not come to agreement on the terms of a balanced budget plan.

4. Public Law 33, 105th Cong., 1st sess. (August 5, 1997).

5. What is perhaps most ironic about this bill and the behavior of Committee Chair Shuster is that when he was first selected as the panel chief, Shuster vowed to put an end to discretionary projects in the transportation reauthorizations (Field 1995). The proclamation was in spite of the fact that Shuster was seen as one of the pioneers of such legislation (Pianin and Babcock 1998).

6. In fairness, these findings were sometimes conditioned on the party or electoral vulnerability of the incumbent, and a slightly older study concluded that variations in federal spending on construction and civilian federal employment had no discernable effect on incumbent vote share (Feldman and Jondrow 1984).

7. As a corollary to this hypothesis, researchers have debated the "universalism" assumption of the benefits hypothesis, which presumes the natural outgrowth of legislative logrolling is that distributive legislation should include benefits going to majorities or super-majorities of congressional districts, similar in many ways to what was crafted during consideration of the transportation example at the beginning of this chapter (Fiorina 1981; Stein and Bickers 1994b; Weingast, Shepsle, and Johnsen 1981; Weingast 1994).

8. The data set has also been quite useful in the above-mentioned universalism debate (e.g., see Stein and Bickers 1994b).

9. Just such an example occurred in 1998, when Senator Patrick Leahey (D-VT) was partially successful in pushing for an amendment to the National Sea Grant College reauthorization bill that declares Lake Champlain a Great Lake in order to qualify Vermont colleges for federal funds through this program (Kamen 1998).

10. Fenno describes the "environmental constraints" on the Interior Committee in very pluralistic terms, noting that the panel deals with "a variegated array of policy subjects . . . none drawing the same cast of clientele characters as another. The Interior Committee's environment is, therefore, profuse with clientele groups—some national, permanent and well known, many local, *ad hoc,* and ephemeral. No one or two or three can be said to dominate any one policy area, let alone the total Committee environment" (Fenno 1973, 37–38).

11. Interview with Robert Walker, Washington, DC, June 23, 1998.

12. This is not the first study of the distribution of federal funds to analyze Appropriations subcommittee membership (Anagnoson 1980; Ferejohn 1974; Heitshusen 2001). However, the Appropriations Committee is usually ignored in studies of the benefits hypothesis.

13. For a complete examination of the congressional budgetary process, see Schick 1980 or Schick 1995.

14. Interviews with Robert Walker, Washington, DC, June 23, 1998, and former Representative David Skaggs, Boulder, CO, October 8, 1999.

15. As described in chapter 3, this technique makes the assumption that the component measures have "equal" effects on a legislator's sense of demand for the benefits provided by a specific subcommittee.

16. State-capital-directed programs are identified through the proportion of total outlays of each individual program going only to congressional districts containing the capitals. Programs that distributed more than 75 percent of their total dollars to state-capital districts were eliminated from the study altogether. Of course, Type I

and Type II errors may occur in this methodology, but there was no obviously better technique for eliminating these programs. I thank Ken Bickers for suggesting this methodology.

17. Removal of state-capital-directed funds does eliminate an entire class of programs from the study—those for which the state distributes the money, such as the Justice Department's Crime Victims Assistance program or the Appalachian Regional Commission's Development Grants. However, there is no obvious way to include such data in this study, and their inclusion in the current form severely biases the analysis.

18. The study was accomplished using Congressional Information Service's (CIS) Congressional Masterfile on CD-ROM.

19. Appropriations legislation can include programs under the purview of several different authorizing committees, or the programmatic jurisdiction of authorizing committees can be divided among a number of Appropriations subcommittees.

20. The procedure is described in Stata 1997. Essentially, the procedure starts by estimating the parameters using ordinary least squares (OLS). From the residuals, any case with a Cook's D value > 1 is dropped. Then case weights are calculated (downweighting observations with larger residuals) and weighted least squares used to estimate new parameters. This process is repeated until the maximum difference in weights drops below .01.

21. Using a Wald test, I examined H_0: $\beta_1 = \beta_3 = \beta_4 = 0$ for the authorizing committee or H_0: $\beta_2 = \beta_3 = \beta_5 = 0$ for the Appropriations subcommittee. The alternate hypothesis is that these parameter estimates are not equal to zero. Findings are only reported where the null hypothesis can be rejected. In most cases, however, regular t-statistics revealed that the coefficients for committee membership and for committee membership interacted with district demand were individually significant.

22. For the Interior Committee, a large proportion, if not a majority, of congressional districts receive no money whatsoever from programs within their purview. For tests of the effect of committee membership, a more appropriate analysis takes account of the left-side or lower-end censoring, so I employ a Tobit model (Maddala 1992, 338–42). Efforts to adjust for extreme outliers on the dependent variable did not produce significantly different results.

Chapter 5
1. The Australian ballot is a government printed ballot that replaced election ballots produced by political parties. Its main advantages were that it allowed voters to cast a secret vote and, to some extent, allowed candidates to break free of party control over campaigns and office-holders.

2. For examinations of the history of the Legislative Reorganization Act of 1946, see Byrd 1988; Davidson 1990; Rundquist 1985.

3. Joint Committee on the Organization of Congress document, *Resolutions and Bills Proposing Changes in Legislative Organization and Operation Introduced in the 78th Congress.* Committee archives, National Archives, Washington, DC.

4. Joint Committee on the Organization of Congress document, *Resolutions and Bills Proposing Changes in Legislative Organization and Operation Introduced in the 79th Congress to March 4.* Committee archives, National Archives, Washington, DC.

5. S. Con. Res. 23, 78th Cong., introduced November 9, 1943.

6. Other members of the La Follette-Monroney Committee included Senators Elbert Thomas (D-UT), Claude Pepper (D-FL), Richard Russell (D-GA), Wallace White (R-ME), C. Wayland Brooks (R-IL), and Representatives Eugene Cox (D-GA), Thomas Lane (D-MA), Earl Michener (R-MI), Everett Dirksen (R-IL), and Charles Plumley (R-VT).

7. U.S. Senate, Report of Joint Committee on the Organization of Congress, 79th Cong., 2nd sess., S. Rept. 1011.

8. Public Law 601, 79th Cong., 2nd sess. (August 2, 1946).

9. U.S. Congress, Joint Committee on the Organization of Congress, *Organization of Congress,* 79th Cong., 1st sess. (1945), 882.

10. Staff Memorandum, Senate Committee on Expenditures in the Executive Branch, #82-1-2, Monroney Archives, University of Oklahoma, p. 2.

11. The number of standing committees dropped in 1927 with the consolidation of eleven expenditures committees into a single Committee on Expenditures in the Executive Departments.

12. In fairness to Wilson's research, although he finds that districts with representation on the Rivers and Harbors Committee do receive more of such federal benefits than districts without a representative on the panel, he argues it is due to area need rather than the committee seat.

13. A few committees from this period were included in the previous analysis, but chapter 3 includes only those whose jurisdiction more or less corresponded with the jurisdiction they eventually assumed after the 1946 reforms.

14. The U.S. Census did not start reporting data at the congressional district level until after the 1960 Census.

15. With only 48 possible different values for 435 different congressional districts, it was often impossible to get an accurate accounting of where the actual committee median should be located in the distribution of random medians that have relatively little variation.

16. The relative flood potential level is the same values as those used for the 1950s data in chapter 3, but remapped for the 1940s congressional districts. Although the Army Corps of Engineers publication from which these values were calculated is believed not to have been published for the period examined here, the important measure for our purposes is the *relative* flood potential between different areas. It is assumed that this flood potential did not change dramatically in most geographic areas from one decade to the next.

17. While this is admittedly not a perfect test for the composition of committees, since it does not measure the committee composition against the *entire* chamber, it is the best possible, given the data limitations. The results of the Wilcoxon tests appear in parentheses in table 6; see Cox and McCubbins (1993) for utilization of this test on committee composition.

18. Federal highway construction programs were often seen as lucrative sources of funds. Not surprisingly, much of the initial planning for the Interstate Highway System came from the National Resources Planning Board, established by Roosevelt in 1938 (Rose 1990, 16, 17).

19. *Congressional Record* (July 25, 1946): H10040. The expression refers to the young slave girl, Topsy, in *Uncle Tom's Cabin,* who claimed to have simply "growed up" without the supervision of parents. I thank Prof. Anna Brickhouse for explanation of this reference.

20. Wadsworth's committee consolidation plan had been the basis for much of the work of the La Follette-Monroney Committee concerning jurisdictional restructuring (Galloway 1946, 176).

21. *Congressional Record* (July 25, 1946) H: 10042.

22. See Ripley (1969) for a study of the assignment compensation patterns of committee restructuring in the Senate as a result of the LRA.

23. In many respects the same experience would occur forty years later with Gramm-Rudman-Hollings (formally known as the Balanced Budget and Emergency

Deficit Control Act of 1985), whose provisions for spending caps were often ineffective (Shuman 1992).

24. See, for example, Wilmerding (1943).

25. A "concurrent resolution" contains no binding legislation, but simply expresses the will of the Congress. Furthermore, it does not require a presidential signature.

26. *Congressional Record* (July 25, 1946) H: 10058.

27. The Senate eventually reintroduced this idea in an appropriation bill in the 80th Congress. While existing in the Senate for many years, the party policy committees never seemed to be as effective in coordinating and defining chamber policy agendas as was hoped. Galloway subsequently stated that "[a]s devices for coordinating legislative policy-making and strengthening party leadership, the Senate policy committees have thus far failed to achieve their full potential. As instruments for promoting more effective liaison and cooperation with the President, they have also been a disappointment, partly because of the lack of similar party policy committees in the House of Representatives. Their limited achievements to date can be attributed, presumably, to their composition, to the fragmentation of power in Congress, and to the deep internal divisions within both of our major political parties" (Galloway 1953, 604).

28. *Congressional Record* (July 25, 1946) H: 10104.

29. See Bennett 1967 and "The Function of Private Bills" 1971 for a description of what is normally considered a private claim and how the laws concerning these matters have further changed since 1946.

30. Representative Emanuel Celler (D-NY) placed a Legislative Reference Service report by George Galloway into the *Congressional Record* (May 12, 1949) A: 2901–2904.

31. U.S. Congress, Joint Committee on the Organization of Congress, Organization of Congress, 79th Cong., 1st sess. (1945), 284.

32. *Congressional Record* (May 12, 1949) A: 2902.

33. The reason for the lagged decrease in private legislation was that under the LRA, claims filed before January 1, 1945, were still admissible before Congress. According to Monroney, well into the 80th Congress, the House was still dealing with the backlog (*Congressional Record* [July 26, 1947] A: 4049).

34. *Congressional Record* (May 12, 1949) H: 10044.

35. Comments by Senator La Follette at hearings entitled, *Evaluation of Legislative Reorganization Act of 1946*, before the Committee on Expenditures in the Executive Departments, United States Senate, 80th Cong., 2nd sess., p. 61.

Chapter 6

1. Davidson, Kovenock, and O'Leary (1966) conducted a study of congressional attitudes toward reforms in the mid-1960s, but did not survey members on their preferences for specific jurisdictional changes.

2. The public records for the Bolling Committee are extensive and include not only hearings testimony and committee reports, but minutes from the public markup of their bill and many of the letters addressed to the committee from legislators and interest groups. In addition, records and correspondences were obtained from the personal archives of Representatives Carl Albert, Richard Bolling, John "Happy" Camp, Lloyd Meeds, Julia Butler Hansen, Brock Adams, and Bolling Committee staff member Walter Oleszek, as well as the Democratic Caucus files from this period.

3. Much of the basic description of the Bolling-Hansen reform effort is taken from these three works, as well as personal interviews and journalistic accounts in *Congressional Quarterly Weekly Report,* the *New York Times,* and the *Washington Post.*

4. A more contentious vote on the "rule" for consideration of this bill that had been reported out of the Rules Committee resulted in a 205–167 split.

5. U.S. House, Select Committee on Committees, "Committee Reform Amendments of 1974: Report of the Select Committee on Committees, U.S. House of Representatives, to Accompany H. Res. 988," 93rd Cong., 2nd sess. (1974), H. Rept. 93-916.

6. According to the special rule passed by the Rules Committee, the Bolling plan (H. Res. 988) was offered as the bill, with the Hansen plan (H. Res. 1248) in order as substitute amendment, and a proposal similar to the original Bolling proposal formulated by the Select Committee's Vice Chair David Martin (R-NE; H. Res. 1321), in order as a substitute amendment to the Hansen amendment.

7. This was the initial vote in the Committee of the Whole, the final vote moments later in the full House was 359–7.

8. Interview with former Representative Lloyd Meeds (member of the Bolling Committee), Washington, DC, June 25, 1998.

9. Interview with William Cable, Washington, DC, June 23, 1998.

10. The method of aggregating county-level outlays data to congressional districts is similar to the one I used to aggregate county-level Census data to congressional districts for the 1940s and 1950s; it is explained in Barone, Ujifusa, and Matthews (1974, xix).

11. Difference-in-means (*t*-tests) were also conducted and produced nearly identical results.

12. As a rough guide to statistical significance I use a *p*-level of .05 or less. However, I provide the actual significance level for each test, so that readers may interpret the findings as they wish.

13. Many of the Bolling Committee letters are printed in U.S. House, Select Committee on Committees, "Letters and Statements from Members, Groups, and Individuals Regarding the Work of the Select Committee on Committees," 93rd Cong., 2nd sess. (1974); however, "Dear Colleague" letters were only available through the private collections of former members of Congress.

14. Congressional press outlets included the *Congressional Quarterly Weekly Report, National Journal, New York Times,* and *Washington Post.*

15. All statements were coded by two research assistants; discrepancies were resolved by the author.

16. One possible reform that could have been included in this list was the creation of an Energy and Environment Committee out of the Interstate and Commerce Committee. However, debate on this alteration varied widely, and there was no clear consensus as to which constituency groups might win or lose as a result of this jurisdictional change. Bolling had hoped to avoid having to decide such an issue within the context of his reform panel (see Davidson and Oleszek 1977).

17. The initial Bolling report refers to U.S. House, Select Committee on Committees, "Committee Structure and Procedures of the House of Representatives: Working Draft of Report of the Select Committee on Committees," 93rd Cong., 1st sess. (1973).

18. See U.S. House, *Committee Reform Amendments of 1974,* H. Rept. 93-916.

19. Details concerning the constituency characteristics of members of Congress come from Census 1973; Congressional Quarterly 1974; and Barone, Ujifusa, and Matthews 1974.

20. From the founding of Hawaii's statehood until the early 1970s, no statewide candidate endorsed by the ILWU lost an election, and the union was so strong that many areas were referred to as "ILWU precincts." Matsunaga eventually ran for and won a Senate seat in 1976.

21. The Hansen proposal did remove one issue from PO's jurisdiction—the National Archives.

22. U.S. House, Select Committee on Committees, "Open Business Meeting of the Select Committee on Committees, House of Representatives: Markup of House Resolution Committee Reform Amendments of 1974," 93rd Cong., 2nd sess. (1974), 233.

23. While education interests were also concerned with this jurisdictional change, many members saw this issue as a means of gaining publicity as policy entrepreneurs and not necessarily as a way to protect district needs and secure campaign support (Davidson and Oleszek 1977, 170).

24. Hansen Committee members James O'Hara (MI), Frank Thompson (NJ), and Phillip Burton (CA) were all senior Democrats on the Education and Labor Committee.

25. The AFL-CIO's Committee on Political Education (COPE) reports voting scores for all members of Congress derived from roll-call votes it deems important to labor-oriented matters (the scale is 0–100, with 100 being the most labor-supportive). The Education and Labor median in the 93rd Congress was 86.33; using the previously employed Monte Carlo technique, this produced a p-value of .02.

26. Zinc and copper mining were the largest employers in Montana outside of farming, and the United Mine Workers controlled Montana Democratic Party politics. Senators Mansfield and Metcalf had both won their elections with the support of the unions, and Melcher knew that he would need the same support if he wished to replace either one. Melcher ran for and won Mansfield's Senate seat in 1976.

27. Davidson and Oleszek report that when the Hansen Committee voted to retain Education and Labor, Landrum stated that he had regretted testifying in favor of its division before the Bolling Committee. However, we should note that he said this before a number of high-ranking Education and Labor members, and Landrum, a member of Ways and Means, was an advocate of the Hansen Committee reinstating much of his committee's lost jurisdiction (Davidson and Oleszek 1977, 210–11).

28. The group also included individuals like Morris Udall, Thomas Rees, and Patricia Schroeder (Davidson and Oleszek 1977, 217).

29. U.S. House, Select Committee on Committees, "Open Business Meeting," 219.

30. Cable interview, June 23, 1998.

31. U.S. House, Select Committee on Committees, "Open Business Meeting," 53.

32. The average percentage of workers using public transportation to commute in these cities was 16.1 percent, as calculated from 1970 Census information on Standard Metropolitan Statistical Areas.

33. The average percentage of workers commuting on public transportation in these cities was 9.1.

34. Seniority is measured using the number of consecutive terms served, including the current term. Democratic Party membership is measured using a dummy variable with Republican affiliation equal to 1 and Democratic affiliation equal to 0. Ideology (liberalism) is measured using the first dimension of Poole and Rosenthal's W-NOMINATE scores. This measure of broad ideological predisposition establishes the location of a member of Congress on an underlying spatial dimension derived from the scaling of all non-unanimous roll-call votes taken during each session of Congress. Like Americans for Democratic Action (ADA) scores, NOMINATE scores rank members on a liberal/conservative space, with a range of scores from −1 (liberal) to +1 (conservative).

35. There was a second roll-call vote on the Aging jurisdiction when John Heinz (R-PA) offered the same amendment to the Martin reform plan on October 8, 1974. That amendment passed by a 299–44 margin with no debate.

36. HISC had long been under attack by liberals who saw the committee mostly in terms of its McCarthy-led witch-hunting activities (Kaplan 1968; Goodman 1968), and had as recently as March 1973 attempted to cut funding to the panel.

37. Government Operations did not particularly want HISC's jurisdiction. In fact, Government Operations Chair Chet Hollifield (D-CA) spoke on the floor in favor of the panel in order to avoid acquiring its work as part of the Hansen proposal.

38. Not surprisingly, constituent ideology (Nixon vote) and member ideology correlate very highly (.71; see Miller and Stokes 1963). When constituent ideology is substituted in this model for legislator ideology, it has exactly the same effect; however, party changes sign—Republicans are less likely to support retaining HISC.

39. Initially only the Bolling proposal provided for the transformation of the Select Small Business Committee into a standing committee. However, an amendment by Orval Hansen (R-ID) to the Hansen proposal was accepted on the House floor on October 3, which called for the same provision in that plan.

40. This accounting of winner and loser committees with respect to jurisdictional changes is similar to Lowe's (1976, 55).

41. Two panels—Agriculture and Government Operations—would have made minor jurisdictional gains under the Bolling plan, but public statements of members did not seem to indicate widespread support on these panels for the added workload.

42. Banking was the only committee that was going to take sizable losses to its jurisdictional boundaries under both plans.

43. The interests of elderly constituents are not expected to have had much influence on members' Hansen vote. After acceptance of the Aging Committee (Young) amendment to the Hansen plan and overwhelming approval of the identical (Heinz) amendment to the Martin plan a few days later, John Heinz also expected that a similar amendment would be offered and approved to the Bolling plan, should it come to a vote (*Congressional Record,* October 8, 1974, H: 34455).

44. The sensitivity analysis is conducted by computing the logit probabilities for each variable individually, using its minimum and maximum values and holding all other variables at their mean or mode (Liao 1994).

Chapter 7

1. Of course, I am not the first to describe this phenomenon (see Aldrich and Rohde 1997b; Rohde 1991). Therefore, I offer only details concerning caucus strength and party polarization that are necessary for a lucid discussion of congressional reforms in this period.

2. Owens (1997) notes the same trend through a similar examination of party unity votes.

3. These ADA scores are simply adjusted for shifting and stretching scales across time and legislative chambers.

4. Aldrich and Rohde observe that according to their measures of intraparty cohesion and interparty division, which depend mostly on scales derived from roll-call votes, many of the same conditions present in 1990s also existed in the 1940s. However, they note that this finding (similarly noted in Cox and McCubbins, chap. 6) is a bit misleading, since the most divisive issue within the Democratic Party at the time, civil rights, was largely kept off the roll-call agenda; hence, it is not likely to characterize an era of conditional party government.

5. For a more detailed examination of the circumstances surrounding the Joint Committee on the Organization of Congress, see Evans and Oleszek 1997 and articles in Thurber and Davidson 1995.

6. Interview with former Representative Lee Hamilton, by telephone, July 19, 2000.

7. U.S. Congress, Joint Committee on the Organization of Congress, *Background Materials: Supplemental Information Provided to Members of the Joint Committee on the Organization of Congress,* 103rd Cong., 1st sess. (1993), Committee Print 103-55, 812–25. See also Davidson (1995b, 31–32).

8. U.S. Congress, Joint Committee on the Organization of Congress, *Operations of the Congress: Testimony of Current Representatives on the Structure of the House of Representatives,* hearing before the Joint Committee on the Organization of Congress, 103rd Cong., 1st sess., February 4, 1993, S. Hrg. 103-11, 4–5.

9. See the following: memorandum, "Freshman Democratic Reform Package," March 31, 1993, p. 7; description of the Freshman Republican reform proposal in Cooper 1993; memorandum, "Response to Freshman Reform Package," April 21, 1993 (facsimile by Representative David Skaggs); memorandum, "DSG Reform Task Force Recommendations to Joint Committee on Organization of Congress," June 24, 1993.

10. Telephone interview with Lee Hamilton, July 19, 2000.

11. The Senate plan was introduced jointly by Senators Boren and Domenici, but the House version was sponsored by Hamilton alone. Dreier refused to cosponsor the legislation because Speaker Foley would not commit to a "generous amendment rule" (Evans and Oleszek 1997, 72).

12. This more salient section of the reform package called for congressional compliance with existing labor legislation.

13. The Project was chaired by Thomas Mann of the Brookings Institution and Norman Ornstein of the American Enterprise Institute; it included the input of Richard Fenno, Lawrence Hansen, Robert Katzmann, Charles Jones, Matt Pinkus, Nelson Polsby, Cokie Roberts, Catherine Rudder, Steven Smith, and Joseph White.

14. Telephone interview with Lee Hamilton, July 19, 2000. See also Evans and Oleszek 1997, 68–69.

15. U.S. Congress, Joint Committee on the Organization of Congress, *Business Meetings on Congressional Reform Legislation,* 103rd Cong., 1st sess. (1993), Committee Hearings 103-320, 200.

16. Joint Committee staff summary of meeting, entitled, "Speaker and Majority Leader Meeting," dated October 13, 1993.

17. Bielenson's amendments also included a ban on proxy votes.

18. Interview with anonymous Democratic staff member, Washington, DC, June 19, 1998.

19. Interview with anonymous congressional staff member, Washington, DC, June 18, 1998.

20. U.S. Congress, Joint Committee on the Organization of Congress, *Organization of the Congress: Final Report of the House Members of the Joint Committee on the Organization of Congress,* 103rd Cong., 1st sess. (1993), Report 103-413, vol. 1, 148–51.

21. Joint Committee staff summary of meeting, entitled, "Speaker and Majority Leader Meeting," dated October 13, 1993.

22. Joint Committee staff summary of meeting, entitled, "Pre-Leadership Meeting of Democratic Leaders," dated October 28, 1993.

23. Interview with anonymous congressional staff member, Washington, DC, June 18, 1998.

24. Interview with Walter Oleszek, Washington, DC, June 25, 1998.

25. For more on the formulation and effect of the *Contract,* see Bader 1996; Gimpel 1996; and McSweeney and Owens 1998.

26. LEGI-SLATE Reports [defunct on-line periodical], "Michael Names GOP Congressional Reform Task Force," March 15, 1993.

27. Evans and Oleszek report that a copy of Dreier's proposals was left in a wastepaper basket and subsequently picked up and reported in the press (1997, 95).

28. Interview with Robert Walker, Washington, DC, June 23, 1998.

29. Interview with anonymous Republican staff member, Washington, DC, June 18, 1998, see also Evans and Oleszek 1997.

30. Walker recalled that this group included Gingrich and Walker, as well as eventual Majority Leader Dick Armey (TX), Majority Whip Tom DeLay (TX), Deputy Whip Dennis Hastert (IN), Conference Chair John Boehner (OH), and either Republican National Congressional Committee Chair Tom Paxon (NY) or Budget Committee Chair John Kasich (OH). Walker could not remember who the seventh person was, but stated that this inner circle consisted of the eventual members of the Speaker's Advisory Group. Both Paxon and Kasich were eventual members of that Group (Sinclair 1998).

31. Such statements were made in interviews with both former Republican and Democratic staff members.

32. Joint Committee staff summary of meeting, entitled, "Bipartisan Leadership Session," dated October 28, 1993.

33. For this measure, I rely on Baumgartner and Jones's coding of the *Congressional Quarterly Almanac.*

34. The Post Office and Civil Service Committee produces a considerably higher number of public laws each year, but most are simply commemorative (e.g., designating a specific week as "Geography Awareness Week," etc.). However, this panel does produce a number of substantive enactments each year. For example, in the 103rd Congress, the Post Office and Civil Service Committee played a significant role in the passage of the Family and Medical Leave Act, reforms in the Hatch Act, and reauthorization of the special counsel law.

35. In fact, until the House post office scandal finally toppled Rostenkowski in the 103rd Congress, the Ethics Committee had not done much since 1989, when it adjudicated allegations of sexual improprieties, extortion, and conspiracy against several legislators.

36. This accounting of multiple referrals specifically focuses on each committee's central legislative functions by examining only public bills and ignoring resolutions (concurrent, joint, etc.) of any kind.

37. Aldrich and Rohde (1995, 5–6) suggest similar notions about committee reforms during the Republican transition.

38. Though it would be more appropriate to examine all Republicans due to serve in the 104th Congress, no equivalent measure of ideology exists for the newly entering freshman class prior to their service. Nevertheless, it was well known that this was a particularly conservative freshman class, and it is quite reasonable to assume that any liberal outlier contingent as compared to the incumbent Republican portion of the caucus would also have been an outlier to the entire GOP caucus for the 104th Congress that included the freshmen.

39. Party unity scores for individual members are taken from the *Congressional Quarterly Almanac* and represent the percentage of party line roll-call votes in a given year in which a representative was present and voted in agreement with a majority of his or her party. The scores used here for 1993 did not include failures to vote as "opposition" to the party.

40. Interview with David Dreier, by telephone, March 12, 2001.

41. *Congressional Quarterly Almanac,* 1993, 208–9.

42. Of the panel's work over the period from 1989 to 1994 (as measured by the

number of hearing days devoted to different subject categories), a larger percentage focused on the environment and wildlife matters than marine transportation.

43. Data on campaign contributions are culled from Federal Election Commission records at http://www.fec.gov/.

44. U.S. Congress, Joint Committee on the Organization of Congress, *Committee Structure,* 103rd Cong., 1st sess., May 13, 1993, S. Hrg. 103-74, 400.

45. Former Representative Lloyd Meeds recounted, ironically, that as a member of the Bolling Committee he had sought the elimination of the Merchant Marine and Fisheries Committee in 1973–74, but in his subsequent occupation as a lobbyist for maritime interests, he labored during the transition period in late 1994 to save the panel from elimination (interview, Washington, DC, June 25, 1998).

46. This measure captures all government employees (federal, state, and local). It is not possible to completely disaggregate federal employees from General Social Survey (GSS) survey data.

47. This difference between postal workers and the general population does not reach the level of statistical significance mostly due to the relatively small number of individuals employed in postal work.

48. "Suspension of the rules" entails suspending regular procedures or remaining debate over a bill and passing the measure with a two-thirds majority.

49. Public Law 94, 103rd Cong., 1st sess. (October 6, 1993), *Congressional Quarterly Almanac, 1993,* 201–3.

50. Telephone interview with David Dreier, March 12, 2001.

51. This difference is found to be statistically significant at the .01 level.

52. Interview with David Dreier, by telephone, March 12, 2001.

53. Interview with Robert Walker, Washington, DC, June 23, 1998.

54. Interview with anonymous Republican staff member, Washington, DC, June 18, 1998.

55. Interview with Robert Walker, Washington, DC, June 23, 1998. See Smith and Lawrence 1997 (170) for a similar argument.

56. Telephone interview with David Dreier, March 12, 2001; see also Drew 1996, 38; Davidson 1995a.

57. *Congressional Quarterly Almanac 1993,* 415–16.

58. Respondents to the GSS survey who identified themselves as having been on active duty military for at least two consecutive months.

59. Interview with anonymous Republican staff member, Washington, DC, June 18, 1998.

60. Telephone interviews with, respectively, Lee Hamilton, July 19, 2000, and with David Dreier, March 12, 2001.

61. Telephone interview with Lee Hamilton, July 19, 2000.

Chapter 8

1. Interview with Walter Oleszek, Washington, DC, June 25, 1998.

2. Telephone interview with David Dreier, March 12, 2001.

3. Again, the examination relies on a technique to identify significant legislation used most effectively in Mayhew 1991.

4. U.S. Congress, Joint Committee on the Organization of Congress, *Business Meetings on Congressional Reform Legislation,* 103rd Cong., 1st sess. (1993), Committee Hearings 103-320, 196.

5. The 107th Congress represented the first time that Republican committee chairs faced the three-term limit instituted at the start of the 104th Congress. The resulting jockeying for replacement chairs caused a battle between Billy Tauzin (LA) and Mike Oxley (OH) for the chair of the Commerce Committee. In order satisfy both suitors,

and to prevent liberal Republican Marge Roukema (NJ) from ascending to the Banking chairmanship, regulation of securities and exchange issues and insurance was shifted to the new Financial Services Committee, and Oxley was made chair (Bresnahan and Pershing 2001).

6. See Davidson 1995b for specific lessons associated with the Republican effort at structural changes for the 104th Congress.

References

Abram, Michael, and Joseph Cooper. 1968. "The Rise of Seniority in the House of Representatives." *Polity* 1:52–85.

Adler, E. Scott. 2002. "Changing Members and Changing Focus: Committee Composition and the Transformation of Issue Agendas on the House Banking and Public Works Committees." In *Policy Dynamics,* edited by Frank Baumgartner and Bryan Jones. Chicago: University of Chicago Press.

Adler, Madeleine Wing. 1969. "Congressional Reform: An Exploratory Case." Ph.D. diss., Department of Political Science, University of Wisconsin, Madison.

Ainsworth, Scott, and Itai Sened. N.d. "Institutional Stickiness and Congressional Reform." Manuscript. Department of Political Science, University of Georgia.

Aldrich, John. 1995. *Why Parties? The Origin and Transformation of Party Politics in America.* Chicago: University of Chicago Press.

Aldrich, John, and David Rohde. 1995. "Theories of the Party in the Legislature and the Transition to Republican Rule in the House." Paper presented at the Annual Meeting of the American Political Science Association, Chicago, IL.

———. 1997a. "Balance of Power: Republican Party Leadership and the Committee System in the 104th House." Paper presented at the Annual Meeting of the Midwest Political Science Association, Chicago, IL.

———. 1997b. "The Transition to Republican Rule in the House: Implications for Theories of Congressional Politics." *Political Science Quarterly* 112:541–67.

———. 1998. "Measuring Conditional Party Government." Paper presented at the Annual Meeting of the Midwest Political Science Association, Chicago, IL.

———. 2000. "The Republican Revolution and the House Appropriations Committee." *Journal of Politics* 62:1–33

———. 2001. "The Logic of Conditional Party Government: Revisiting the Electoral Connection." In *Congress Reconsidered,* edited by Lawrence Dodd and Bruce Oppenheimer. Washington, DC: Congressional Quarterly Press.

Alston, Chuck. 1993. "Democrats Flex New Muscle with Trio of Election Bills." *Congressional Quarterly Weekly Report,* March 20, 643–45.

Alvarez, Michael, and Jason Saving. 1997a. "Congressional Committees and the Political Economy of Federal Outlays." *Public Choice* 92:55–73.

————. 1997b. "Deficits, Democrats, and Distributive Benefits: Congressional Elections and the Pork Barrel in the 1980s." *Political Research Quarterly* 50:809–32.

Anagnoson, J. Theodore. 1980. "Politics in the Distribution of Federal Grants: The Case of the Economic Development Administration." In *Political Benefits,* edited by Barry Rundquist. Lexington, MA: Lexington Books.

————. 1982. "Federal Grant Agencies and Congressional Election Campaigns." *American Journal of Political Science* 26:547–61.

Anderson, Donnald. 1989. *Guide to the Records of the United States House of Representatives at the National Archives, 1789–1989.* House Document No. 100-245. Washington, DC: GPO.

APSA. 1945. *The Reorganization of Congress: A Report of the Committee on Congress of the American Political Science Association.* Washington, DC: Public Affairs Press.

Arnold, R. Douglas. 1979. *Congress and the Bureaucracy.* New Haven, CT: Yale University Press.

————. 1990. *The Logic of Congressional Action.* New Haven, CT: Yale University Press.

Associated Press. 1995. "Republicans Pledge Bold, Quick Action; Democrats Brace for Difficult Transition to Minority in Congress." *Atlanta Journal/Constitution* (January 3), A/1.

Bader, John. 1996. *Taking the Initiative: Leadership Agendas in Congress and the "Contract with America."* Washington, DC: Georgetown University Press.

Bailey, Stephen, and Howard Samuel. 1952. *Congress at Work.* New York: Henry Holt.

Balz, Dan, and Ronald Brownstein. 1996. *Storming the Gates: Protest Politics and the Republican Revival.* Boston: Little, Brown.

Barnett, Pamela. 2001. "House GOP Proposes New Financial Services Committee." *National Journal's Congress Daily* (January 2). Access from http://nationaljournal.com/pubs/congressdaily/top.htm#.

Barone, Michael, Grant Ujifusa, and Douglas Matthews. 1974. *The Almanac of American Politics, 1974.* Boston: Gambit.

Baumann, David. 1999. "A Spending Bonanza, Thanks to Kosovo." *National Journal* (April 24), 1110–11.

Baumgartner, Frank, and Bryan Jones. 1998. "Congressional Hearings and Enactments Data Set." Seattle: Department of Political Science, University of Washington.

Baumgartner, Frank, Bryan Jones, and Michael Rosenstiehl. 1997. "The Co-Evolution of Issues and Structures in Congress." Department of Political Science, University of Washington.

Baumgartner, Frank, Bryan Jones, Michael Rosenstiehl, and Ronald Lorenzo. 1994. "Committee Jurisdictions in Congress, 1980–1991." Paper presented at the Annual Meeting of the American Political Science Association, New York City.

Bennett, Marion. 1967. "Private Claims Acts and Congressional References." *JAG Law Review* (Nov–Dec): 9–19, 39.

Berman, Daniel. 1964. *In Congress Assembled: The Legislative Process in the National Government.* New York: Macmillan.

————. 1966. *A Bill Becomes a Law: Congress Enacts Civil Rights Legislation.* 2nd ed. New York: Macmillan.

Bickers, Kenneth, and Robert Stein. 1990. U.S. Domestic Assistance Programs Database: 1983–1990. Bloomington: Indiana University. Now includes 1991–1997 data. Access from http://www.indiana.edu/~iupolsci/bio_bickers.html.

———. 1991. *Federal Domestic Outlays, 1983–1990: A Data Book.* Armonk, NY: M. E. Sharpe.

Binder, Sarah. 1997. *Minority Rights, Majority Rule: Partisanship and the Development of Congress.* New York: Cambridge University Press.

Black, Duncan. 1958. *The Theory of Committees and Elections.* London: Cambridge University Press.

Born, Richard. 1976. "Cue-taking within State Party Delegations in the U.S. House of Representatives." *Journal of Politics* 38:71–94.

Bovitz, Gregory. 1999. "Porkbusters in Congress: The Electoral Politics of Terminating Distributive Programs." Ph.D. diss. Department of Political Science, University of California, San Diego.

Brady, David, Kara Buckley, and Douglas Rivers. 1999. "The Roots of Careerism in the U.S. House of Representatives." *Legislative Studies Quarterly* 24:489–510.

Bresnahan, John, and Ben Pershing 2001. "Committee Contests Going Down to Wire." *Roll Call On-line,* January 4.

Brown, George. 1922. *The Leadership of Congress.* Indianapolis: Bobbs-Merrill.

Browne, William. 1995. *Cultivating Congress: Constituents, Issues and Interests in Agriculture Policymaking.* Lawrence, KS: University Press of Kansas.

Bullock, Charles. 1971. "The Influence of State Party Delegations on House Committee Assignments." *Midwest Journal of Political Science* 15:525–46.

———. 1976. "Motivations for U.S. Congressional Committee Preferences: Freshmen of the 92nd Congress." *Legislative Studies Quarterly* 1:201–12.

Burger, Timothy. 1994a. "Ax to Fall on Three House Panels: DC, Post Office, Merchant Marine." *Roll Call* (November 17), 1.

———. 1994b. "House Committees On Chopping Block?" *Roll Call* (November 7), 3.

Burns, James McGregor. 1949. *Congress on Trial: The Legislative Process and the Administrative State.* New York: Harper.

Butler, David, and Bruce Cain. 1992. *Congressional Redistricting: Comparative and Theoretical Perspectives.* New York: Macmillan.

Byrd, Robert. 1988. "Congressional Reform: The Legislative Reorganization Act of 1946." In *The Senate, 1789–1989: Addresses on the History of the United States Senate,* edited by Robert Byrd. Washington, DC: GPO.

Calvert, Randall. 1995. "The Rational Choice Theory of Social Institutions: Cooperation, Coordination, and Communication." In *Modern Political Economy: Old Topics, New Directions,* edited by Jeffrey Banks and Eric Hanushek. New York: Cambridge University Press.

Cannon, Clarence. 1963. Cannon's Procedure in the House of Representatives. 87th Cong., 2nd sess. Washington, DC: GPO.

Canon, David, Garrison Nelson, and Charles Stewart. 1994. "Committees in the United States Congress, 1946–1994. Dataset."

Carmines, Edward, and James Stimson. 1989. *Issue Evolution: Race and the Transformation of American Politics.* Princeton, NJ: Princeton University Press.

Carsey, Thomas, and Barry Rundquist. 1999. "Targeting Distributive Benefits: Comparing Health, Agriculture, Transportation, Crime and Defense Spending." Paper presented at the Annual Meeting of the American Political Science Association, Atlanta, GA.

———. 2001. *Congress and the Distributive Politics of Military Procurement.* Norman: University of Oklahoma Press.

Chamberlain, Lawrence. 1967. The President, Congress, and Legislation. New York: AMS Press. [Focuses c. 1946.]

Clymer, Adam. 1994. "Gingrich Moves Quickly to Put Stamp on House." *New York Times* (November 17), A1.

Cohen, Linda, and Roger Noll, eds. 1991. *The Technology Pork Barrel.* Washington, DC: Brookings Institution.

Cohen, Richard. 1999. "Crackup of the Committees." *National Journal,* July 31, 2210–17.

Collie, Melissa. 1988. "The Legislature and Distributive Policy Making in Formal Perspective." *Legislative Studies Quarterly* 13:427–58.

Congressional Quarterly. 1974. *Congressional Districts in the 1970s.* Washington, DC: Congressional Quarterly Press.

Cooper, Joseph. 1970. "The Origins of the Standing Committees and the Development of the Modern House." *Rice University Studies* 56:1–167.

Cooper, Joseph, and David Brady. 1981. "Institutional Context and Leadership Style: The House from Cannon to Rayburn." *American Political Science Review* 75:411–25.

Cooper, Joseph, and Garry Young. 1997. "Partisanship, Bipartisanship, and Cross-partisanship in Congress Since the New Deal." In *Congress Reconsidered,* edited by Lawrence Dodd and Bruce Oppenheimer. Washington, DC: Congressional Quarterly Press.

Cooper, Kenneth. 1993. "GOP Freshmen Seek to Abolish Key Panel as Part of House Overhaul." *Washington Post* (March 31),

———. 1994a. "GOP Plan to Cut House Ethics Panel Criticized." *Washington Post* (November 18), A12.

———. 1994b. "GOP Plans Shake-Up of House Committees." *Washington Post* (December 3), A1.

Cowart, Susan Cooper. 1981. "Representation of High Demand Constituencies on Review Committees." *Public Choice* 45:427–34.

Cox, Gary, and Mathew McCubbins. 1993. *Legislative Leviathan: Party Government in the House.* Berkeley: University of California Press.

Crawford, William. 1993. *United States Military Road Atlas.* Falls, Church, VA: Military Living Publications.

Damore, David, and Thomas Hansford. 1999. "The Allocation of Party Controlled Campaign Resources in the House of Representatives, 1989–1996." *Political Research Quarterly* 52:371–85.

Davidson, Roger. 1990. "The Legislative Reorganization Act of 1946." *Legislative Studies Quarterly* 15:357–73.

———. 1995a. "Building a Republican Regime on Capitol Hill." *APSA Legislative Studies Section Newsletter, Extension of Remarks* 19:1–2, 12.

———. 1995b. "Congressional Committees in the New Reform Era." In *Remaking Congress: Change and Stability in the 1990s,* edited by James Thurber and Roger Davidson. Washington, DC: Congressional Quarterly Press.

———. 1999. "Building the Republican Regime: Leaders and Committees." In *New Majority or Old Minority? The Impact of Republicans on Congress,* edited by Nicol Rae and Colton Campbell. Lanham, MD: Rowman and Littlefield.

Davidson, Roger, David Kovenock, and Michael O'Leary. 1966. *Congress In Crisis: Politics and Congressional Reform.* Belmont, CA: Wadsworth.

Davidson, Roger, and Walter Oleszek. 1977. *Congress against Itself.* Bloomington: Indiana University Press.

de Boinville, Barbara. 1982. "Origins and Development of Congress." Washington, DC: Congressional Quarterly Press.

Deckard, Barbara. 1972. "State Party Delegations in the U.S. House of Representatives—A Comparative Study of Group Cohesion." *Journal of Politics* 34:199–222.

Deering, Christopher. 1999. "Learning to Legislate: Committees in the Republican Congress." In *New Majority or Old Minority? The Impact of Republicans on Congress,* edited by Nicol Rae and Colton Campbell. Lanham, MD: Rowman and Littlefield.

Deering, Christopher, and Steven Smith. 1997. *Committees in Congress.* Washington, DC: Congressional Quarterly Press.

Democratic Study Group. 1974. "The Bolling Committee Reform Proposals." Washington, DC. Personal archives of Walter Oleszek, of the Congressional Research Service.

Denzau, Arthur, and Robert Mackay. 1983. "Gatekeeping and Monopoly Power of Committees: An Analysis of Sincere and Sophisticated Behavior." *American Journal of Political Science* 27:740–61.

Deschler, Lewis. 1977. *Deschler's Precedents of the U.S. House of Representatives.* Washington, DC: GPO.

Dewar, Helen. 1998. "One Big Win but Many More Losses." *Washington Post* (October 23), A16.

Diermeier, Daniel. 1995. "Commitment, Deference, and Legislative Institutions." *American Political Science Review* 89:344–55.

Dion, Douglas. 1997. *Turning the Legislative Thumbscrews: Minority Rights and Procedural Change in Legislative Politics.* Ann Arbor: University of Michigan Press.

Dodd, Lawrence, and Richard Schott. 1979. *Congress and the Administrative State.* New York: John Wiley and Sons.

Drew, Elizabeth. 1996. *Showdown: The Struggle between the Gingrich Congress and the Clinton White House.* New York: Simon and Schuster.

Ehrenhalt, Alan. Various years. *Politics in America: Members of Congress in Washington and at Home.* Washington, DC: Congressional Quarterly Press.

Epstein, David. 1997. "An Informational Rationale for Committee Gatekeeping Power." *Public Choice* 91:271–99.

Eulau, Heinz, John Wahlke, William Buchanan, and Leroy Ferguson. 1959. "The Role of the Representative: Some Empirical Observations on the Theory of Edmund Burke." *American Political Science Review* 53:742–56.

Evans, C. Lawrence. 1995. "Committees and Health Jurisdictions in Congress." In *Intensive Care: How Congress Shapes Health Policy,* edited by Thomas Mann and Norman Ornstein. Washington, DC: American Enterprise Institute and the Brookings Institution.

Evans, C. Lawrence, and Walter Oleszek. 1995. "Reform Redux: Jurisdictional Change and the New Republican House." Paper presented at the Annual Meeting of the Midwest Political Science Association, Chicago, IL.

———. 1997. *Congress under Fire: Reform Politics and the Republican Majority.* Boston: Houghton Mifflin Company.

Feldman, Paul, and James Jondrow. 1984. "Congressional Elections and Local Federal Spending." *American Journal of Political Science* 28:147–64.

Fenno, Richard. 1966. *The Power of the Purse: Appropriations Politics in Congress.* Boston: Little, Brown.

———. 1973. *Congressmen in Committees.* Boston: Little, Brown.

———. 1978. *Home Style: House Members in Their Districts.* Glenview, IL: Scott, Foresman.

Ferejohn, John. 1974. *Pork Barrel Politics: Rivers and Harbors Legislation, 1947–1968.* Stanford, CA: Stanford University Press.

Field, David. 1995. "Shuster Vows End to Pork Projects." *Washington Times* (January 23), A9.

Fiellin, Alan. 1970. "The Group Life of a State Delegation in the House of Representatives." *Western Political Quarterly* 23:305–20.

Fiorina, Morris. 1981. "Universalism, Reciprocity, and Distributive Policymaking in Majority Rule Institutions." *Research in Public Policy Analysis and Management* 1:197–221.

———. 1989. *Congress: Keystone of the Washington Establishment.* New Haven, CT: Yale University Press.

Follett, Mary Parker. 1896. *The Speaker of the House of Representatives.* New York: Crowell.

Ford, Henry Jones. 1898. *The Rise and Growth of American Politics: A Sketch of Constitutional Development.* New York: Macmillan.

"The Function of Private Bills." 1971. In *Guide to the Congress of the United States: Origins, History, and Procedure.* Washington, DC: Congressional Quarterly Press.

Galloway, George. 1942. "Congress—Problem, Diagnosis, Proposals." *American Political Science Review* 36:1091–1103.

———. 1946. *Congress at the Crossroads.* New York: Thomas Y. Crowell.

———. 1951. "The Operation of the Legislative Reform Act of 1946." *American Political Science Review* 45:41–68.

———. 1953. *The Legislative Process in Congress.* New York: Thomas Y. Crowell.

———. N.d. "On Reforming Congress." Located in Joint Committee on the Organization of Congress Archives, National Archives, Washington, DC.

Galloway, George, and Sidney Wise. 1976. *History of the House of Representatives.* New York: Thomas Y. Crowell.

Gamm, Gerald, and Kenneth Shepsle. 1989. "Emergence of Legislative Institutions: Standing Committees in the House and Senate, 1810–1825." *Legislative Studies Quarterly* 14:39–66.

Gillespie, Ed, and Bob Schellhas. 1994. *Contract with America: The Bold Plan by Rep. Newt Gingrich, Rep. Dick Armey, and the House Republicans to Change the Nation.* New York: Times Books.

Gilligan, Thomas, and Keith Krehbiel. 1989. "Asymmetric Information and Legislative Rules with a Heterogeneous Committee." *American Journal of Political Science* 33:459–90.

———. 1990. "Organization of Informative Committees by a Rational Legislature." *American Journal of Political Science* 34:531–64.

Gimpel, James. 1996. *Legislating the Revolution: The Contract with America in Its First 100 Days.* Boston: Allyn and Bacon.

Goodman, Walter. 1968. *The Committee.* New York: Farrar, Strauss, and Giroux.

Goodwin, George. 1970. *The Little Legislatures: Committees of Congress.* Amherst: University of Massachusetts Press.

Gore, Albert. 1943. "Congress Can Save Itself." *Collier's Magazine,* January 16, 13, 32–33.

Goss, Carol. 1972. "Military Committee Membership and Defense-Related Benefits in the House of Representatives." *Western Political Quarterly* 25:215–33.

Groseclose, Tim. 1994a. "The Committee Outlier Debate: A Review and a Reexamination of Some of the Evidence." *Public Choice* 80:265–73.

———. 1994b. "Testing Committee Composition Hypotheses for the U.S. Congress." *Journal of Politics* 56:440–58.

Groseclose, Tim, and David King. 1998. "Little Theatre: Committees in Congress." In *Great Theatre: The American Congress in the 1990s,* edited by Herbert Weisberg and Samuel Patterson. New York: Cambridge University Press.

Groseclose, Tim, Steven Levitt, and James Snyder. 1999. "Comparing Interest Group Scores across Time and Chambers: Adjusted ADA Scores for the U.S. Congress." *American Political Science Review* 93:33–50.

Gryski, Gerard. 1991. "The Influence of Committee Position on Federal Program Spending." *Polity* 23:443–59.

Gugliotta, Guy. 1994. "New Priorities Reflected by GOP Nomenclature, Committees' Titles, Jurisdictions Shuffled." *Washington Post* (December 3), A4.

Hall, Richard, and Bernard Grofman. 1990. "The Committee Assignment Process and the Conditional Nature of Committee Bias." *American Political Science Review* 84:1149–66.

Hall, Richard, and Gary McKissick. 1997. "Institutional Change and Behavioral Choice in House Committees." In *Congress Reconsidered,* edited by Lawrence Dodd and Bruce Oppenheimer. Washington, DC: Congressional Quarterly Press.

Halvorson, Jon, and Harold Elder. 1998. "Is the Geographic Distribution of Federal Expenditures Linked to Congressional Seniority?" Paper presented at the Annual Meeting of the Public Choice Society, New Orleans.

Hansen, John Mark. 1991. *Gaining Access: Congress and the Farm Lobby, 1919–1981.* Chicago: University of Chicago Press.

Harris, Charles. 1995. *Congress and the Governance of the Nation's Capital: The Conflict of Federal and Local Interests.* Washington, DC: Georgetown University Press.

Harris, Joseph. 1946. "The Reorganization of Congress." *Public Administration Review* 6:267–82.

Heitshusen, Valerie. 2001. "The Allocation of Federal Money to House Committee Members: Distributive Theory and Policy Jurisdictions." *American Politics Research* 29:79–97.

Heller, Robert. 1945. "Strengthening the Congress." Washington, DC: National Planning Association.

Henderson, Thomas. 1970. *Congressional Oversight of Executive Agencies: A Study of the House Committee on Government Operations.* Gainesville: University of Florida Press.

Herrnson, Paul. 1998. *Congressional Elections: Campaigning at Home and in Washington.* Washington, DC: Congressional Quarterly Press.

Hibbing, John. 1991. *Congressional Careers: Contours of Life in the U.S. House of Representatives.* Chapel Hill: University of North Carolina Press.

Higgs, Robert. 1987. *Crisis and Leviathan: Critical Episodes in the Growth of American Government.* New York: Oxford University Press.

Hill, Jeffrey, and Kenneth Williams. 1993. "The Decline of Private Bills: Resource Allocation, Credit Claiming, and the Decision to Delegate." *American Journal of Political Science* 37:1008–31.

Hird, John. 1991. "The Political Economy of Pork: Project Selection at the U.S. Army Corps of Engineers." *American Political Science Review* 85:429–56.

Hogg, Robert, and Allen Craig. 1995. *Introduction to Mathematical Statistics.* Englewood Cliffs, NJ: Prentice Hall.

Hook, Janet, and David Cloud 1994. "A Republican-Designed House Won't Please All Occupants." *Congressional Quarterly Weekly Report,* December 3, 3430–35.

Hooton, Cornell. 1997. "Politics versus Policy in Public Works Grants: A Critical Test of the Simple Model." *American Politics Quarterly* 25:75–103.

Hosansky, David 1994. "GOP Bid to Reform Committees Faces Intraparty Skepticism." *Congressional Quarterly Weekly Report,* November 19, 3324–25.

———. 1997. "Requests for Road Money Pour In." *Congressional Quarterly Weekly Report,* March 8, 584.

"House Committee Reform Proposals Drawing Opposition." 1974. *Congressional Quarterly Weekly Report,* February 2, 195.

Howell, William, E. Scott Adler, Charles Cameron, and Charles Riemann. 2000. "Measuring the Institutional Performance of Congress in the Post-war Era: Surges and Slumps in the Production of Legislation, 1945–1994." *Legislative Studies Quarterly* 25:285–312.

Huntington, Samuel. 1965. "Congressional Responses to the Twentieth Century." In *The Congress and America's Future,* edited by David Truman. New York: American Assembly.

Hurwitz, Mark, Roger Moiles, and David Rohde. 2001. "Distributive and Partisan Issues in Agriculture Policy in the 104th House." *American Political Science Review* 95:911–22.

Ippolito, Dennis. 1981. *Congressional Spending.* Ithaca, NY: Cornell University Press.

Jaccard, James, Robert Turrisi, and Choi Wan. 1990. Interaction Effects in Multiple Regression. Newbury Park, CA: Sage.

Jacobson, Gary. 1987. "The Marginals Never Vanished: Incumbency and Competition in Elections to the U.S. House of Representatives, 1952–82." *American Journal of Political Science* 31:126–41.

———. 1997. *The Politics of Congressional Elections.* New York: Longman.

Jacoby, Mary, and Gabriel Kahn. 1994. "Future of Twenty-two House Panels." *Roll Call* (November 14), A1, A16–A20.

Jantscher, Gerald. 1975. Bread upon the Waters: Federal Aids to the Maritime Industries. Washington, DC: Brookings Institution.

Jenkins, Jeffery. 1998. "Property Rights and the Emergence of Standing Committee Dominance in the Nineteenth-Century House." *Legislative Studies Quarterly* 23:493–521.

Jones, Charles. 1961. "Representation in Congress: The Case of the House Agriculture Committee." *American Political Science Review* 55:358–67.

———. 1968. "Joseph G. Cannon and Howard W. Smith: An Essay on the Limits of Leadership in the House of Representatives." *Journal of Politics* 30:617–46.

Julnes, George, and Lawrence Mohr. 1989. "Analysis of No-Difference Findings in Evaluation Research." *Evaluation Research* 13:628–55.

Kahn, Gabriel. 1994. "On House Panels, Challenges Galore." *Roll Call* (November 10), 1, 34.

Kamen, Al. 1998. "Break Out the Champlain." *Washington Post* (March 25), A19.

Kaplan, Lewis. 1968. "The House Un-American Activities Committee and Its Opponents: A Study of Congressional Dissonance." *Journal of Politics* 30:647–71.

Katz, Jonathan, and Brian Sala. 1996. "Careerism, Committee Assignments, and the Electoral Connection." *American Political Science Review* 90:21–33.

Kernell, Samuel. 1977. "Toward Understanding Nineteenth-Century Congressional Careers: Ambition, Competition, and Rotation." *American Journal of Political Science* 21:669–93.

Kernell, Samuel, and Michael McDonald. 1999. "Congress and America's Political Development: The Transformation of the Post Office from Patronage to Service." *American Journal of Political Science* 43:792–811.

Kiewiet, D. Roderick, and Mathew McCubbins. 1991. *The Logic of Delegation: Congressional Parties and the Appropriations Process.* Chicago: University of Chicago Press.

King, David. 1997. *Turf Wars: How Congressional Committees Claim Jurisdictions.* Chicago: University of Chicago Press.

Kingdon, John. 1966. "A House Appropriations Subcommittee: Influences on Budgetary Decisions." *Southwestern Social Science Quarterly* 47:68–78.

———. 1995. *Agendas, Alternative, and Public Policies.* New York: HarperCollins.

Koszczuk, Jackie 1998. "On the Hill and at Home, GOP Is Torn by Internal Strife." *Congressional Quarterly Weekly Report,* April 4, 859.

Krehbiel, Keith. 1985. "Obstruction and Representativeness in Legislatures." *American Journal of Political Science* 29:643–59.

———. 1990. "Are Congressional Committees Composed of Preference Outliers?" *American Political Science Review* 84:149–63.

———. 1991. *Information and Legislative Organization.* Ann Arbor: University of Michigan Press.

———. 1993. "Where's the Party?." *British Journal of Political Science* 23:235–66.

———. 1999. "Paradoxes of Parties in Congress." *Legislative Studies Quarterly* 24: 31–64.

La Follette, Robert Jr. 1943. "A Senator Looks at Congress." *The Atlantic Monthly,* July, 91–96.

Lawrence, Eric, Forrest Maltzman, and Paul Wahlbeck. 1999. "Dispensing Opportunity and Power? Speaker Cannon and the Politics of Committee Assignments." Paper presented at the Annual Meeting of the American Political Science Association, Atlanta, GA.

Lee, Frances. 1998. "Representation and Public Policy: The Consequences of Senate Apportionment for the Geographic Distribution of Federal Funds." *Journal of Politics* 60:34–62.

Lee, R. Alton. 1990. *Eisenhower and Landrum-Griffin: A Study in Labor-Management Politics.* Lexington, KY: University Press of Kentucky.

Lehman, William. 2000. *Mr. Chairman: The Journal of a Congressional Appropriator.* New York: University Press of America.

LeLoup, Lance. 1980. *The Fiscal Congress: Legislative Control of the Budget.* Westport, CT: Greenwood Press.

Levine, Arthur 1975. "Getting to Know Your Congressman: The $500 Understanding." *Washington Monthly,* February, 47–59.

Levitt, Steven, and James Poterba. 1999. "Congressional Distributive Politics and State Economic Performance." *Public Choice* 99:185–216.

Levitt, Steven, and James Snyder. 1995. "Political Parties and the Distribution of Federal Outlays." *American Journal of Political Science* 39:958–80.

———. 1997. "The Impact of Federal Spending on House Election Outcomes." *Journal of Political Economy* 105:30–53.

Liao, Tim Futing. 1994. *Interpreting Probability Models: Logit, Probit and Other Generalized Linear Models.* Thousand Oaks, CA: Sage.

Londregan, John, and James Snyder. 1994. "Comparing Committee and Floor Preferences." *Legislative Studies Quarterly* 19:233–66.

Lowe, David. 1976. "The 'Impossible Task': Organizational Innovation, Congressional Reform, and the Bolling Committee." Ph.D. diss. Department of Political Science, Johns Hopkins University, Baltimore, MD.

Lowi, Theodore. 1964. "American Business, Public Policy, Case-Studies, and Political Theory." *World Politics* 16:677–715.

Luce, Robert. 1932. "Petty Business in Congress." *American Political Science Review* 26:815–28.

Maass, Arthur. 1983. *Congress and the Common Good.* New York: Basic Books.

Maddala, G. 1992. *Introduction to Econometrics.* New York: Macmillan.

Makinson, Larry, and Joshua Goldstein. 1996. *Open Secrets: The Encyclopedia of Congressional Money and Politics.* Washington, DC: Congressional Quarterly Press.

Maltzman, Forrest. 1997. *Competing Principals: Committees, Parties, and the Organization of Congress.* Ann Arbor: University of Michigan Press.

Maltzman, Forrest, and Steven Smith. 1994. "Principals, Goals, Dimensionality, and Congressional Committees." *Legislative Studies Quarterly* 19:457–76.

Maney, Patrick. 1978. *"Young Bob" La Follette: A Biography of Robert M. La Follette, Jr., 1895–1953.* Columbia: University of Missouri Press.

Mann, Thomas, and Norman Ornstein. 1993. *A Second Report of the Renewing Congress Project.* Washington, DC: American Enterprise Institute and Brookings Institution.

Martis, Kenneth. 1982. *The Historical Atlas of United States Congressional Districts, 1789–1983.* New York: Free Press.

Masters, Nicholas. 1961. "Committee Assignments in the House of Representatives." *American Political Science Review* 55:345–57.

Mayhew, David. 1974a. *Congress: The Electoral Connection.* New Haven, CT: Yale University Press.

———. 1974b. "Congressional Elections: The Case of the Vanishing Marginals." *Polity* 6:295–317.

———. 1991. *Divided We Govern: Party Control, Lawmaking, and Investigations, 1946–1990.* New Haven, CT: Yale University Press.

McConachie, Lauros. 1898. *Congressional Committees: A Study of the Origins and Development of our National and Local Legislative Methods.* New York: Crowell.

McCubbins, Mathew, and Thomas Schwartz. 1985. "The Politics of Flatland." *Public Choice* 46:45–60.

McSweeney, Dean, and John E. Owens. 1998. *The Republican Takeover of Congress.* New York: St. Martin's Press.

Merriam, Charles, and Louise Overacker. 1928. *Primary Elections.* Chicago: University of Chicago Press.

Miller, Warren, and Donald Stokes. 1963. "Constituency Influence in Congress." *American Political Science Review* 57:45–56.

Monroney, A. S. Mike. 1945. "Streamlining Congress." *Personnel Administration* 7:7–10.

———. 1949. "The Legislative Reorganization Act of 1946: A First Appraisal." In *The Strengthening of American Political Institutions,* edited by A. S. Mike Monroney et al. Port Washington, NY: Kennikat Press.

Mooney, Christopher, and Robert Duval. 1993. *Bootstrapping: A Nonparametric Approach to Statistical Inference.* Newbury Park, CA: Sage.

Moore, Michael K., and John R. Hibbing. 1996. "Length of Congressional Tenure and Federal Spending." *American Politics Quarterly* 24:131–49.

Morrow, William. 1969. *Congressional Committees.* New York: Scribner's.

Moulton, Harold. 1912. *Waterways versus Railways.* New York: Houghton Mifflin.

Munger, Frank, and Richard Fenno. 1962. *National Politics and Federal Aid to Education.* Syracuse, NY: Syracuse University Press.

Munger, Michael. 1988. "Allocation of Desirable Committee Assignments: Extended Queues versus Committee Expansion." *American Journal of Political Science* 32:317–44.

Nelson, Garrison. 1994. *Committees in the U.S. Congress, 1947–1992: Committee*

Histories and Member Assignments. Vol. 2. Washington, DC: Congressional Quarterly Press.

North, Douglass. 1981. *Structure and Change in Economic History.* New York: W. W. Norton.

Oppenheimer, Bruce. 1997. "Abdicating Congressional Power: The Paradox of Republican Control." In *Congress Reconsidered,* edited by Lawrence Dodd and Bruce Oppenheimer. Washington, DC: Congressional Quarterly Press.

Ornstein, Norman, ed. 1975. *Congress in Change: Evolution and Reform.* New York: Praeger.

Ostrom, Elinor. 1986. "An Agenda for the Study of Institutions." *Public Choice* 48: 3–25.

Ota, Alan. 1998a. "Congress Clears Huge Transportation Bill, Restoring Cut-Off Funding to States." *Congressional Quarterly Weekly Report,* May 23, 1385.

———. 1998b. "Some Controversial Riders on Transportation Spending Fall by the Wayside." *Congressional Quarterly Weekly Report,* October 24, 2899.

———. 1998c. "What the Highway Bill Does." *Congressional Quarterly Weekly Report,* July 11, 1892.

Outland, George. 1945. "We Must Modernize Congress." *Reader's Digest,* February.

Owens, John E. 1997. "The Return of Party Government in the U.S. House of Representatives: Central Leadership-Committee Relations in the 104th Congress." *British Journal of Political Science* 27:247–72.

Owens, John R., and Larry L. Wade. 1984. "Federal Spending In Congressional Districts." *Western Political Quarterly* 37:404–23.

Patterson, James. 1967. *Congressional Conservatism and the New Deal: The Growth of the Conservative Coalition in Congress, 1933–1939.* Lexington: University of Kentucky Press.

Pearson, Drew, and Jack Anderson. 1968. *The Case against Congress: A Compelling Indictment of Corruption on Capitol Hill.* New York: Simon & Schuster.

Perkins, John. 1944. "Congressional Self-Improvement." *American Political Science Review* 38:499–511.

Perkins, Lynette. 1980. "Influences of Members' Goals on Their Committee Behavior: The U.S. House Judiciary Committee." *Legislative Studies Quarterly* 5:373–92.

Pershing, Ben. 2000. "Panel Decisions Loom in January." *Roll Call On-line,* December 18.

Pianin, Eric. 1998. "Bringing Home the Pork Can Pay Off at the Polls." *Washington Post Weekly Edition* (June 15), 10–11.

Pianin, Eric, and Charles Babcock. 1998. "Working the System." *Washington Post National Weekly* (April 13), 8.

Pincus, Walter. 1994. "GOP Promises Exit in Committee Maze: Gingrich Plans Cutbacks in Panels, Staffs." *Washington Post* (November 30), 225.

Pitney, John, and William Connelly. 1996. "'Permanent Minority' No More: House Republicans in 1994." In *Midterm: The Elections of 1994 in Context,* edited by Philip Klinkner. Boulder, CO: Westview Press.

Plott, Charles. 1968. "Some Organizational Influences on Urban Renewal Decisions." *American Economic Review* 58:306–21.

Polsby, Nelson. 1968. "The Institutionalization of the House of Representatives." *American Political Science Review* 63:144–68.

Poole, Keith, and Howard Rosenthal. 1985. "A Spatial Model for Legislative Roll Call Analysis." *American Journal of Political Science* 29:357–84.

———. 1997. *Congress: A Political-Economic History of Roll Call Voting*. New York: Oxford University Press.

Porter, David. 1980. *Congress and the Waning of the New Deal*. Port Washington, NY: Kennikat Press.

Price, Douglas. 1977. "Careers and Committees in the American Congress: The Problem of Structural Change." In *The History of Parliamentary Behavior*, edited by William O. Aydelotte. Princeton, NJ: Princeton University Press.

Rae, Nicol. 1998. *Conservative Reformers: The Republican Freshman and the Lessons of the 104th Congress*. Armonk, NY: M. E. Sharpe.

Ray, Bruce. 1980a. "Congressional Promotion of District Interest: Does Power on the Hill Really Make a Difference." In *Political Benefits*. Lexington, MA: Lexington Books.

———. 1980b. "The Responsiveness of the U.S. Congressional Armed Services Committees to Their Parent Bodies." *Legislative Studies Quarterly* 5:501–16.

Rice, John. 1995. *Mathematical Statistics and Data Analysis*. Belmont, CA: Duxbury Press.

Rich, Michael. 1991. "Targeting Federal Grants: The Community Development Experience, 1950–1986." *Publius* 21:29–49.

Rieselbach, Leroy. 1978. *Legislative Reform: The Policy Impact*. Lexington, MA: Lexington Books.

———. 1994. *Congressional Reform: The Changing Modern Congress*. Washington, DC: Congressional Quarterly Press.

Riker, William. 1980. "Implications from the Disequilibrium of Majority Rule for the Study of Institutions." *American Political Science Review* 74:432–47.

Ripley, Randall. 1969. "Power in the Post–World War II Senate." *Journal of Politics* 31:465–92.

Ritt, Leonard. 1976. "Committee Positions, Seniority, and the Distribution of Government Expenditures." *Public Policy* 24:463–89.

Robinson, James. 1963. *The House Rules Committee*. Indianapolis, IN: Bobbs-Merrill.

Rohde, David. 1991. *Parties and Leaders in the Postreform House*. Chicago: University of Chicago.

Roman, Nancy. 1994a. "Bonior Launches Attack on Gingrich, Rips Talk of Killing House Ethics Panel." *Washington Times* (November 18), A3.

———. 1994b. "Dingel Panel Cuts Would Anger Heir to Chairmanship." *Washington Times* (November 16), A3.

Rose, Mark. 1990. *Interstate: Express Highway Politics, 1939–1989*. Knoxville: University of Tennessee Press.

Rosenbaum, Walter. 1981. *Energy, Politics and Public Policy*. Washington, DC: Congressional Quarterly Press.

Rundquist, Barry, and Thomas Carsey. 1998. "Is Distributive Politics Effective: An Exploratory Study of Health Policy." Paper presented at the Annual Meeting of the American Political Science Association, Boston, MA.

Rundquist, Barry, and John Ferejohn. 1975. "Observations on a Distributive Theory of Policymaking: Two American Expenditure Programs Compared." In *Comparative Public Policy: Issues, Theories and Methods*, edited by Craig Kiske, William Loehr, and John McCamant. New York: John Wiley and Sons.

Rundquist, Barry, Jeong-Hwa Lee, and Ching-Jyuhn Luor. 1995. "States vs. Districts as Units of Analysis in Distributive Studies: An Exploration." Paper presented at the Annual meeting of the Midwest Political Science Association, Chicago, IL.

Rundquist, Barry, Jeong-Hwa Lee, and Jungho Rhee. 1996. "The Distributive Politics of Cold War Defense Spending: Some State Level Evidence." *Legislative Studies Quarterly* 21:265–82.

Rundquist, Paul. 1985. "The Legislative Reorganization Act of 1946—A View from Forty Years." Paper presented at the Annual Meeting of the American Political Science Association, New Orleans, LA.

Schick, Allen. 1980. *Congress and Money: Budgeting, Spending and Taxing.* Washington, DC: The Urban Institute.

———. 1995. *The Federal Budget: Politics, Policy, Process.* Washington, DC: Brookings Institution.

Schickler, Eric. 2001. *Disjointed Pluralism: Institutional Innovation and the Development of the U.S. Congress.* Princeton, NJ: Princeton University Press.

Schickler, Eric, Eric McGhee, and John Sides. 2001. "Remaking the House and Senate: Personal Power, Ideology, and the 1970s Reforms." Paper presented at the annual meeting of the Midwest Political Science Association, Chicago, IL.

Schickler, Eric, and Andrew Rich. 1997. "Controlling the Floor: Parties as Procedural Coalitions in the House." *American Journal of Political Science* 41:1340–75.

Schlesinger, Joseph. 1966. *Ambition and Politics: Political Careers in the United States.* Chicago: Rand McNally.

Seelye, Katharine. 1998. "As Congress Session Ends, a Question of Legacy." *New York Times* (October 18), 28.

Select Committee on Committees. 1974. "Committee Reform Amendments of 1974: Explanation of H. Res. 988 as Adopted by the House of Representatives, October 8, 1974." Washington, DC: GPO.

Sellers, Patrick. 1997. "Fiscal Consistency and Federal District Spending in Congressional Elections." *American Journal of Political Science* 41:1024–41.

Shaiko, Ronald, and Marc Wallace. 1999. "From Wall Street to Main Street: The National Federation of Independent Business and the New Republican Majority." In *After the Revolution: PACs, Lobbies, and the Republican Congress,* edited by Robert Biersack, Paul Herrnson, and Clyde Wilcox. Boston: Allyn and Bacon.

"Shaping New-Style Congress: Opposition to Major Changes." 1946. *U.S. News and World Report* (October 18), 27–28.

Sheppard, Burton. 1985. *Rethinking Congressional Reform: The Reform Roots of the Special Interest Congress.* Cambridge, MA: Schenkman Books.

Shepsle, Kenneth. 1978. *The Giant Jigsaw Puzzle.* Chicago: University of Chicago Press.

———. 1979. "Institutional Arrangements and Equilibrium in Multidimensional Voting Models." *American Journal of Political Science* 23:27–60.

———. 1986. "Institutional Equilibrium and Equilibrium Institutions." In *Political Science: The Science of Politics,* edited by Herbert Weisberg. New York: Agathon Press.

Shepsle, Kenneth, and Barry Weingast. 1981. "Structure-Induced Equilibria and Legislative Choice." *Public Choice* 37:503–19.

———. 1984a. "Political Solutions to Market Problems." *American Political Science Review* 78:417–34.

———. 1984b. "When Do Rules of Procedure Matter?" *Journal of Politics* 46: 206–21.

———. 1994. "Positive Theories of Congressional Institutions." *Legislative Studies Quarterly* 19:149–80.

Shuman, Howard. 1992. *Politics and the Budget: The Struggle between the President and the Congress.* Englewood Cliffs, NJ: Prentice Hall.

Sinclair, Barbara. 1997. *Unorthodox Lawmaking: New Legislative Processes in the U.S. Congress.* Washington, DC: Congressional Quarterly Press.

———. 1998. "Leading the Revolution: Innovation and Continuity in Congressional

Party Leadership." In *The Republican Takeover of Congress,* edited by Dean McSweeney and John E. Owens. New York: St. Martin's Press.

———. 1999. "Partisan Imperatives and Institutional Constraints: Republican Party Leadership in the House and Senate." In *New Majority or Old Minority? The Impact of Republicans on Congress,* edited by Nicol Rae and Colton Campbell. Lanham, MD: Rowman and Littlefield.

Skowronek, Steven. 1982. *Building a New American State: The Expansion of National Administrative Capabilities, 1877–1920.* New York: Cambridge University Press.

Smith, Steven, and Eric Lawrence. 1997. "Party Control of Committees in the Republican Congress." In *Congress Reconsidered,* edited by Lawrence Dodd and Bruce Oppenheimer. Washington, DC: Congressional Quarterly Press.

Stanwood, Edward. 1903. *American Tariff Controversies in the Nineteenth Century.* Boston: Houghton Mifflin.

Stata. 1997. *Stata Reference Manual, Release 5.* College Station, TX: Stata Press.

Stein, Robert. 1981. "The Allocation of Federal Aid Monies: The Synthesis of Demand Side and Supply Side Explanations." *American Political Science Review* 75: 334–43.

Stein, Robert, and Kenneth Bickers. 1994a. "Congressional Elections and the Pork Barrel." *Journal of Politics* 56:377–99.

———. 1994b. "Universalism and the Electoral Connection: A Test and Some Doubts." *Political Research Quarterly* 47:295–317.

———. 1995. *Perpetuating the Pork Barrel: Policy Subsystems and American Democracy.* New York: Cambridge University Press.

Stewart, Charles. 1989. *Budget Reform Politics: The Design of Appropriations Process in the House of Representatives, 1865–1921.* New York: Cambridge University Press.

———. 1992. "The Growth of the Committee System, from Randall to Gillett." In *The Atomistic Congress: An Interpretation of Congressional Change,* edited by Allen Hertzke and Ronald Peters. Armonk, NY: M. E. Sharpe.

———. 1995. "Structure and Stability in House Committee Assignments, 1789–1947." Paper presented at the Annual Meeting of the Midwest Political Science Association, Chicago, IL.

Sundquist, James. 1981. *The Decline and Resurgence of Congress.* Washington, DC: Brookings Institution.

Svorny, Shirley. 1996. "Congressional Allocation of Federal Funds: The Job Training Partnership Act of 1982." *Public Choice* 87:229–42.

Swift, Elaine. 1987. "The Electoral Connection Meets the Past: Lessons from Congressional History, 1789–1899." *Political Science Quarterly* 102:625–45.

Tarbell, Ida. 1912. *The Tariff in Our Times.* New York: Macmillan.

Thurber, James A., and Roger H. Davidson. 1995. *Remaking Congress: Change and Stability in the 1990s.* Washington, DC: Congressional Quarterly Press.

Tiefer, Charles. 1989. *Congressional Practice and Procedure: A Reference, Research, and Legislative Guide.* Westport, CT: Greenwood Press.

Tin, Annie. 1994. "GOP Takes the Reins of Power: Small Business." *Congressional Quarterly Weekly Report,* November 12, 3268.

Tullock, Gordon. 1981. "Why So Much Stability?" *Public Choice* 37:189–202.

Unekis, Joseph, and Leroy Rieselbach. 1984. *Congressional Committee Politics: Continuity and Change.* New York: Praeger.

United States Bureau of the Census. 1960. *Congressional District Atlas.* Washington, DC: GPO.

———. 1973. *Congressional District Data Book: Ninety-third Congress (A Statistical Abstract Supplement).* Washington, DC: GPO.

United States Department of Defense. Various years. *Map Book of Major Military Installations (1955–1982), State/District Atlas of Major Military Installations (1983–present).* Washington, DC: Office of the Secretary of Defense, Washington Headquarters Service.

VandeHei, Jim. 1998. "Shuster Steered Highway Funds to Punish Foes." *Roll Call* (April 2).

Victor, Kirk. 1995. "Mr. Smooth." *National Journal* (July 8), 1761.

Wallace, Robert. 1960. *Congressional Control of Federal Spending.* Detroit, MI: Wayne State University Press.

Wawro, Gregory. 2000. *Legislative Entrepreneurship in the U.S. House of Representatives.* Ann Arbor: University of Michigan Press.

Webster, Gerald. 1991. "Congress and the Changing Distribution of Federal Outlays." *The Professional Geographer* 43:49–61.

Weingast, Barry. 1994. "Reflections on Distributive Politics and Universalism." *Political Research Quarterly* 47:319–27.

Weingast, Barry, and William Marshall. 1988. "The Industrial Organization of Congress; or, Why Legislatures, Like Firms, Are Not Organized as Markets." *Journal of Political Economy* 96:132–63.

Weingast, Barry, Kenneth Shepsle, and Christopher Johnsen. 1981. "The Political Economy of Benefits and Costs: A Neoclassical Approach to Distributive Politics." *Journal of Political Economy* 89:642–64.

Weisman, Jonathan. 1997. "Battle over Highway Funding Ends with Stopgap Bill." *Congressional Quarterly Weekly Report,* November 15, 2838.

Weisskopf, Michael. 1996. "Campaign '96—Small Business Lobby Becomes a Big Player in Campaigns." *Washington Post* (August 9), A1.

Welch, Susan, and John Peters. 1977. *Legislative Reform and Public Policy.* New York: Praeger.

West, Darrell, and Burdett Loomis. 1999. *The Sound of Money: How Political Interests Get What They Want.* New York: W. W. Norton.

White, Joseph. 1989. "The Function and Power of the House Appropriations Committee." Ph.D. diss. Department of Political Science, University of California, Berkeley.

Wilmerding, Lucius Jr. 1943. *The Spending Power: A History of the Efforts of Congress to Control Expenditures.* New Haven, CT: Yale University Press.

Wilson, Rick. 1985. "What Was It Worth to Be on a Committee in the House, 1889 to 1913?" *Legislative Studies Quarterly* 11:47–63.

———. 1986. "An Empirical Test of Preferences for the Political Pork Barrel: District Level Appropriations for River and Harbor Legislation, 1889–1913." *American Journal of Political Science* 30:729–54.

Wilson, Woodrow. [1885] 1981. *Congressional Government: A Study in American Politics.* Baltimore, MD: Johns Hopkins University Press.

Young, Roland. 1943. *This Is Congress.* New York: A. A. Knopf.

Zelizer, Julian. Forthcoming. *The Cost of Democracy: A History of America's Congress, 1945–2000.* Cambridge: Cambridge University Press.

Index